Teaching in Multilingual Classrooms

A Teacher's Guide to Context, Process, and Content

Hilda Hernández
California State University, Chico

Merrill,
an imprint of Prentice Hall
Upper Saddle River, New Jersey   Columbus, Ohio

Library of Congress Cataloging-in-Publication Data
Hernández, Hilda.
    Teaching in multilingual classrooms : a teacher's guide to context,
process, and content/by Hilda Hernández.
        p. cm.
    Includes bibliographical references and indexes.
    ISBN 0-675-21358-4
    1. Education, Bilingual—United States. 2. Language arts—United States.
3. Language teachers—United States. 4. Multicultural education—United
States.   I. Title.
LC3731.H47   1997
371.97'0973—dc20
                                           96-21265
                                              CIP

Cover art: *Synchros,* © Marko Spalatin/1995
Editor: Debra A. Stollenwerk
Production Editor: Linda Hillis Bayma
Design Coordinator: Julia Zonneveld Van Hook
Text Designer: Ed Horcharik
Cover Designer: Thomas Mack
Production Manager: Patricia A. Tonneman
Electronic Text Management: Marilyn Wilson Phelps, Matthew Williams, Karen L. Bretz,
    Tracey Ward
Illustrations: Christine Haggerty
Director of Marketing: Kevin Flanagan
Advertising/Marketing Coordinator: Julie Shough

This book was set in Zapf Calligraphic BT by Prentice Hall and was printed and bound by
Quebecor Printing/Book Press. The cover was printed by Phoenix Color Corp.

© 1997 by Prentice-Hall, Inc.
Simon & Schuster/A Viacom Company
Upper Saddle River, New Jersey 07458

Photo credits: All photos provided by the author.

Printed in the United States of America

10 9 8 7 6 5 4 3 2 1

ISBN: 0-675-21358-4

Prentice-Hall International (UK) Limited, *London*
Prentice-Hall of Australia Pty. Limited, *Sydney*
Prentice-Hall of Canada, Inc., *Toronto*
Prentice-Hall Hispanoamericana, S. A., *Mexico*
Prentice-Hall of India Private Limited, *New Delhi*
Prentice-Hall of Japan, Inc., *Tokyo*
Simon & Schuster Asia Pte. Ltd., *Singapore*
Editora Prentice-Hall do Brasil, Ltda., *Rio de Janeiro*

To my parents and grandparents for teaching me how special it is to be bilingual

To my brother, Frank, for epitomizing the best of teaching in multilingual classrooms

Preface

Teaching in multilingual classrooms is in some ways analogous to building bridges. There are inextricable ties spanning language and culture as well as home, school, and community. And from an instructional perspective, the connections between language, literacy, and academic development are most critical. The purpose of this book is to help teachers see and appreciate the broad panorama of teaching and learning in classrooms characterized by linguistic and cultural diversity.

In this book I approach classrooms that are multilingual and multicultural from a tripartite perspective that encompasses context, process, and content. *Context* is the world in which teachers teach and students learn. The cultural, linguistic, and instructional *process*es involved are perhaps less visible than more concrete aspects of schooling but no less important. *Content* is the substance—the more formal dimension of curriculum and instruction. From this perspective, teachers can better understand major areas related to teaching English language learners. They can make connections to their own classrooms, whatever the level, setting, or school population. They can incorporate and apply the principles presented in their teaching and in the learning environment they create.

This is a book for all teachers of students from diverse language backgrounds: elementary and secondary, beginning and experienced, prospective specialists and nonspecialists. It is for those preparing to enter the profession as well as for educators continuing their professional development at the graduate level. It is for teachers in settings that are urban, suburban, and rural.

Organization of the Text

The text is divided into five parts. Part 1 consists of an introductory chapter designed to provide the basis for the nine that follow. The first chapter describes multilingual classrooms and explains why a focus on context, process, and content is central to providing effective instructional programs for language minority students.

Parts 2, 3, and 4 are the heart of this book. Chapters 2 to 9 explore different dimensions of context, process, and content related to multilingual classrooms. Combining theory and practice, they offer a synthesis of contemporary scholarship complemented by strategies and techniques that teachers can readily apply in K–12 classrooms. Each chapter begins with a statement of objectives and concludes with a summary of the major ideas presented.

Part 2 contains two chapters that examine the societal, home, and community contexts in which students acquire and learn language and culture. In Chapter 2, the focus is on the societal context—the rich diversity of ethnic and language groups in the United States, contemporary immigration patterns, and differing perceptions on diversity. This sets the stage for the exploration of home and community contexts in Chapter 3, more specifically, the language of the home, parents' perceptions of school and their involvement in the education of their children, and strategies for making connections between home, school, and community.

The three chapters in Part 3 focus on the processes of language acquisition and acculturation as well as on the dynamics of processes manifest within the instructional environment of the classroom. Chapter 4 looks at how students adapt to a new culture developmentally and as individuals. Chapter 5 deals with language proficiency, second language acquisition, and the implications of theory and research on classroom practice. This overview of linguistic and cultural processes prepares teachers to examine students' orientation to the school and classroom, social and interactional dynamics, and classroom language and discourse in Chapter 6.

Part 4 contains three chapters that address content. Chapters 7 and 8 both examine language and literacy development. Chapter 7 deals primarily with the foundations of language and literacy development—considerations such as language functions and accuracy, comprehension, cultural background and cognitive strengths, basic issues in literacy instruction, and critical literacy. Chapter 8 complements this discussion by highlighting approaches and strategies appropriate to different levels of development. In Chapter 9, attention is directed toward promoting academic competence through content instruction that is language-sensitive.

Part 5 consists of a concluding chapter that brings together major threads throughout the text. Chapter 10 assists teachers in assessing learning and evaluating the features of programs in their own schools. This is done by first considering cultural and linguistic diversity as factors involved in formal and informal assessment. Attention is then directed to the essential characteristics of schools that empower language minority students and to guidelines for self-assessment.

Acknowledgments

I gratefully acknowledge the contributions that others have made in the preparation of this book. First, I am deeply indebted to John McNamara for the artistry of the photographs that so beautifully enhance this text. It has been a genuine pleasure to collaborate on a second project with my former colleague from James Logan High School, Union City, California. I also want to thank the teachers, parents, and students from the New Haven Unified School District in Union City, California, for allowing their photographs to be included as part of this book. If a picture is worth a thousand words, theirs certainly speak volumes. Very special thanks go to my brother Frank Hernández for creating the part opening art and chapter 7 organizers that grace this text. The writing samples featured in the organizers were done by second-grade students in Frank's class at Searles Elementary School, New Haven Unified School District, Union City, California. In addition to being a gifted artist, he is a real expert on teaching in multilingual classrooms.

I sincerely appreciate the contributions of those who reviewed the text at various stages of development. Especially warm thanks to reviewers John Attinasi, California State University, Long Beach; Jean E. Benton, Southeast Missouri State University; Lupe Cadenas, California State University, Los Angeles; Minerva L. Caples, Central Washington University; Donna Cole, Wright State University; Alan Crawford, California State University, Los Angeles; Stephen Díaz, California State University, San Bernardino; Christian Faltis, Arizona State University; Beatrice S. Fennimore, Indiana University of Pennsylvania; Andrew P. Hanson, California State University, Chico; Hee-Won Kang, California State University, Fresno; Walter G. McIntire, University of Maine at Orono; Amado M. Padilla, Stanford University; Elizabeth Quintero, University of Minnesota, Duluth; and Ron Wilhelm, University of North Texas. Their suggestions and ideas helped me to better shape my vision into one that others can share.

I also want to express my gratitude to colleagues at California State University, Chico, for their interest, advice, and support. For suggestions based on various drafts of the chapters and manuscript, I am most grateful to Jerry Converse, Margaret Korte, Jim Overholt, Paula Selvester, and Sara Trechter. I also acknowledge the very useful and insightful comments provided by student teachers in the basic credential programs, special education and language development candidates in the specialist programs, and, most of all, my graduate students in foreign/second language education. Particular thanks to Paula Villa for her feedback. I thank all of my students—past and present—for everything they have taught me about teaching in multilingual classrooms around the world.

Very special thanks to David Faherty, my administrative editor at Merrill Publishing Company on my first book, for getting me started on this one, and Debbie Stollenwerk, my administrative editor at Merrill/Prentice Hall, for seeing me through the project from the beginning to the end. She was everything that I needed in an editor and more; I particularly appreciated her patience in allowing the vision to come together as I knew it would and the support she provided at every point along the way. Her positive outlook and sense of humor were always welcome. Thanks, too, go to Penny Burleson for her assistance and Marilyn Prudente for her editing. Especially warm thanks to Linda Bayma, my production editor, for cheerfully keeping this whole enterprise on track toward final publication.

For their generosity, I thank the individuals, publishers, and school, state, and government agencies who granted permission for the use of materials reproduced in this book. Their contributions are most gratefully acknowledged.

Finally, I thank my family, whose love, support, and encouragement made this book possible.

Brief Contents

Contents

PART FOUR
Content   121

Chapter 7
Language and Literacy Development: Foundations   123

Chapter 8
Language and Literacy Development: Approaches and Strategies   161

Chapter 9
Teaching Content: Developing Academic Language and Competence 201

PART FIVE
In the Final Analysis 229

Chapter 10
Assessment and Evaluation 231

Appendix
Legal Responsibilities of Education Agencies Serving Language Minority Students 249

P A R T

1 Introduction

1

Multilingual Classrooms

If I can reach the children of today I touch the children of tomorrow.

Francis Xavier Trujillo

Multilingual classrooms are multicultural classrooms. They are classrooms characterized by cultural and linguistic diversity. Teaching effectively in a multilingual classroom means creating a learning environment in which teachers promote English language development, provide full access to the core curriculum, and foster communication, collaboration, and critical thinking. In short, teachers provide the kind of instruction that enables students to empower themselves.

The intent of this text is to provide teachers and prospective teachers—elementary and secondary—with the basic knowledge and strategies required to work more effectively in classrooms that are multicultural *and* multilingual. Affirming the cultural and linguistic heritage of each individual is requisite, but alone it is not enough. Elementary teacher Winnie Porter reminds us of what it means to teach in today's multilingual classrooms: "The realities are that it's not just academics anymore—it's the whole child, and that means what *their* home is like, and *their* culture and their language" (quoted in Olsen & Mullen, 1990, 76). Teaching students from diverse ethnolinguistic backgrounds presents its own unique set of challenges and rewards. It is an increasingly important dimension of multicultural education for all classroom teachers.

This chapter begins by explaining why a focus on context, process, and content is central to the implementation of educational programs that empower language minority students. It goes on to present a rationale for focusing particular attention on language minority students within the framework of education that is multicultural, articulating primary goals for English language learners and identifying corresponding areas of teacher competency.

After completing this chapter, you will be able to

1. examine context, process, and content in relation to multilingual classrooms
2. examine basic assumptions underlying multicultural education for multilingual populations
3. identify related goals and teacher competencies

Context, Process, and Content

Context, process, and content are central dimensions in any discussion of education that is multicultural. As used in this text, they provide a tripartite framework for looking at education from a multicultural perspective—an approach that is powerful, conceptually sound, and yet intuitive for most teachers. As an organizing structure, context, process, and content encompass the most basic and critical areas of research and theory as well as practice. They facilitate an integrated examination of dynamic classroom, home, and community factors that influence the linguistic and academic development of language minority students. From a practical standpoint, teachers are accustomed to viewing classrooms in terms of context, process, and content. These dimensions are common to all classrooms, regardless of grade level or subject matter. To be effective, teaching must take each of these areas into account.

Context, process, and content have been addressed elsewhere in relation to multicultural education (Hernández, 1989, 1992). In this text, they are further developed with regard to multilingual populations. The sections that follow provide an overview.

Context

Shulman (1986) observes that teaching occurs within many contexts: individual, group, class, school, home, and community. Each is embedded within a larger context: individuals interact within groups, groups exist within classrooms, classrooms function within schools, and so on. As teachers and students operate within these multiple contexts, they are constantly "influenced by the larger contexts in which the class is embedded—the school, the community, the society, the culture" (Shulman, 1986, 20).

Understanding context is critical to understanding education. "We can only understand students and classroom practices in the context of the school, the school in the context of the community, and the community in the context of the culture and political economy of the United States and its relation to its neighbors" (Mehan, Trueba, & Underwood, 1985, 49). In the schooling of language minority students, the contexts outside are no less critical than those within the classroom.

Beyond the boundaries of the school, cultural background factors, particularly as they relate to home and family life, are among the most important. "As children begin to identify with the social world around them—their family, peers and community—their experience becomes embedded in an intricate web of cultural meanings and historical conditions" (Matute-Bianchi, 1985, 36). Within the home, for example, parents are central figures. Parental involvement in the educational process is almost "synonymous with *empowerment*" (Underwood, 1986, 124). Enhancing children's academic performance means bringing parents into the process effectively as real partners. This embraces a wide range of areas from family socialization patterns and literacy practices in the home to parental expectations and knowledge of the school system (see Hernández, 1992). These are just a few of the factors that Valdés refers to as "non-instructive features" of linguistic minority groups (1986).

Clearly, understanding the dynamics of multilingual classrooms requires that teachers regard the broader contexts that impact on their classrooms. For example, Sleeter and Grant (1991) advocate the bridging of academic knowledge with the cultural knowledge that students already possess. "Students who achieve and succeed in school experience a meshing or overlap between the knowledge taught in school and the knowledge that has personal meaning to them" (p. 51).

Process

In the classroom, context can be described in terms of both process and content. Classrooms are highly organized, social, and cultural learning environments. Within each classroom, social, interactional, and organizational processes provide the channels through which sociocultural factors influence students' academic performance and personal development. To influence the quality of schooling for language minority students in general and to provide optimal learning environments in particular, teachers must examine the dynamic processes that are central to classroom life (Hernández, 1992).

Classroom processes are those facets of teaching and learning that encompass interaction, organization, social aspects, and management (Shulman, 1986). Thus, process comprises the less formal and visible aspects of classroom life. These dimensions explain how and why individual students experience classroom life differently—why the meaning of certain classroom events is shared by all participants whereas others are interpreted in divergent ways based upon students' social, linguistic, and cultural backgrounds.

Interaction between teachers and students is one of the most critical features of the classroom learning environment. Classrooms are pervasive language environments in which "classroom dialogue . . . *is* the educational process, or, at least, the major part of it for most children" (Stubbs, 1976, 68). Current research focuses on the multiple manifestations of language in the classroom as a key to understanding social and cultural dimensions of teaching and learning (Hernández, 1992). For example, behaviors appropriate to the immigrant home may be misinterpreted or negatively perceived in the classroom setting (Valdés, 1986).

Interpersonal relationships are manifest through interaction in other aspects of the social context. As an example, teacher attitudes and expectations influence student perceptions and performance, and they are difficult to change. "It is not that we are mean people, way down deep, but that in fact the society has done such a good job of socializing us that we just brutally expect certain kinds of things and are thoroughly mystified by other kinds of things" (Valdés, 1986, 54). Changing the patterns that teachers use to interact with language minority students in different situations requires that teachers examine their actual experiences with students and the factors that influence these experiences.

The key to creating a climate conducive to high levels of performance is through interaction, social context, and organization (Hernández, 1992). In the final analysis, "it is in the classroom itself that the climate must be created to provide for the academic achievement of language minority students" (Chávez, 1985, 34).

Content

Content is the "substance" of teaching and of learning, for it is in and through content that teachers and students interact (Shulman, 1986). Content encompasses everything from subject matter, formal curriculum, and instructional methods and materials to the specific set of skills, processes, and understandings transmitted. "The content and the purposes for which it is taught are the very heart of the teaching-learning processes" (Shulman, 1986, 8). Content may be organized into lessons, units, semesters, or years. Conceptually, it may be presented as facts, concepts, principles, generalizations, and the like.

If language minority students are to succeed academically, attention must be focused on content. First and foremost, schools must provide all students full access to a quality education—quality in every sense of the term. Knowledge is power, and education, by definition, should empower.

> Knowledge helps us envision the contours and limits of our own existence, what is desirable and possible, and what actions might bring about those possibilities. Knowledge helps us examine relationships between what is ethical and what is desirable; it widens our experience; it provides analytic tools for thinking through questions, situations, and problems. Knowledge that empowers centers around the interests and aims of the prospective knower. Apart from the knower, knowledge has no intrinsic power; in interaction with the knower's desires and purposes, knowledge has meaning and power. (Sleeter & Grant, 1991, 50)

All students must have access to a curriculum that provides depth and breadth of knowledge, a curriculum that is also relevant, stimulating, and practical (Berliner, 1990; Underwood, 1986). Students will not be prepared to enter higher education and perform successfully without mastery over the contents of a curriculum that comprises many subjects, skills, and attitudes. Those who enter the work force upon graduation from high school will be inadequately prepared to perform successfully. Those who never finish high school will be at an even greater disadvantage.

Educators have observed that as contemporary classrooms become increasingly multilingual, approaches developed with the special needs of "prototypical" student populations in mind often fail to address the actual needs of large segments of learners (Underwood, 1986). Teachers need instructional strategies and techniques that work effectively with students from diverse linguistic and cultural backgrounds and in different situations. They also want better ways to evaluate both language development and subject matter competency in the second language. The treatment and delivery of content should adhere to the precepts of multicultural education. Curricular content and instructional materials need to provide multicultural perspectives that reflect the dynamic cultural pluralism that is a fact of life in multilingual classrooms. This includes but is not limited to groups defined by nationality, ethnicity, gender, age, socioeconomic status, religion, and so on. Instruction needs to facilitate communication and interaction with those from different cultures within the classroom and enhance connections with local neighborhoods and communities and beyond. In the process, instruction should validate the status of all students as capable learners.

Teaching effectively in multilingual classrooms requires an understanding of the dynamics of context, process, and content (Hernández, 1992). Outside the classroom, teachers must know how to connect with the homes and communities of their students. They also need to be able to use their knowledge of the linguistic and cultural milieu of their students in ways that enhance their educational experience. Whatever we teach, we are teachers of English. As such, "it is our responsibility to understand our own language and its interaction with other languages in the community" (Dauenhauer, 1980, 29). Within the multilingual classroom, teachers must strive to create optimal learning environments that provide all students with full access to the curriculum and a quality education.

Basic Assumptions

The concepts and strategies presented in this book are based upon a set of assumptions presented in *Multicultural Education: A Teacher's Guide to Content and Process* (Hernández, 1989, 9–12). These assumptions encompass the following premises:

- It is increasingly important for political, social, educational, and economic reasons to recognize that the United States is a culturally diverse society.
- Multicultural education is for all students.
- Multicultural education is synonymous with effective teaching.
- Teaching is a cross-cultural encounter.
- The educational system has not served all students equally well.
- Multicultural education is synonymous with educational innovation and reform.
- Next to parents, teachers are the single most important factor in the lives of children (Baker, 1983).
- Classroom interaction between teachers and students constitutes the major part of the educational process for most students (Stubbs, 1976).

Certain issues are particularly salient in multilingual classrooms and warrant special attention (Richard-Amato & Snow, 1992). In order to facilitate consideration of context, process, and content specific to multilingual classrooms, the original set of assumptions has been enhanced to include four additional premises.

Premise 1 *To achieve academically, students in multilingual classrooms need to develop high levels of language proficiency for both communicative and academic purposes.* First and foremost, language is for communication. All students must develop the functional language skills that enable them to meet basic social and personal needs through interaction with other people. However, language is also for academic purposes. It is inextricably linked to cognitive and academic development. To fully develop cognitive abilities, students need a command of language that allows them to deal with a full range of content and topics with appropriate fluency and accuracy. Achieving these outcomes requires that the language used in the classroom setting be contextualized, meaningful, and purposeful.

Premise 2 *The academic achievement of language minority students is contingent upon the interaction of sociocultural factors manifest in the context of home, school, and community.* Academic achievement reflects the sociocultural factors that characterize the contexts in which schooling takes place and the processes enacted within the classroom and between the home, school, and community. "If the voices of difference are to find a place in the everyday interactions of public schools, educators of bicultural students must create the conditions for all students to experience an ongoing process of culturally democratic life" (Darder, 1991, 101).

Premise 3 *Regular classroom teachers have a professional responsibility to meet the educational needs of all learners in multilingual classrooms.* Across the nation, multilingual classrooms are increasingly a reality. They are virtually the norm in many areas in states like California, Texas, New York, Florida, Illinois, New Mexico, Arizona, New Jersey, Massachusetts, and Minnesota. Services to students whose primary language is other than English are less than adequate in many schools. Title VII programs, for example, serve only a small fraction of second language learners. This means that regular classroom teachers have a critical role to play in creating learning environments sensitive to the linguistic, cultural, and social needs of students whose primary language is not English. If language minority students are to succeed academically, this is a responsibility that cannot be abdicated.

Knowledge and skills related to the schooling of language minority students must no longer remain the exclusive purview of specialists in English as a second language (ESL), English language development, and bilingual education. For a variety of reasons, many regular classroom teachers have been seemingly content to relegate responsibility for teaching language minority students to the "experts." Some openly resist class or course assignments designated for language minority students. Referring to teachers at the secondary level, Minicucci and Olsen (1993) describe patterns in which language minority students are increasingly segregated from their English-speaking peers: There is pressure "from mainstream content area teachers who don't *want* LEP [limited English proficient] students in their 'regular' classes" (p. 18).

As professionals, we can no longer tolerate the delegation of primary responsibility for the schooling of language minority students to a relative handful of teachers, however well prepared these teachers may be. Implementation of effective ESL and bilingual programs requires highly specialized professional preparation and the support of other teachers as well as administrators, parents, and community members. It makes no sense politically, socially, educationally, and economically not to provide regular classroom teachers with professional preparation that addresses teaching in multilingual classrooms. Meeting the needs of language minority students must be a responsibility shared by all educators.

Premise 4 *Regular classroom teachers can and do make a difference in the education of language minority students.* If English language learners are to succeed academically, regular classroom teachers must be better prepared to work with them. Bilingual and ESL programs cannot operate effectively in isolation, and teachers with specialized professional preparation cannot do it alone. "The pattern of content areas offered and not offered to LEP students varies greatly from school to school. Thus, a LEP student's access to particular subject matter is determined largely by what school he or she attends, and in many cases these students simply do not receive required core academic content courses" (Minicucci & Olsen, 1993, 18).

Through their efforts in and out of the classroom, regular classroom teachers can do a great deal to promote effective instruction for language minority students. A broad spectrum of strategies and techniques used in effective programs for language minority students are accessible to nonspecialists—regular classroom teachers and specialists in other areas such as media, reading, and special education. Administrators and counselors also benefit from familiarity with these concepts and approaches. The use of appropriate strategies and techniques requires a basic knowledge of language, culture, and pedagogy and a change in

Teachers who embrace cultural and linguistic diversity are really at the forefront of educational reform.

attitude. Their use by regular classroom teachers and others is intended to complement existing, effective bilingual and ESL programs. They are not a substitute for such programs.

Goals and Competencies

Teachers who make a positive difference in the schooling of second language learners have several things in common. First, they embrace cultural and linguistic diversity. Second, they have a clear view of the educational goals that will ultimately empower all of their students. Third, they are cognizant of the competencies and skills required to effectively teach English language learners.

Teachers who embrace cultural and linguistic diversity are really at the forefront of educational reform. As junior high school teacher Kate Duggan observes, the process of developing expertise is a reflective one:

> Most of us begin to teach as we were taught. And because nothing in our teacher training taught us otherwise, we model traditional teaching. . . . [W]hen I began teaching in an urban public school it simply didn't work. My first week I knew it wasn't working. My old discipline techniques didn't work. Trying to pour information into their heads, standing in front of the room talking at them just didn't work. I had to start all over. What should I do? The first test I gave, 82% of the kids in one class

Teaching, to be effective, must meet students' academic, linguistic, intellectual, social, and individual needs.

flunked. I went home and cried. I didn't know what to do. I began to realize it might have something to do with me and my teaching. I began asking questions of myself, of them. I began trying things and seeking new approaches. That's when I became a *real* teacher. (quoted in Olsen & Mullen, 1990, 61)

It is no surprise that constant questioning and searching about teaching is a common element among highly effective teachers of second language learners (Olsen & Mullen, 1990). Teachers' own words speak volumes about the challenges and rewards of working with second language learners. Listen to what high school teacher David Christiano has to say about the cultural and social dynamics involved:

So I think about it all the time—the positive aspects of racial and ethnic identity versus the degree of acculturation needed in order to survive together in a society. *How can we survive and be an integrated society and still retain the richness of our identities in a positive and not an exclusive way?* And that's what I try to find a way to do in my teaching. And it permeates what I do with my class. (quoted in Olsen & Mullen, 1990, 70).

A high school English teacher, Gayle Byrne, sums it up with this image of what she wants to do in her teaching: "to ensure that every child has the whole rainbow of crayons with which to draw their lives" (quoted in Olsen & Mullen, 1990, 97).

Four goals are basic to providing second language learners with the quality education to which they are legally entitled. The first is for students to develop a full range of oral and literacy proficiencies in English. The second is to ensure equal access to the core curriculum and promote the academic achievement of students to the highest level of their ability. The third is to foster critical thinking skills and the requisite feelings and attitudes that enable students to be thoughtful and productive individuals. The fourth is to facilitate the two-way acculturation process that Cortés (1991) defines as *multiculturation* and to support primary language development in ways that are feasible and appropriate.

The primary purpose of this book is to help classroom teachers in multilingual settings develop the competencies needed to provide an effective educational program for English language learners—that is, to achieve the four basic goals just stated. Through the framework provided by context, process, and content, this book addresses the major areas identified as most important by teachers in the field (Olsen & Mullen, 1990). These are language development, curriculum (academic content), climate, and culture. Included within these areas are the following important characteristics:

an understanding of
- current methods and approaches used to promote second language development and their underlying theoretical assumptions
- processes involved in the development of communicative and literacy skills in a second language
- the interrelationship of factors—psychological, social, cultural, and educational—in the process of second language acquisition and their effect on academic achievement

the ability to
- evaluate, develop, and modify instructional materials to meet the needs of second language learners
- develop a curriculum that integrates language development, critical thinking, and content
- develop a curriculum that includes literature and materials from diverse cultures
- promote high expectations of student performance

skills in
- using instructional strategies and techniques that promote English language development
- adapting content area instruction to facilitate cognitive development
- building lessons based on student experiences
- dealing with issues related to cultural awareness, ethnicity, prejudice, respect, and racism

_____ **Summary**

Context, process, and content are central to the creation of classroom environments in which the unique abilities of each learner are fully developed. Creating such learning environments requires a commitment to embracing diversity—an affirmation of the linguistic and cultural heritage of each individual—and knowing how to enable students to empower themselves. It also entails a clear understanding of the educational goals that are especially critical for learners whose primary language is not English. These include development of a full range of oral and literacy proficiencies; development of critical thinking, communicative, and collaborative skills; and academic achievement through full access to the core curriculum.

Teaching, to be effective, must meet the academic, linguistic, intellectual, social, and individual needs of all students in culturally and linguistically diverse classrooms. It must enable students to experience education in the fullest sense of the term, to be enriched through "the formation of habits of judgment and the development of character, the elevation of standards, the facilitation of understanding, the development of taste and discrimination, the stimulation of curiosity and wondering, the fostering of style and a sense of beauty, the growth of a thirst for new ideas and visions of the yet unknown" (Scheffler, cited in Bracey, 1993, 110).

References

Baker, G. C. (1983). Planning and organizing for multicultural instruction. Reading, MA: Addison-Wesley.

Berliner, D. (1990). *Research on teaching: Insight and promising direction*. Lecture, California State University, Chico.

Bracey, G. W. (1993). The third Bracey report on the condition of public education. *Phi Delta Kappan, 75*(2), 104–117.

Chávez, R. (1985). Classroom learning environments. In H. Mehan, H. Trueba, & C. Underwood (Eds.), *Proceedings of the Linguistic Minority Project Conference: Vol. 1. Schooling language minority youth* (pp. 33–35). Lake Tahoe, CA: University of California Linguistic Project.

Cortés, C. E. (1991). E pluribus unum: Out of many one. *California perspectives: An anthology from the immigrant students project* (Vol. 1, pp. 13–16). San Francisco: California Tomorrow.

Darder, A. (1991). *Culture and power in the classroom: A critical foundation for bilingual education*. New York: Bergin & Garvey.

Dauenhauer, R. L. (1980). *Conflicting visions in Alaskan education* (Occasional Paper No. 3). Fairbanks: Center for Cross-Cultural Studies, University of Alaska.

Hernández, H. (1989). *Multicultural education: A teacher's guide to content and process*. Upper Saddle River, NJ: Merrill/Prentice Hall.

Hernández, H. (1992). The language minority student and multicultural education. In C. A. Grant (Ed.), *Research and multicultural education: From the margins to the mainstream* (pp. 141–152). London: Falmer Press.

Matute-Bianchi, E. (1985). Cultural membership and school achievement. In H. Mehan, H. Trueba, & C. Underwood (Eds.), *Proceedings of the Linguistic Minority Project Conference: Vol. 1. Schooling language minority youth* (pp. 36–38). Lake Tahoe, CA: University of California Linguistic Project.

Mehan, H., Trueba, H., & Underwood, C. (Eds.). (1985). *Proceedings of the Linguistic Minority Project Conference: Vol. 1. Schooling language minority youth*. Lake Tahoe, CA: University of California Linguistic Project.

Minicucci, C., & Olsen, L. (1993). Caught unawares: California secondary schools confront the immigrant student challenge. *Multicultural Education, 1*(2), 16–19, 38.

Olsen, L., & Mullen, N. A. (1990). *Embracing diversity* (California Tomorrow Immigrant Students Project Research Report). San Francisco: California Tomorrow.

Richard-Amato, P. A., & Snow, M. A. (Eds.). (1992). *The multicultural classroom: Readings for content-area teachers*. White Plains, NY: Longman.

Shulman, L. (1986). Paradigms and research programs in the study of teaching: A contemporary perspective. In M. C. Wittrock (Ed.), *Handbook of research on teaching* (3rd ed., pp. 3–36). New York: Macmillan.

Sleeter, C. E., & Grant, C. A. (1991). Mapping terrains of power: Student cultural knowledge versus classroom knowledge. In C. E. Sleeter (Ed.), *Empowerment through multicultural education* (pp. 49–67). Albany: State University of New York Press.

Stubbs, M. (1976). *Language, schools and classrooms*. London: Methuen.

Underwood, C. (Ed.). (1986). *Proceedings of the Linguistic Minority Project Conference: Vol. 2. Schooling language minority youth* (pp. 102–108, 124). Berkeley: University of California Linguistic Minority Project.

Valdés, G. (1986). Individual background factors related to the schooling of language minority students, session 2 and open forum 2. In C. Underwood (Ed.), *Proceedings of the Linguistic Minority Project Conference, Vol. 2. Schooling language minority youth* (pp. 34–59). Lake Tahoe, CA: University of California Linguistic Minority Project.

P A R T

2 Context

2

The Societal Context

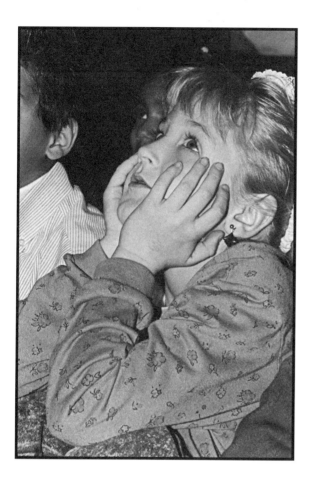

Teachers realize we are America's future; they want to teach us the best they can.

High school student

Multilingual classrooms are characterized by the presence of students for whom English is not the primary language. They reflect the cultural, ethnic, and linguistic diversity that has been the hallmark of this nation. Many people do not realize how significant a proportion of our entire population is bilingual or even multilingual. According to the Census Bureau, "one in seven U.S. residents speaks a language other than English at home. . . . That's 31.8 million people" (Elam, Rose, & Gallup, 1993, 146).

This chapter begins by providing a general description of the student populations that make multilingual classrooms linguistically and culturally diverse. As is evident in the sections that follow, there is more to the picture of linguistic, ethnic, and cultural diversity than numbers. We will begin by looking more closely at the demographics of our multilingual population in general and by major groupings. After doing so, attention is directed toward profiling our immigrant and refugee populations and examining societal perceptions on linguistic diversity.

After completing this chapter, you will be able to

1. recognize the rich linguistic, cultural, and ethnic diversity of our language minority student population
2. identify major issues facing different ethnolinguistic communities
3. characterize recent immigration patterns
4. consider different perspectives on linguistic diversity

Linguistic and Ethnic Diversity

The profile of cultural and linguistic diversity in our nation is striking and dynamic. There are two primary sources of multilinguality in the United States (Waggoner, 1988). The first comprises populations speaking languages other than English originally living in territories later acquired by the United States (e.g., Native Americans, Hispanics, Hawaiians, some French). The second is voluntary immigration (e.g., immigrants, refugees, unofficial immigrants).

The growth of multilingualism in recent decades is clearly evident in data from the 1990 census. The largest non-English language groups in the United States, according to government figures, are given in Table 2-1.

What do we know about people who speak languages other than English in their homes? Waggoner's (1993) analysis of the 1990 census data reveals some interesting information. For example:

• The majority of persons who speak a language other than English at home are native born, not immigrants.

• Spanish speakers comprise almost half of those speaking non-English languages; over 1 million people speak Chinese languages, French, German, and Italian.

Table 2-1   The largest non-English language groups in the United States

Language	1990 population
Arabic	355,000
Chinese languages	1,319,000
French	1,930,000
German	1,548,000
Greek	388,000
Hungarian	148,000
Italian	1,309,000
Japanese	428,000
Korean	626,000
Polish	723,000
Portuguese	431,000
Russian	242,000
Spanish	17,345,000
Vietnamese	507,000
Yiddish	213,000
Other	4,333,000
Total	31,845,000

Source: *Numbers and Needs*, cited in *NCBE Forum* (March, 1993, 4)

- Between 1980 and 1990, the most dramatic growth in numbers was in Asian immigrant languages such as Vietnamese, Thai, Lao, Korean, and Chinese.

- Geographically, there were at least 300,000 home speakers of non-English languages in 18 states, 8.6 million in California alone.

- Among the school-age population, 1.9 million students in California speak a non-English language at home; almost 1 million students in Texas and about 700,000 in New York do the same.

- Among the school-age population, 6.3 million students are home speakers of non-English languages. These children and adolescents now represent one in seven students and the proportion is increasing.

It is difficult to generate accurate data as to the actual number of K–12 students in U.S. schools who speak a language other than English. First, definitions of what constitutes an "English language learner"—be it under this term or another—vary considerably. In 1980, for example, identification procedures differed to such an extent that estimates ranged from 1.7 to 5.3 million students (*Numbers and Needs*, cited in *NCBE Forum*, 1993). Second, the disproportionate undercounting of minorities and undocumented immigrants is responsible for other errors in the data (Waggoner, 1993). In addition, figures reported by school districts to state and federal agencies fail to include enrollments in private schools and counts of those students who are not enrolled.

Students who are Native American, Hispanic, Asian Pacific American, African American, or members of other groups comprise a dynamic and complex ethnolinguistic mosaic.

Major Ethnolinguistic Groups

In communities across the nation, the ethnolinguistic picture that emerges is one of great diversity. The challenge facing educators today is one of adding English to students' linguistic repertoire while supporting full development of the primary language within the home and community and, whenever possible, in the classroom. The sections that follow highlight some of the issues that confront major ethnic groups.

Native Americans

First among the ethnic languages are those of the Native American peoples. At the time the Europeans arrived, more than 500 languages were spoken in North America by the resident population (Lawrence, 1978, 314). These people included more than a million Native Americans—Apache, Navajo, Kickapoo, Cheyenne, Pawnee, Crow, Comanche, Washo, Natchez, Arawak, Taino, Carib, Chickasaw, Choctaw, Cherokee, Creek, Shawnee, Lenni Lenape, Mohegan, Ottawa, Cayuga, Mohawk, Delaware, Seneca, and others—living in the area now defined as the continental United States (Castellanos, 1992). These North American estimates would be larger if Alaska Natives were included. When Alaska was purchased from Russia by the United States, more than 99% of its population comprised Tlingit, Haida, and Athabascan Indians; Yup'ik, Chugach, and Inupiat Eskimos; Aleuts; and Creoles. "As late as 1880, the United States Census estimated that of a total population of 33,426, only 430 whites [were living] in the Territory" (Alaska Federation of Natives, 1989, 69). To put the numbers of Native Americans in perspective, Thornton estimates the pre-Columbian population of the United States at over 5 million while Dobyns suggests that there were 18 million people in the region north of Mexico (cited in Lomawaima, 1995).

The contemporary profile of Native Americans is still characterized by diversity. Lomawaima (1995) cites figures indicating that 510 tribes are currently recognized by the federal government, including at least 200 Alaska Native villages. Native American communities reflect tremendous linguistic, religious, geographic, historic, and economic diversity. "Native people are not all the same. A fluent member of a Cherokee Baptist congregation living in Tahlequah, Oklahoma, is different from an English-speaking powwow-dancing Lakota born and raised in Oakland, California, who is different from a Hopi fluent in Hopi, English, Navajo, and Spanish who lives on the reservation and supports her family by selling 'traditional' pottery in New York, Santa Fe, and Scottsdale galleries. The idea of being generically 'Indian' really was a figment of Columbus's imagination" (p. 332).

For educators, this diversity of cultures, languages, and experiences means that approaches and strategies are unlikely to be generalizable across Native American peoples (Lomawaima, 1995). To be appropriate and relevant, content, curriculum, and methods must be developed locally, so that they meet the needs of children in poor urban schools as well as those in tribal homelands. Research on Indian education reveals multiple challenges. These include the need to (a) address drop-out rates that are disproportionately high, (b) develop classroom materials and methods that are culturally relevant and appropriate to learning and interactional styles, and (c) deal with language policy and renewal (Lomawaima, 1995).

As an example, many Native American languages are endangered. As late as 1978, there were 250 Native American languages (Lawrence, 1978). More recent estimates are lower. "For the whole USA and Canada together, . . . of 187 languages, I calculate that 149 are no longer being learned by children; that is, of the Native North American languages still spoken, 80% are moribund" (Kraus, cited in Hinton, 1992, 25). California has more endangered languages than any other area, for 90 to 95 % of the native languages in California are "no longer learned by children" (Hinton, 1992, 25). The challenges of language maintenance and renewal are a concern in many communities "as truly fluent speakers grow fewer and older, and younger generations grow up inundated by the constant English chatter transmitted via cable, satellite dish, and videos" (Lomawaima, 1995, 341).

Despite the difficulties, there are many efforts within Native American homes, communities, and beyond to reverse this trend by those committed to teaching, learning, and recording native languages. These include advocacy for bilingual-bicultural education programs and educational development efforts involving linguists and speakers of native languages with advanced graduate degrees (Hinton, 1992; Lawrence, 1978). Technology-assisted solutions are also being explored (Berg & Ohler, 1990).

Hispanic Americans

From the time the Spanish arrived, first in Puerto Rico and then Florida, across the Southwest and beyond, Hispanics established a strong cultural, political, economic, social, and linguistic presence in the United States. Currently, the United States ranks among the world's nations with the largest Spanish-speaking populations, with Hispanics comprising almost 10% of the total population (Leadership Education for Asian Pacifics [LEAP], 1992). García's (1995, 374) synthesis of Hispanic demographics reveals that the 18.8 million Hispanics in the United States are distributed as follows:

ORIGIN	NUMBER (MILLIONS)	PERCENT
Mexico	11.8	62.8
Puerto Rico	2.3	12.2
Central and South America	2.1	11.2
Cuba	1.0	5.3
Other	1.6	8.5

Over 80% of all Hispanics reside in eight states: Arizona, California, Colorado, Florida, Illinois, New Mexico, New York, and Texas. Approximately 200,000 Hispanics immigrate to the United States legally every year and estimates are that a similar number immigrate illegally (García, 1995, 374).

Linguistically, 11 million Hispanics report that they speak Spanish at home (García, 1995, 374). However, among immigrants as well as native born, the pattern of English acquisition and subsequent language shift from Spanish to English is striking ("The Veltman Report," cited in Nicolau & Valdivieso, 1992). Of those who arrive in the United States before the age of 14, more than half make English their usual, everyday language. By the time immigrants have lived in the United States for 15 years, three out of four use English on a regular daily basis. Most children of immigrant parents—70%—become English speakers for all practical purposes. Their children, in turn, learn English as their first language. According to Nicolau and Valdivieso, this shift to English is accelerated in urban areas, slower in rural settings. (For a methodological critique of the Veltman study, see Waggoner, 1989.)

The data on academic underachievement are revealing and troubling. Nieto (1995) reports that the United States spends less money on the education of Latino students than on any other group. Of all Hispanic students, 85% live in urban districts and 70% attend segregated schools. "Hispanic children reside primarily in central city, metropolitan, and rural areas in highly populated pockets of racial and ethnic segregation" (Kozol, cited in García, 1995, 375).

Forty percent of all Hispanics leave school before graduation, and over one third (35%) are retained at least once while in school. Puerto Ricans claim the "dubious distinction" of being among the most undereducated ethnic groups in the United States (Nieto, 1995, 388). Nieto identifies the drop-out rate as "the major educational dilemma facing the Puerto Rican community" (p. 388). Mexican Americans and other Hispanic groups share similar concerns. Except for Native Americans, Latinos are more likely than other minority groups to be retained one, two, or more grades and to drop out before completing high school (Nieto, 1995). Students' ability to understand the language of instruction has been a long-standing issue for Puerto Ricans, Mexican Americans, and other Hispanics. For example, after Spain ceded Puerto Rico to the United States following the Spanish-American War in 1898, the children of Puerto Ricans were almost immediately mandated by Congress to learn the English language and adopt American culture. "No doubt contributing to the early drop-out crisis were practices such as placing students behind their peers or in 'special' classes (such as those for the mentally retarded or slow learners) because they were Spanish speaking" (Sánchez Korrol, cited in Nieto, 390).

For Puerto Ricans and Mexican Americans, key elements in educational reforms designed to promote equal educational opportunity for Hispanic students strike similar themes. For Puerto Ricans, bilingual education, family and community involvement, cultural and linguistic maintenance, and reevaluation of school policies and practices are at the forefront (Nieto, 1995). These are not unlike the implications emerging from analysis of theory, research, policy, and practice on educating Mexican American students (García, 1995). Development of full proficiency in English and maintenance of the primary language are paramount. Equally critical are high expectations for academic achievement and programmatic adjustments sensitive to individual and cultural differences.

Asian and Pacific Islander Americans*

Historical accounts dating back to the Ch'i dynasty indicate that the first Asian to reach America was Hwui Shan, a Chinese priest, who in 498 A.D. sailed down the Pacific coast, and spent 40 years among Native American peoples (LEAP, 1991a, 1). Today the Asian Pacific American population—comprising almost 30 major ethnic groups—is the fastest growing group in the United States, with a projected increase of over 400% between 1990 and 2050 (LEAP, 1992, 2). Over the last decade, California, New York, New Jersey, and Pennsylvania experienced a growth rate of over 100% in the Asian Pacific American school-age population (Pang, 1995, 412).

Asian Pacific American demographics reflect considerable diversity and substantial growth. For example:

• In 1990, the five largest Asian ethnic groups were Chinese, and then Filipino, Japanese, Asian Indian, and Korean. By the end of the decade, predictions indicate that the largest groups will be Filipino, then Chinese, Vietnamese, Korean, Asian Indian, and Japanese (LEAP, 1991a, 8–9; 1992, 3). Also desig-

---

*As used by the U.S. government, "Asian and Pacific Islander" is a term that encompasses 59 ethnic groups from Bangladeshi to Yapese (LEAP, 1991b).

nated as Asian Pacific Americans are people belonging to smaller groups, such as those of Hawaiian, Guamanian, Samoan, Cambodian, Hmong, Laotian, Indonesian, Bangladeshi, Burmese, Indochinese, Javanese, Singaporean, and Sri Lankan heritage (Pang, 1995).

- By the year 2020, more than half of the Asian Pacific American population will be foreign born. This is expected to hold true for Pacific Asian American ethnic groups—Chinese, Korean, Asian Indian, Filipino, Vietnamese—except Japanese Americans (LEAP, 1993, 3).

- The Asian Pacific American school-age population is now estimated at around 1.7 million students (Kiang & Lee, cited in Pang, 1995, 412). For more than half of these children, the first language they bring to school is not English (Trueba et al., cited in Pang, 1995, 415).

- Pang (1995) notes that students of mixed parentage (e.g., Asian Pacific American, Asian Latino Americans, Asian Black Americans, Asian Native Americans) should also be acknowledged, for interracial marriages date back centuries, "since the first Filipino immigrants made Louisiana their home in 1763 and wed outside their ethnic community" (Cordova, cited in Pang, 1995, 412).

A number of language and educational factors make Asian Pacific Americans such a diverse and complex population, among which are students' place of birth (i.e., U.S. born or immigrant), intragroup conflicts, socialization practices, and language differences (Pang, 1995). For example, the degree of cultural assimilation into mainstream society and the extent to which students identify along ethnic lines are influenced by whether they were born in the United States or migrated for economic or political reasons. "The longer Asian Pacific Americans live in the United States, the stronger is a shift toward a bicultural existence, especially in young people" (p. 415). Students often experience conflict with members of other ethnic groups as well as with those within the Asian Pacific American population itself. Intragroup conflict may stem from animosities or social class differences traced back to the "old country." It is also attributed to fear of being mistakenly identified as an immigrant and ascribed the status of a foreigner, or from a lack of understanding the language, culture, and beliefs of other students. Teachers cannot assume that native born students of the same ethnic background as immigrant students will automatically make ideal "buddies" for newcomers. Rather, Pang suggests that teachers ask students to volunteer for the role, thus reducing the potential for conflict when students are not comfortable taking on the responsibility.

The languages spoken by Asian Pacific Americans are as diverse as the people (Pang, 1995). They derive from five distinct language roots and differ phonetically, grammatically, and structurally. Written forms may employ Chinese characters or ideographs or use a Romanized alphabet. Languages may be monosyllabic (e.g., Laotian) or polysyllabic (e.g., Japanese). In contrast with English, they may be tonal languages in which speakers listen for differences in tone that convey differences in the meaning of words (e.g., Cantonese).

Socialization practices and the role of parental support in academic achievement are other critical factors for educators working with Asian Pacific American students (Pang, 1995). On the positive side, for many students, perceptions of parental support and the desire to please parents are predictive of academic performance. On the down side, within some groups, the pressure of parental expectations that children perform exceptionally well may heighten test anxiety among high-achieving students while negatively affecting the self-concept and self-esteem of those who are not academically inclined. Issues will vary across as well as within groups. In some groups, for example, parents are likely to assume a very active role in providing training at home to compensate for what they regard as limitations in the academic preparation their children receive at school. Within other groups, however, parents may have only limited familiarity with school policies, practices, and culture.

In the final analysis, as with other groups, the strengths and needs of Asian Pacific American students are complex and varied. "Understanding the great diversity among Asian Pacific Americans is crucial. . . . Creation of alternatives in curriculum, policies, materials, counseling, and instructional strategies demands a change in the educators' attitudes toward, and knowledge of, Asian Pacific American students" (Pang, 1995, 423).

African Americans

In their analysis of historical and sociocultural influences on African American education, Lee and Slaughter-Defoe (1995) observe that "any discussion of African American education within a multicultural context must use as a primary filter the implications of African American cultural knowledge, values, and language" (p. 357). As with all groups, the cultural context for learning is critical. African American families and communities are characterized by a diversity of Caribbean, Latin American, African, and African American experiences. For educators, this variety in linguistic, cultural, and social experiences means that educational environments within each community are different, and that approaches to policies and practice are varied. Moreover, in the years to come, the diversity of these communities is likely to increase even further as growing numbers of African American children are schooled with other student populations (Lee & Slaughter-Defoe, 1995).

Research studies since 1980 reveal major concerns in African American education with regard to disproportionate retention, drop-out and suspension rates; disproportionate and inappropriate representation in special education programs; and inequitable resource allocations (Lee & Slaughter-Defoe, 1995). Teacher quality, behavior, expectations, and interaction patterns are also recurring themes. Clearly, consideration of the complex factors influencing the academic achievement of African American children needs to include culture, language, and literacy.

In response to the problems created by the traditional emphasis schooling has placed on cultural assimilation over cultural heritage, many contemporary approaches designed to improve the education of African American students draw upon a strong cultural foundation (Lee & Slaughter-Defoe, 1995). Practices reflective of this cultural paradigm stress cultural solidarity, community self-reliance, and greater incorporation of cultural knowledge, practices, and values in the educational process. Language is an important part of this paradigm.

In addition to the many languages other than English represented within this group, many African Americans speak a variety of English referred to as Black English, African American English, or African American Language (Lee & Slaughter-Defoe, 1995; LeMoine, 1993). There are standard and vernacular forms. Although standard Black English is closer syntactically to standard English than the vernacular, both varieties share common characteristics of phonology, intonation, and modes of discourse such as call and response, signification, tonal semantics, and narrative sequencing (Smitherman et al., cited in Lee & Slaughter-Defoe, 1995, 357).

Despite the primacy of language in communication and the construction of knowledge, research on the implications of Black English for teaching and learning is limited (Lee & Slaughter-Defoe, 1995). With respect to literacy, for example, we know that there is no substantive support for claims that use of Black English interferes with learning to read (Hall & Guthrie, cited in Lee & Slaughter-Defoe, 1995). We also know that teachers can effectively draw upon the strengths of Black English (e.g., expository structure, topic-associative narrative) to enhance literacy and academic competence. To date, however, insights drawn from the research on different language varieties and their impact on teaching and learning have not significantly influenced instruction at the classroom level (Lee, cited in Lee & Slaughter-Defoe, 1995).

Within our society, we ascribe relatively higher or lower status to language varieties, and Black English (especially the vernacular variety) is generally regarded as less prestigious (Lee & Slaughter-Defoe, 1995). This has educational implications. For children whose primary language is Black English, there are indications that the kind of natural language learning climate most typically associated with instruction for language minority students is best. As an example, LeMoine (1993) argues that many African American students born into homes where African American language is spoken enter kindergarten with limited proficiency in mainstream American English. "Because of the rule-governed linguistic differences between the two communication systems, these students will need to acquire mastery of mainstream American English as a second language" (LeMoine, 1993). Along similar lines, Farr advocates that schools emphasize bidialectism or bilingualism and biculturalism in responding to the powerful bonds that exist between linguistic competence, social competence in a given community, and self-concept (cited in Lee & Slaughter-Defoe, 1995).

Other Ethnolinguistic Groups

This picture of linguistic diversity would not be complete without recognizing that many other groups also contribute to the nation's multilingual mosaic. The largest non-English language groups were identified earlier in Table 2-1. In addition, the United States is home to many persons speaking other languages such as Persian (202,000), French Creole (188,000), Armenian (150,000), Hungarian (148,000), and Dutch (143,000), to name a few* (U.S. Dept. of Commerce, 1995, 53). A look at immigration figures by country of birth for 1971 to 1993 reveals a broad spectrum of coun-

---

*Figures include individuals 5 years old and over.

tries not represented within the major categories discussed previously. These include but are not limited to immigrants from countries such as Armenia, Azerbaijan, Belarus, France, Germany, Greece, Iran, Iraq, Israel, Italy, Jordan, Lebanon, Moldova, Poland, Portugal, Romania, Russia, Syria, Turkey, Ukraine, Uzbekistan, and the former Yugoslavia (U.S. Dept. of Commerce, 1995, 11). These figures also reveal striking differences in the regional distribution of ancestry groups. For example, the Northeast is home to more people of French Canadian, Greek, Hungarian, Italian, Lithuanian, Portuguese, Russian, Slovak, and Ukrainian ancestry than any other region. The Midwest boasts the largest numbers of persons of Croatian, Czech, Dutch, Finnish, German, Norwegian, Swedish, and Swiss heritage, while the South attracts more with French backgrounds. Finally, the West is most popular among those who are Danish, Scandinavian, and Yugoslavian (U.S. Dept. of Commerce, 1995, 53).

Newspaper accounts from across the country indicate that the educational issues facing these groups are as diverse as the groups themselves. For some ethnolinguistic groups, language and religion are closely intertwined. For example, "most recent [Muslim] Arab immigrants [largely Palestinian in Lakewood, Ohio] insist that only Arabic be spoken at home because they want their children to retain their cultural heritage and the language of their Muslim religion" (Fuetsch, 1995, 19A).

As with other groups, there are differential patterns of academic achievement. Immigration from Eastern Europe and the former Soviet Union has increased significantly since 1988, with many of the newcomers settling in New York, California, Illinois, and Florida (Millar, 1996, 29). Of the 7,200 students in New York City's program for English language learners, Russian ranks third behind Spanish and Chinese as the pupils' most common primary language. There are anecdotal accounts that suggest that many of these students are doing well. There is also some concern that these students may be stereotyped as a new "model" minority:

> Across the country, teachers and school administrators report that some of the highest intellectual honors—National Merit Scholarships, science awards, math competitions and chess championships—are being scooped up by immigrants from Eastern Europe and the former Soviet Union. The students, teachers say, also tend to get top grades in subjects like English literature and American history. (Millar, 1996, 29)

In the final analysis, cultural, ethnic, and linguistic diversity are more than an American tradition. They are part of a larger global reality in which only a few relatively small countries can be described as truly unilingual. Crawford (1992) puts this multilingual heritage into perspective when he observes that

> not a single major power lacks for minority tongues. Multilingualism is the norm, not the exception, for the simple reason that languages greatly outnumber human societies. In a world with approximately 160 national flags and some 6,000 languages, the odds weigh heavily against unilingualism. (p. 238)

Immigration

Today's multilingual classrooms are a reflection of migration trends on a global scale. World migration is increasing at a magnitude unprecedented in history.

"From 1989 to 1992, the number of people living outside their country of origin doubled, from 50 million to 100 million" ("The Global Migration," 1993, 19). Overall, the foreign-born population in the United States was just under 8% in 1993. By comparison, it was around 23% in Australia, nearly 16% in Canada, and about 8.5% in Germany (U.S. Dept. of Commerce, 1995, 850). The 1993 United Nations Population Fund report indicates that most migrants are escaping poverty, violence, drought, and environmental destruction. Almost half are women.

In the 1980s, estimates indicate that 7,338,000 legal immigrants entered the United States. Estimates of undocumented immigrants are more problematic. For example, reporting on a 1992 study commissioned by the California state legislature, Minicucci and Olsen (1993) note that "an estimated 70% of the immigrants in California are undocumented. For students, this means fear, legal and economic pressures, and transiency" (p. 17). The Bureau of the Census estimates the undocumented population at between 3.5 and 4 million people* (U.S. Dept. of Commerce, 1995, 12).

Nationwide, demographic patterns reveal that the wave of immigration that began in the late sixties and extends into the present is different from those that preceded it (Kellogg, 1988). First, this latest immigration is one of the largest in our history. The number of immigrants has dramatically increased in the eighties and well into the nineties. Second, this wave of immigration comes largely from Asia (e.g., Vietnam, the Philippines, Korea, China, India, Laos, Cambodia, and Japan) and Latin America (e.g., Mexico, El Salvador, Guatemala, Nicaragua, and Honduras). Third, unlike earlier waves of immigration, relatively few of the new immigrants (in the period since 1960) come from Europe. Finally, settlement patterns reflect high concentrations of immigrants in certain areas, minimal settlement in others. Eighty percent of the immigrants have settled in 10 states. This helps to account for the fact that half of the nation's population growth in the 1980s was in California, Texas, and Florida.

In analyzing the demographic characteristics of the immigrant population, Kellogg emphasizes youth, linguistic diversity, and educational background. As a group, immigrants are younger than the U.S. population as a whole (Walker, cited in Kellogg, 1988). The median age for selected immigrant groups illustrates this point. Southeast Asians are among the youngest. The median age is 13 for Hmong immigrants, 18 for Cambodians, 19 for Laotians, and 21 for Vietnamese. Hispanic immigrants are also young, with the average age for Mexicans estimated to be 23; for Dominicans, 26; and Central Americans, 27. Among other immigrant groups, the median age is 27 for Jamaicans, 29 for Haitians, and 39 for Cubans. That immigrants are younger has important implications for the educational system. Immigrants are coming during their "prime working and child-bearing years" (p. 202). The fact that a significant proportion of new immigrants is of school age suggests that educators must be prepared to address both short- and long-term needs.

The linguistic diversity reflected in recent immigration patterns is also striking (Kellogg, 1988). In the past, the languages of many immigrants shared common features with English, such as Latin roots, a Roman alphabet, and literary

---

*These figures include immigrants who became residents before 1982, those who entered the country illegally, and nonimmigrant overstays.

traditions. Today, major immigrant groups speak languages whose linguistic origins are totally different from English, languages that do not share the alphabet used in our schools (e.g., Cambodian, Laotian, Thai). Until recently, some languages (e.g., Haitian Creole and Hmong) did not have written forms.

There are also tremendous variations among immigrant groups in terms of educational levels (Kellogg, 1988). The educational levels of many new immigrants—Filipino, Haitian, and Vietnamese, for example—surpasses those of previous groups (Walker, cited in Kellogg, 1988). While significant numbers of recent immigrants already have some literacy skills in English when they arrive in the United States, others are illiterate even in their native language.

Perceptions of Diversity

As the demographic data demonstrate, linguistic diversity is a reality in our nation. Within our society, how it is perceived differs widely. Some consider cultural and linguistic diversity as a problem. Others see it as a right. Still others regard the richness of our cultural and linguistic mosaic as a resource. How linguistic diversity is perceived makes a difference in language planning, education, and many other areas. Ruíz (1988) has identified three different orientations toward linguistic diversity: "language-as-problem," "language-as-right," and "language-as-resource." Which of these views best describes your perspective?

The language-as-problem orientation stems in part from the association of linguistic diversity with disadvantage, most especially poverty, handicap, limited social mobility, and low educational achievement. The sorts of programs designed in the 1960s to address socially undesirable conditions treated language as an underlying problem. Thus, the Bilingual Education Act (BEA) of 1968 and the state statutes on bilingual education that have followed start with the assumption that non-English language groups have a handicap to overcome. "The BEA, after all, was conceived and formulated in conjunction with the War on Poverty. Resolution of this problem—teaching English, even at the expense of the first language—became the objective of school programs now generally referred to as transitional bilingual education" (Ruíz, 1988, 7).

Over time, this "connection of non-English language heritage and bilingualism with social problems has become entrenched in popular thought" (p. 7). This view is inherent in federal and state legislation. The "original BEA made poverty a requirement for eligibility in bilingual programs, and although this was dropped in the 1974 version, it remains a popular notion that bilingual education is for the poor and disadvantaged" (p. 9). The association of language and language diversity with social problems is also manifest in the widely held belief that "multilingualism leads ultimately to a lack of social cohesiveness; with everyone speaking their own language, political and social consensus is impossible" (p. 10). Diversity, however, does not, in and of itself, imply disunity (Ruíz, 1988).

This orientation contrasts markedly with the language-as-right orientation. From this second perspective, language issues are equated with issues of civil and minority rights and, in the schools, with instruction in the mother tongue. "It is essential that for short term protections and long term guarantees, we be able to translate the interests of language-minority groups into rights-language" (Ruíz, 1988, 12–13). One outcome of the legal process has been to introduce legalistic language (e.g., compliance, enforcement, entitlements, requirements, protection) and attitudes that result in a confrontational posture that alienates segments of the public. "This atmosphere creates a situation in which different groups and authorities invoke their rights against each other: children vs. schools; parents vs. school boards; majority vs. minority groups; some minority groups vs. others; state rights vs. federal authority; and so on" (p. 13). Gains in some districts are tempered by responses in others that take the form of noncompliance and legal manipulation. Federal regulations are often disregarded with impunity.

The third orientation, language as resource, recognizes the nation's deficiency in language capability. "Not only are we not developing language skills in the population to any great extent; we are doing almost nothing to encourage non-English language maintenance" (Ruíz, 1988, 15). Arguments from this position favor development of the nation's multilingual capacity. These include international capabilities (e.g., military preparedness, national security, diplomacy, global economic interdependence, international communications) as well as social and educational benefits (e.g., enhancing conceptual skills, cross-cultural awareness, intergroup relations). When language is seen as a resource to be developed and conserved, perceptions of language minority communities change as they become sources of valued expertise. This, in turn, contributes to "greater social cohesion and cooperation" (p. 17).

The view of language as a valued resource underscores the need to promote development of the nation's multilingual capacity.

In the final analysis, how teachers regard the language diversity they see in the classroom will be conveyed to students through the way they deal with context, process, and content. Will your students see their languages as a problem, a right, or a resource? What message will you convey?

Summary

Since their inception, schools in the United States have served students whose primary language is not English (Kloss, 1977). Millions of children and adolescents—native and foreign born—have shared in this experience. They continue to do so today in considerable numbers. Demographic patterns suggest that the current wave of immigration is different from those earlier in our history. This wave of immigration is one of the largest. Highly concentrated, it is primarily from Asia and Latin America. In addition, there are significant numbers of English language learners who are native born. Language minority students who are Native American, Hispanic, Asian Pacific American, African American, and members of other groups comprise a dynamic and complex ethnolinguistic mosaic.

For society as a whole, linguistic diversity has different faces. Perceptions differ. Whether the nation's multilingual heritage is regarded as a problem, a right, or a resource depends upon one's orientation. Does it denote a disadvantage, is it a matter of equity, or is the richness of our multilingual population a resource to be valued and fully developed? In the classroom, teachers' actions will convey what they believe.

References

Alaska Federation of Natives. (January, 1989). *The AFN report on the status of Alaska Natives: A call for action.* Anchorage: Author.

Berg, P. K., & Ohler, J. (1990). Strategic plans for use of modern technology in the education of American Indian and Alaska Native students, Chapter 13. Manuscript draft, Indian Nations At-Risk Task Force, U.S. Department of Education.

Castellanos, D. (1992). A polyglot nation (1983). In J. Crawford (Ed.), *Language loyalties* (13–19). Chicago: University of Chicago Press.

Crawford, J. (1992). *Hold your tongue: Bilingualism and the politics of English only.* Reading, MA: Addison-Wesley.

Elam, S. M., Rose, L. C., & Gallup, A. M. (1993). The 25th annual Phi Delta Kappa Gallup Poll of the public's attitudes toward the public schools. *Phi Delta Kappan, 75*(2), 137–152.

Fuetsch, M. (1995, November 29). Absorbing a different culture. *Plain Dealer*, Lakewood edition, p. 19A.

García, E. E. (1995). Educating Mexican American students: Past treatment and recent developments in theory, research, policy, and practice. In J. A. Banks & C. A. McGee Banks (Eds.), *Handbook of research on multicultural education* (pp. 372–387). New York: Macmillan.

The global migration. (1993, October). *Parade*, pp. 17, 19.

Hinton, L. (1992, Fall). Keeping the languages alive. *News from Native California*, pp. 25–31.

Kellogg, J. B. (1988). Forces of change. *Phi Delta Kappan, 70*(3), 199–204.

Kloss, H. (1977). *The American bilingual tradition*. Rowley, MA: Newbury House.

Lawrence, G. (1978). Indian education: Why bilingual-bicultural? *Education and urban society*, *10*(3), 305–320.

LEAP. (1991a). *Asian Pacific American experience in the United States, A Brief Chronological History: 498–1991*. Los Angeles: Author.

LEAP. (1991b). *Asian and Pacific Islander Americans by national and ethnic origins*. Los Angeles: Author.

LEAP. (1992). *The state of Asian Pacific America: A public policy report, policy issues to the year 2020* (Executive summary). Los Angeles: Author.

LEAP. (1993). *The state of Asian Pacific America: A public policy report, policy issues to the year 2020* (Executive summary of a book co-published by the LEAP Asian Pacific American Public Policy Institute and the UCLA Asian American Studies Center). Los Angeles: Author.

Lee, C. D., & Slaughter-Defoe, D. T. (1995). Historical and sociocultural influences on African American education. In J. A. Banks & C. A. McGee Banks (Eds.), *Handbook of research on multicultural education* (pp. 348–371). New York: Macmillan.

LeMoine, N. (1993, August 8). *Mainstream English as a second language: Focus on linguistically different African American students*. Paper presented at the Tenth Annual Summer Seminar for Foreign Language Teachers, University of California Santa Barbara.

Lomawaima, K. T. (1995). Educating Native Americans. In J. A. Banks & C. A. McGee Banks (Eds.), *Handbook of research on multicultural education* (pp. 331–347). New York: Macmillan.

Millar, H. (1995, November 14). At the head of the class? *New York Times*, p. 29C.

Minicucci, C., & Olsen, L. (1993). Caught unawares: California secondary schools confront the immigrant student challenge. *Multicultural Education*, *1*(2), 16–19, 38.

NCBE Forum. (1993, March). Washington, DC: National Clearinghouse for Bilingual Education, p. 4.

Nicolau, S., & Valdivieso, R. (1992). Spanish language shift: Educational implications (1988). In J. Crawford (Ed.), *Language loyalties* (317–322). Chicago: University of Chicago Press.

Nieto, S. (1995). A history of the education of Puerto Rican students in U.S. mainland schools: "Losers," "outsiders," or "leaders"? In J. A. Banks & C. A. McGee Banks (Eds.), *Handbook of research on multicultural education* (pp. 388–411). New York: Macmillan.

Pang, V. O. (1995). Asian Pacific American students: A diverse and complex population. In J. A. Banks & C. A. McGee Banks (Eds.), *Handbook of research on multicultural education* (pp. 412–424). New York: Macmillan.

Ruíz, R. (1988). Orientations in language planning. In S. L. McKay & S. C. Wong (Eds.), *Language diversity: Problem or resource? A social and educational perspective on language minorities in the United States* (pp. 3–25). New York: Newbury House.

U.S. Department of Commerce. (1995). *Statistical Abstracts of the United States 1995* (115th ed.). Washington, DC: Government Printing Office.

Waggoner, D. (1988). Language minorities in the United States in the 1980s: The evidence from the 1980 census. In S. L. McKay & S. C. Wong (Eds.), *Language diversity: Problem or resource? A social and educational perspective on language minorities in the United States* (pp. 69–108). New York: Newbury House.

Waggoner, D. (1989). Spanish language futures in the United States: A methodological critique (Research note). *NABE Journal*, *13*(3), 253–261.

Waggoner, D. (1993). The growth of multilingualism and the need for bilingual education: What do we know so far? *Bilingual Research Journal*, *17*(1–2), 1–12.

3

The Home and Community Context

The world each person creates for himself [or herself] is a distinctive world. . . . Every communication, interpersonal or intercultural, is a transaction between these private worlds.

Dean Barnlund

Although the cultures of school, home, and community are certain to differ in significant ways, it is what happens as students, parents, teachers, administrators, and community members interact that is of paramount importance. As cultural "brokers," teachers must bridge and link the linguistically and culturally different worlds of home, school, and community. Those who are advocates for English language learners appreciate the need for collaboration. "Unless the boundaries between classrooms and communities can be broken, and the flow of cultural patterns between them encouraged, the schools will continue to legitimate and reproduce communities of townspeople who control and limit the potential progress of other communities and who themselves remain untouched by other values and ways of life" (Heath, 1983, 369).

This chapter focuses on areas that must be addressed if the social and cultural contexts of home, school, and community are to be considered an integral part of the multilingual classroom equation. After completing this chapter, you will be able to

1. appreciate the home language and the implications of language shift
2. recognize how children's acquisition of a second language affects parent-child relationships in the home environment
3. recognize parents' perceptions toward school and their children's success in school
4. identify parent involvement patterns
5. identify strategies that promote a cooperative and collaborative relationship between home and school
6. recognize special features of classroom and community language use and apply these insights to making connections between school and community

Home and Family

Teachers typically regard the home environment as a powerful influence in shaping the child as a member of the classroom community. Indeed it is. What is often overlooked, however, is the relationship between home and school and the impact that schooling has on the home. In the sections that follow, we explore the implications of language shift in the home, parents' perceptions of education, and their involvement in their children's education.

The Language of the Home

What happens to the languages that students bring with them to school? Are they likely to be maintained or will they be quickly replaced by English? Few teachers realize that from a historical perspective, "language has been among the most vulnerable ethnic traits" (Crawford, 1992, 125). Hence, for the vast majority of students, the question is not whether they will learn English; it is a virtual certainty that they will develop some level of English language proficiency. The real question is how rapidly they will lose the primary language and what the immediate and long-term effects will be both at home and at school.

Crawford (1992) addresses these and other questions as he examines current patterns of minority language use. His findings challenge "conventional wisdom." For example, Crawford concludes that *"there is no evidence that linguistic assimilation is slowing down"* (p. 127). Rather, it appears that the process is accelerating and that a substantial shift to English and loss of the native language begins with the children of immigrants. This means that the language shift that had traditionally taken three generations—from immigrant grandparents who remained dominant in the native language and developed survival skills in English to their bilingual children to their grandchildren who spoke almost exclusively English—now transpires over the course of two.

Furthermore, the rate at which immigrant groups abandon their native language and adopt English as the basic language varies considerably (Crawford, 1992, 127). For example, among immigrants arriving in the 1960s, those making the most rapid shift into English by the mid-seventies were Scandinavians, Germans, Japanese, Filipinos, Koreans, and Arabs. Those shifting into English most slowly were Chinese, Hispanic, Greek, and Portuguese. Somewhere in the middle of this range were those who spoke French, Italian, and Polish. Social and economic factors appear to be particularly critical in determining how rapidly groups adopted English, as are age and region. The younger the immigrant is upon arrival in the United States, the greater the likelihood that English will eventually be the individual's dominant or only language. With respect to region, anglicization rates for Hispanics in urban barrios exceed those found in rural areas like southern Texas (p. 128).

Teachers may question whether students in their classrooms are likely to experience accelerated loss of their primary language. In general, it appears that a number of factors—societal, cultural, and linguistic—combine to create the conditions that inhibit language maintenance and foster language loss (Conklin & Lourie, cited in Scarcella, 1990). Clearly, some language minority students are more susceptible to language loss than others. Teachers can identify many of the factors involved, and this information may provide insights as to the dynamics of language maintenance and attrition for language groups in their community. As the factors suggest, each language group faces its own unique set of conditions.

Conklin and Lourie (Scarcella, 1990, 30–31) report that a variety of factors contribute to accelerated language loss. Linguistic factors include language groups characterized by a small and dispersed number of speakers, a remote and inaccessible homeland, and occupational dislocation (particularly from rural to urban areas). Not surprisingly, when there is little or no prospect of returning to the homeland, conditions will favor language loss. Cultural factors can also encourage language shift. Ethnic groups who experience greater cultural and religious congruency with middle American society are more likely to anglicize. Language loss is more likely when (a) institutions requiring use of the mother tongue are lacking, (b) the emphasis on family and community ties is weak, and (c) ethnic identity is defined by factors other than language (e.g., religion). In addition, children tend to lose the primary language sooner when a group places greater emphasis on education and is accepting of English-only education. Finally, there are factors related to the nature of the language itself that also contribute to its loss. A language is abandoned more rapidly if it is nonstandard and/or unwritten and of little global importance. If there is a non-Latin writing system and no tradition of literacy, the likelihood of language loss is also increased.

Although critical, these are not the only factors that influence what happens to the home language. Schooling contributes to the dynamics of language maintenance and loss, and the implications extend far beyond academics. In many families, children develop language proficiency in the second language before their parents do. When this happens, it may create unexpected problems within the home—for parents and children alike. In his autobiography, Richard Rodríguez (1982) shares a personal account of what happened in his home. He describes how interaction between his parents and siblings changed after the shift from Spanish to English in the home:

> The family's quiet was partly due to the fact that, as we children learned more and more English, we shared fewer and fewer words with our parents. Sentences needed to be spoken slowly when a child addressed his mother or father. (Often the parent wouldn't understand.) The child would need to repeat himself. (Still the parent misunderstood.) The young voice, frustrated, would end up saying, "Never mind"—the subject was closed. Dinners would be noisy with the clinking of knives and forks against dishes. My mother would smile softly between her remarks; my father at the other end of the table would chew and chew at his food, while he stared over the heads of his children. (p. 23)

The scenario that Rodríguez describes is being repeated in other homes. This contributes to language loss, as "adult language use in the home plays the most significant role in passing on mother-tongue skills to the next generation. Yet more and more immigrant parents are inclined to speak English with their children" (Crawford, 1992, 128).

Wong Fillmore (1992) is particularly concerned about what happens when children learn English in preschool programs. Reporting on a study of 1,100 families in states across the nation—Native Americans, Arabs, Latinos, east and southeast Asians, and others—Wong Fillmore finds that "as immigrant children learn English, the patterns of language use change in their homes. The younger they are when they learn English, the greater the effect. The evidence also suggests that these children are losing their native languages as they learn English" (p. 6). This study found that children in preschool programs increase their use of English with parents and other siblings at home. Moreover, the younger children are when they begin preschool, the faster and more completely they seem to lose their primary language. This happens even when the parents are unable to speak English. In some families, the transition takes place so quickly that it dramatically changes communication patterns in the home. "Nearly two-thirds of the families (64.4%) that had children in English-only preschools reported that their children were no longer using the family language much at home" (p. 6).

Wong Fillmore asks what happens to family relations when the language children give up happens to be the only one the parents speak. In many families, the switch from one language to another has serious implications. This is understandable since parents speaking little or no English rely on the native language to support and influence their children. When the role of the home language is diminished, English does not serve as a substitute. Anecdotal information gleaned from interviews conducted in the study suggests serious consequences, such as breakdowns in communication, alienation, and family disintegration. In one family, all four teenagers are unable to speak the only language their parents know. In many families, parents are mystified over their children's loss of the home language (pp. 6–7).

Contrary to conventional wisdom, teachers are advised to convey the message that parents should insist on using the native language at home (Wong Fillmore, 1992). First, abandoning the native language and shifting into English does not appear to promote English language development. Despite the parents' best intentions, native speakers of English will provide their children with better models for the new language. However, parents (and siblings proficient in the native language) can make a significant contribution by modeling the native language and helping children to develop high levels of proficiency in the home language. In fact, failure to do so may impede ultimate language development, particularly for younger learners. Second, if the parents are considerably less proficient in English than their children, a shift into English can affect parent-child communication. As we have seen, the implications for the children at home and school are significant. Third, maintenance and development of the native language is critical to second language learners as individuals and to society in general. It serves no purpose for individuals who constitute a significant linguistic and cultural resource to abandon their primary languages at a time in which policymakers are charting a course to build an "internationally literate citizenry" (Baliles, 1989, vii). In a Task Force Report on International Education, for example, the nation's governors asserted that:

> It is time to learn languages.
>
> It is time to learn geography.
>
> It is time to change our thinking about the world around us. For we cannot compete in a world that is a mystery "Beyond our Borders." (Baliles, 1989, v)

Bilingualism is an integral part of academic achievement for the twenty-first century. Language minority students can—and should—be at the forefront.

Parents' Perceptions

David C. Lam, then Lieutenant Governor of British Columbia, Canada, recounts his youngest daughter's first day of school after the family's immigration to Canada. When she entered the second grade class at Jamieson Elementary School, her repertoire in English was limited to a few words, among them "good morning" and "I am Doreen Lam." This is what happened:

Bilingualism is an integral part of academic achievement for the twenty-first century.

She went to school and all day she imitated. She pretended that she knew what was going on. But her teacher knew. At the end of the day, the teacher asked her to stay behind in order that she might help her. But to a little girl of six and one-half, she considered that being detained and punished. So, what could a young child do? She cried. And she cried, not just a little sobbing. She cried like Archie Bunker's daughter, Gloria. She really cried.

The teacher tried to explain to her, "I just wanted to help you." But, have you ever seen a duck talking to a chicky? They don't communicate. The teacher was trying to help her, but this little girl, our daughter, just kept crying. And in a moment of desperation, with compassion, the teacher suddenly cried too.

At that moment, two people were crying. Then they stopped and hugged each other. Our daughter came home and told her mother, and mother cried. Then mother told me, and I cried!

We are forever grateful to that teacher. Instead of ignoring or rejecting our daughter, she showed compassion and care, which built confidence.*

Lam goes on to describe his daughter's success in school—winning an award in public speaking, being elected vice-president of student council, receiving a university scholarship. He also reminds teachers of how important their role is in the lives of English language learners: "Your students, a group of new people, look to you, not just to learn a new language, but to learn a new culture in a new land with a new framework of values. What you pass on may affect the rest of

---

*From "Who Are We?—A Parent Speaks," by David C. Lam, 1992, *Elementary Education Newsletter* (p. 1). Copyright © 1992 by Teachers of English to Speakers of Other Languages, Inc. Used with permission.

these persons' lives" (Lam, 1992, 1). Lam's observations are as pertinent to teachers in the United States (and other countries) as they are to those in Canada.

When the parents of second language learners are asked about their perceptions of school, how do they respond? Whereas it is obvious that no one individual or group can speak for all parents, it is helpful to realize that "immigrants and refugees, on the whole, are more determined than nonimmigrants of comparable class background to use education as a strategy for upward social mobility" (Gibson, cited in Schram, 1994, 67). Delgado-Gaitán's (1987) ethnographic study of three Mexican immigrant families is illustrative. In addition to teaching their children to behave cooperatively and in ways consistent with family values, to respect adult authority, and to assume appropriate household responsibilities, the parents expected their children to succeed in school, to comply with teacher expectations, and to attain occupational or professional positions that exceeded those of the parents. All three families recognized that learning English and completing school was essential if their children were to succeed. "While these families show a great deal of concern to maintain their cultural values of respect and cooperation and their Spanish language, we also see their urgency in having their children learn English and any other competencies that will lead to success" (Delgado-Gaitán, 1987, 155). Of particular concern to Delgado-Gaitán was the revelation that despite the parents' strong desire that their children succeed in school and in careers, only one family seemed to understand what was required for achieving the level of success they wanted for their children. The families essentially knew what the goal was, but did not seem to be aware of exactly how to guide their children toward the occupational or professional career they had defined.

This is one important opportunity for collaboration that is often overlooked by teachers. These parents needed the kinds of information and assistance in career planning that schools can offer. Beginning in the elementary grades, teachers can provide direction and support through units on career opportunities, by inviting parents and community members as guest speakers, and by making the exploration of alternative career paths an integral part of excursions and field trips (F. Hernández, 1992). Parents of older students will need assistance in operationalizing the aspirations they have for their children. For many parents, this will include awareness of academic requirements and expectations, consideration of professional and vocational options, access to financial aid, and so on.

Parent Involvement

One thing is clear. Teachers of language minority students need to be willing to reach out to the parents. Sometimes teachers do so with misgivings, not knowing how parents will respond. Sometimes they have doubts about how to proceed, whether their efforts will be successful. They are not alone. Amy Thele had questions too.

Amy Thele (1992) is a teacher in Fresno, California. Her pupils are from migrant families; they have no telephones at home. After none of the parents attended back-to-school night, Thele decided to make home visits. "I knew that this was a good step to take, and yet part of me was nervous and afraid. What if they resented the fact that I didn't speak Spanish? What if they felt I was invading their privacy? What if they saw me only as another public official poking around in their territory, asking questions, and being too inquisitive? Fearful or not, I had to go through with it" (p. 5).

Thele's account of her home visits is a poignant one.

> The first family I visited was Erica's. I knew my [children] came from poor families, but after this visit I felt some comfort in knowing that, although their homes were small, they were probably all like Erica's—clean, safe, and warm. However, nothing could have prepared me for the visits to the homes located in a dilapidated trailer park. The homes for many of my kids were cramped, run down, one-room trailers with no heat, indoor toilets, and electrical wires exposed everywhere.
>
> I learned a lot that first day. My feelings went from anger—anger at a system that allowed those living conditions to exist; to respect—respect for those families who continued to work their hardest and try their best to provide for their children. They weren't giving up, they didn't seem to despair, and they never once treated me with suspicion.*

Thele reported that after making the home visits, all except three parents went to the school for parent conferences. They also provided support in other ways. Thele recalls that parents she "never expected to see turned out to watch their children at our Christmas assembly. They slipped into the auditorium quietly and exited quickly. They were not the parents with video cameras, or the ones who posed for pictures after the show. But I knew who they were, and so did their children" (p. 5).

This is one teacher's experience. When we look at the collective experience of many schools, insights emerge that are contributing to a rethinking of what parent involvement really means, particularly for language minority students among the at-risk populations. For example, Vandegrift and Greene (1992) evaluated parent involvement programs in 55 elementary and secondary schools involved in the Arizona At-Risk Pilot Project. On the basis of their experiences, they contend that schools need to define parent involvement in ways that are more appropriate to the population they serve. "Schools don't always know what parent involvement *really* means" (p. 57).

Traditional definitions of parent involvement imply that parents are both supportive and active. By this yardstick, parents are expected to display high levels of commitment to their children and their children's education while participating in observable activities that support the school. With at-risk populations, however, a wider range of involvement patterns are typical. Support and participation appear to fall along a continuum of involvement, with parents grouped into the four basic categories described in Figure 3-1.

In the first category, parents are both supportive and active participants. In addition to providing their children with encouragement and assistance with

---

*From "Home Visits," by Amy Thele, 1992, in *Elementary Education Newsletter* (p. 5). Copyright © 1992 by Teachers of English to Speakers of Other Languages, Inc. Used with permission.

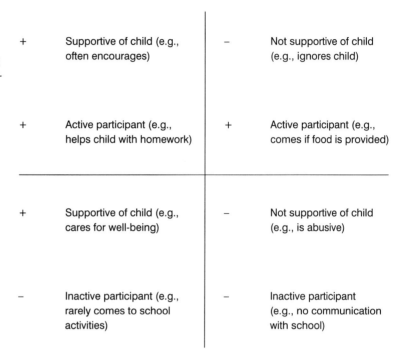

Figure 3-1 Categories of parent involvement
Source: From "Rethinking Parent Involvement" by J. A. Vandegrift and A. L. Greene, 1992, *Educational Leadership*, *50*(1), pp. 57–59. Copyright © 1992 by ASCD. Reprinted by permission. All rights reserved.

homework, these parents are visible on school committees and responsive to notes and telephone calls. Vandegrift and Greene caution that schools should not use this model as the basis for assessing the effectiveness of parent involvement efforts. Alternative avenues are needed, because for many parents, this is not a comfortable role. A second group of parents—strongly supportive of their children and their well-being—are not inclined to participate in school activities. For them, teachers find that newsletters highlighting suggested home activities, home visits, and "make-and-take" workshops work well. Amy Thele's account suggests that many of the parents in her class would fall into this category. A third category, perhaps the most difficult to identify, are parents who create a positive image (by participating in selected school activities such as parent-teacher conferences and attendance at social events) that belies the lack of support they actually offer their children. At school, these parents are visible. At home, their children may be ignored, mistreated, or even abused. In one school, attempts to reach some of these parents included the dramatization of negative parental behaviors in skits acted out by their own children. Even more difficult to reach are parents in the final group—those who are neither supportive of the child nor willing to participate. In working with these parents, teachers need to focus on communication, identifying, if possible, the reasons for the parents' non-supportive, nonactive behavior.

Reporting on parent attitudes and practices in inner-city schools, Dauber and Epstein (cited in Whitehead, 1993) report that the strongest and most consistent predictors of parent involvement at school and at home are the specific school programs and teacher practices that encourage and guide parent involvement. Regardless of parent education, family size, student ability, or school level (elementary or middle school), parents are more likely to become partners in their children's education if they perceive that the schools have strong practices to involve parents at school, at home on homework, and at home on reading activities. (p. 22)

Promoting parent involvement means "garnering parent support—for their children and for education" and improving communication—"meeting parents where they are" (Vandegrift & Greene, 1992, 58, 59). This means changing how schools relate to parents and, in turn, how parents respond to school initiatives. Vandegrift and Greene tell about one school that decided to offer workshops on "Good Parenting Skills" without seeking input from the parents. Not surprisingly, sessions offered in English were not well attended by parents who were primarily Spanish speaking and had not asked for parenting skills. Then a decision was made to interview the parents. It turns out that what the parents wanted was to learn English. In response, the school initiated English as a second language (ESL) classes. This effort was successful. One teacher describes the outcome as follows: "Most parents starting out in the class have only a 2nd or 3rd grade education. Now they are reading in Spanish and English. These parents are excited about reading with their children" (p. 59).

Two key factors are essential for effective parent involvement (Vandegrift & Greene, 1992). The first element is to know your parents. This means assessing the needs of parents and getting to know them individually. It also requires personalizing communications between the school and home, that is, establishing rapport between parents and someone at the school (e.g., teacher, aide, community liaison). The second is to provide as many different opportunities for involvement as possible and to build up to high levels of commitment and participation gradually. "Doing so ensures an appropriate match between a parent's level of commitment and willingness *and ability* to be involved" (p. 59). Other strategies and techniques recommended in the literature include providing child care, transportation, translation of communications sent home (e.g., newsletters, notices, report cards), interpreters, meetings scheduled at convenient times, and a school staff that conveys acceptance and support (Whitehead, 1993, p. 24).

For the parents of English language learners, language is only one of the barriers between home and school. Not knowing how to deal with the culture of the school frustrates and isolates many parents. Delgado-Gaitán (1990) studied the role of 20 Spanish-speaking parents in their children's development of literacy at home and in their education at school. The Mexican parents in her study cared deeply about their children's education, but they lacked the "necessary skills to participate as the school required" (p. 161). When the parents became involved in defining their own goals and structuring the nature of their involvement, participation was meaningful and empowering.

Informed parents are likely to be more involved parents. Figure 3-2 (see pp. 44–45) provides a useful overview of basic education information that schools can provide the parents of language minority students. This is not intended to be a comprehensive list of questions that all schools should address, but rather a place to start in developing handouts or a handbook appropriate to the needs of a given community. The questions exemplify the type of information that parents need and want. Teachers will want to add, delete, and modify as needed.

Making Connections

For students and parents alike, school can be an "alien" place, alien in language and culture, in values and experiences. Recognizing parents as participants in the educational enterprise is critical. Essential, too, are connections that teachers can promote in other ways.

An "Alien" Place

A graphic image of the relationship between home and school is captured by Delgado-Gaitán and Trueba (1991) in an ethnographic study conducted in a California community they refer to by the pseudonym Secoya. What emerges from their examination of the influence of Hispanic home language and culture on children's learning and their experiences integrating culturally is a picture that is of both concern and interest to teachers. The experiences of Hispanic children of immigrant parents may be very different from those of children who are not language minorities. As a cohort, little could be generalized about the children from immigrant families; some did well in school, others did not. What the researchers did find, however, was a sharp contrast between the children's interactions in the classroom and those at home and within their community. In fact, opportunities for the development of language and higher cognitive skills were greater at home and within the community than at school (pp. 142–146).

For example, it is not uncommon for children—older siblings in particular—to function in adult roles by serving as translators for their parents during the initial phase of adjustment. As intermediaries between the family and representatives of public institutions, these children were asked to shoulder responsibilities well beyond their years. Similar patterns have been reported within the Hmong community in LaPlaya (a pseudonym) (Trueba, Jacobs, & Kirton, 1990). The problems of communication in dealing with the medical establishment are illustrative. When conveying symptoms, Hmong children experience difficulties that go well beyond language due to limitations in their knowledge of illness and critical vocabulary.

> Both parents and medical personnel had unreasonable expectations of what children can do in adult situations. Parents expect children to be their advocates—questioning, complaining, and fighting for adequate care. They ask their children to withhold information and to hide family secrets from disapproving Americans. Medical personnel, on the other hand, expect children to elicit from their parents complete descriptions of symptoms that would be indiscreet to discuss across gender and generational boundaries. Doctors and nurses expect children to be able to relay the seriousness of instructions and exert influence on their parents to comply. (p. 54)

Enrollment and attendance, General information, Transportation
- When should my child enroll in school?
- Will my child be able to attend a neighborhood school?
- How is my child's grade level determined?
- Do American schools accept course credits earned in foreign countries?
- How is the noon meal provided for students?
- How much will I have to pay for my child's schooling?
- What do I do when my child is absent from school?
- Will my child ride a school bus from home to school and back?
- What happens if my child misses the bus?
- If my child qualifies for special education and cannot ride the regular school bus, what can be done?
- What can I do to protect my child while he or she is riding the school bus?
- Is there a fee for transportation on a school bus between home and school?

Basic school program and services, Other education programs, Curriculum
- What is a minimum day?
- What subjects are taught in elementary grades (K–6)?
- What subjects are taught at the high school level?
- What high school requirements will my children have to meet?
- What is independent study?
- What other programs may operate in my child's school?
- How does the school determine each child's language proficiency?
- What program options are available for students whose primary language is not English (e.g., bilingual education, English as a second language, etc.)?
- How long does an English language learner stay in one of these programs?
- May parents request the placement of their child into one of these programs?
- May parents request that their child be withdrawn from one of these programs?
- What is advanced placement?
- What is alternative education (e.g., continuation education, vocational education, work experience education, adult education, opportunity education)?
- Who may need alternative education (e.g., continuation education, vocational education, work experience education, adult education, opportunity education)? Is my child eligible? What are the benefits?
- Is there a child development program available for my child? Is my child eligible? What are the benefits?

Figure 3-2   Basic education information for language minority parents
Source: From *A Handbook on California Education for Language Minority Parents* (English Version, pp. E-iii–E-14), 1989, California Department of Education Publications, 515 L Street #250, Sacramento, CA 95814. Copyright © 1989 by California Department of Education. Adapted by permission.

This may have implications for the children. Hispanic children serving in this capacity often internalize racism at a very early age, sharing the fear, rejection, and/or suspicion of the parents and witnessing instances of unfair treatment in the adult world (Delgado-Gaitán & Trueba, 1991, 146).

All too often, classroom activities have failed to recognize or capitalize upon the collective skills developed in the home and the leadership skills developed in

- What are year-round schools?
- What is summer school?
- How can summer school attendance help my child?
- How do I know if my child is gifted or talented?
- What kind of evidence is used to identify that a child is gifted and talented?
- What types of programs are offered for gifted and talented students?

Grades, Promotions, Testing
- What does an elementary student's report card include?
- What does a high school student's report card include?
- What do the report card symbols mean?
- What is a _____ grade (e.g., citizenship, work habit, etc.)?
- What should I do when I receive my child's report card?
- How often are report cards issued?
- What are the requirements for promotion to the next grade?
- What procedures are involved in grade retention?
- What does the law require for graduation?
- If a student does not complete all required courses or satisfy all requirements for graduation, are there other ways to obtain a high school diploma or its equivalent?
- What areas of student progress are assessed? How is this done?

Parental involvement in the schools
- Why should I become involved in my child's schooling?
- How can I support my child's education at home?
- What are some of the ways in which I can participate in my child's school?
- What rights do I have as a parent?

Structure of the public school system
- What is the structure of the public school system?
- What major agencies have an effect on the public schools?
- Who controls the schools in your school district?
- What is the structure of the typical elementary school?
- What is the structure of a typical high school?
- How are school districts financed?
- Why should parents understand the structure of public schools?

the home and neighborhood. As a result, school is an "alien place"—alien in terms of its failure to incorporate "children's cultural knowledge, values and language to enable them to learn by building on their own knowledge" (Delgado-Gaitán & Trueba, 1991, 143). If what is learned in school lacks meaningful context, it has "little value and application for the children in their home and community" (p. 148).

The Primary Language

Teachers working with second language learners—including those who are not bilingual—need to convey the message that students' primary languages and their cultural background are accepted and valued. This is critical to both language acquisition and self-esteem.

> To devalue a minority child's language is to devalue the child—at least, that's how it feels on the receiving end. The longtime policy of punishing Chicano students for speaking Spanish is an obvious example. While such practices are now frowned upon, more subtle stigmas remain. Children are quick to read the messages in adult behavior, such as a preference for English on ceremonial occasions or a failure to stock the school library with books in Chinese. The "early-exit" approach to bilingual education, with its haste to push children into all-English tracks, may have a similar effect. Whatever the cause, minority students frequently exhibit an alienation from both worlds. Jim Cummins calls it *bicultural ambivalence*: hostility toward the dominant culture and shame toward one's own. (Crawford, 1992, 212–213)

Research reveals that encouraging students to use their primary language in school is not enough to ensure that they will do so (Wong Fillmore & Valadez, 1986, 669). In a setting such as a school, speakers of languages other than the dominant language in the community often find it difficult or awkward to use their native language to talk with each other. Even when second language learners interact with classmates who are bilingual, the speakers will almost invariably shift into English.

Whether or not students are bilingual, teachers need to convey the message that their primary language is accepted and valued. From an academic, linguistic, and affective standpoint, this is sound practice. Not to do so can bring serious consequences for many students. For example, cultural conflict is central to some of the English literacy problems experienced by Indochinese and other minority students. "In subtle and intangible ways cultural values affect students' ability to engage successfully in English literacy activities and interpret meaning from text. School experience and the acquisition of English literacy bring about changes in the minority language and culture that create devastating conflicts, unless students are given the opportunity to integrate cultural values" (Trueba et al., 1990, 104).

The primary language is one of the most critical elements in the integration of cultural values, and teachers need to look for ways to actively promote use of the primary language within their classrooms and beyond. Díaz, Moll, and Mehan (1996) illustrate one strategy that effectively integrates the study of social issues within the classroom and community with the development of literacy and thinking skills in both languages. This strategy was implemented successfully in an ESL classroom in a secondary school in which there was no support in the curriculum for literacy development in the primary language. In directing students through their examination of campus and community attitudes toward language, the teacher used surveys and questionnaires as a technique for soliciting people's opinions toward English and their primary language. To promote literacy development, information collected from the Spanish-speaking community was reported using essays written in English.

On the first day, the teacher framed the assignment by requiring that all of the students ask these three questions (Díaz et al., 1996):

A. What language do you speak best?

B. What language do you read and write best?

C. Do any members of your family who live with you speak another language besides English? (p. 214)

Two other questions were made optional:

D. Would you be willing to take classes to become bilingual?
E. What career do you foresee in your future in which you would benefit by being bilingual? (p. 214)

For the survey, each student was required to interview other people:

A. Two adults not working on campus.
B. Two adults who do work on campus.
C. Three students whose first language is English.
D. Three students whose first language is other than English. (p. 214)

As homework, students were to develop 3 additional questions related to the topic. These were discussed the next day, generating 10 additional questions for possible use in the student questionnaires:

1. Would you prefer to live around bilingual people in a bilingual community?
2. Are your closest friends bilingual?
3. (a) Would you like to go to the university? (b) Do you know that the best university requires four years of second-language training?
4. Which language do you like the best of the ones you don't speak?
5. What language do you speak with your friends? Why?
6. How many teachers do you have that speak some Spanish?
7. Do you think you would like to return to live where you learned your first language?
8. Which language does your closest friend speak with you?
9. Do you think speaking another language is important?
10. Is it comparatively hard for you to learn another language? (p. 215)

The teacher guided the process from interviewing through essay writing to reporting the results. Formula paragraphs modeled the structure to be used in the essays. The following are two unedited student essays (Díaz et al., 1996):

Student A: The people in my cummunity think that being bilingual is very important for several good reasons. Firts, I felt very proud doing the Survey. the people in our communinity feel very proud at them self that they speak Spanish and Eanglish because they can talk with there friends in any of those two lenguages. Secondly, the people I ask Some were bilingual students and adults 60% were bilingual people and 40% weren't bilingual people. Also, I ask a teacher and a student if they would be wiling to work as a bilingual person and they said no and than I ask a Student this qiestion Do you think Speaking Another lenguage is important and he said no that amazed me because I never herd one person that thinks that speaking another lenguage ain't important. finally, I ask a teacher that What career was he interested in that would require a second language and he said no common and he told this I don't know What lauguage I'm interestes that would require a 2nd lenguage because I don't know it and I ask two Students this question what career are yo interested in that would require a 2nd lenguage and 50% said Fransh 10% said Germen 10% said Italian and 20% said no coman as you can see I was having fun. (p. 217)

Student B: I found that people in our community feel good about belingualism for several good reasons. They think it it very important because they can communicate with other people. The people I ask are 60% students, 40% adults, 70% are Spanish speakers, 20% were English speakers, 70% can write and read English, 20% can write and read Spanish well. Most of the people told me that in there house can speak English and Spanish. The people I ask the questions, answers me very polite and they said the questions were very interesting. Some person said that these project was very good for me and interesting for him. When he said that I feel very good about the work I was doing. The most interesting thing that I found wat that the people like the project. Most of the people said that they were willing to take classes to become totally belingual because it could help them right now and in the future. The students I ask said that they have only friends that speak only Spanish and English not othey language. The adults I ask said that been belingual is very important for them because they can communicate with more people and they can have more opportunitis for some jobs that othey people do I fee very good about the way people answer me (pp. 217–218).

Díaz et al. (1996) use this task as an example of how teachers can draw upon skills that students have developed in their first language and use them in support of academic goals in the second. In doing so, instruction is responsive to community dynamics. In working within this particular community, the researchers found that writing, schooling, and social issues were complex, related phenomena (p. 211). Establishing connections between the community and classroom were critical to student success. Díaz et al. emphasize that this activity is also consistent with Vygotsky's notion of creating zones of proximal development (see Chapters 6 and 7), as students move from teacher guidance to self-direction, from social to individual experience.

Summary

Creating a supportive learning environment requires an understanding of cultural, social, and linguistic factors that lie beyond the classroom. For teachers of language minority students, making connections between home, school, and community is an imperative, not an option. With respect to home-school relationships, teachers should be cognizant of the implications of language shift and the impact that children's accelerated loss of the primary language can have on communication within families. They also need to be aware of parents' perceptions of schooling and the expectations they have for their children. Knowledge of the home is critical if parent involvement efforts are to be effective in promoting support for students. In the final analysis, school can be an alien place for students whose linguistic and cultural backgrounds differ from the mainstream. Constructing a less alien environment invokes images of building bridges between home, school, and community—linkages that convey the message that the students, their languages, and their cultures are accepted, valued, and incorporated.

References

Baliles, G. L. (1989). Chairman's overview. In *America in transition* (Report of the Task Force on International Education). Washington, DC: National Governors' Association.

Crawford, J. (1992). *Hold your tongue: Bilingualism and the politics of English only.* Reading, MA: Addison-Wesley.

Delgado-Gaitán, C. (1987). Parent perceptions of school: Supportive environments for children. In H. Trueba (Ed.), *Success or failure? Learning and the language minority student* (pp. 131–155). Cambridge, MA: Newbury House.

Delgado-Gaitán, C. (1990). *Literacy for empowerment.* New York: Falmer Press.

Delgado-Gaitán, C., & Trueba, H. T. (1991). *Crossing cultural borders: Education for immigrant families in America.* London: Falmer Press.

Díaz, S., Moll, L. C., & Mehan, H. (1996). Sociocultural resources in instruction: A context-specific approach. In *Beyond language: Social and cultural factors in schooling language minority students* (pp. 187–230). Los Angeles: Evaluation, Dissemination and Assessment Center, School of Education, California State University, Los Angeles.

Heath, S. B. (1983). *Ways with words.* New York: Cambridge University Press.

Hernández, F. (1992, September). *California history and its multicultural heritage for elementary school instruction.* Paper presented at the annual conference of the California Historical Society, Sacramento, CA.

Lam, D. C. (1992). Who are we?—A parent speaks (excerpt from speech at opening plenary session, TESOL '92). *TESOL Elementary Education Newsletter, 15*(1), 1.

Rodríguez, R. (1982). *Hunger of memory.* New York: Bantam Books.

Scarcella, R. C. (1990). *Teaching language minority students in the multicultural classroom.* Englewood Cliffs, NJ: Prentice-Hall.

Schram, T. (1994). Players along the margin. In G. D. Spindler & L. Spindler (Eds.), *Pathways to cultural awareness: Cultural therapy with teachers and students* (pp. 61–91). Thousand Oaks, CA: Corwin Press.

Thele, A. (1992). Home visits. *TESOL Elementary Education Newsletter, 15*(1), 5.

Trueba, H. T., Jacobs, L., & Kirton, E. (1990). *Cultural conflict and adaptation: The case of Hmong children in American society.* London: The Falmer Press.

Vandegrift, J. A., & Greene, A. L. (1992). Rethinking parent involvement. *Educational Leadership, 50*(1), 57–59.

Whitehead, B. J. (1993). *An educational guide for parents of language minority students at Johnson Park School.* Unpublished master's thesis, California State University, Chico.

Wong Fillmore, L. (1992). When learning a second language means losing the first. *Educator, 6*(2), 4–11.

Wong Fillmore, L., & Valadez, C. (1986). Teaching bilingual learners. In M. C. Wittrock (Ed.), *Handbook of research on teaching* (3rd ed., pp. 648–685). New York: Macmillan.

P A R T

3 Process

4

Cultural Processes

*Teachers do not empower or
disempower anyone, nor do schools.
They merely create the conditions
under which people can* empower
themselves, *or not.*

R. Ruíz

The teacher's role in society is a critical one. As agents of cultural transmission, teachers are at the forefront in the process of ensuring that culture is effectively transmitted from one generation to the next: "we designate the school a mandated cultural process and the teacher a cultural agent" (Spindler & Spindler, 1994, 2). Moreover, in Western society, schools represent the "most massive interference crossculturally" in learning. "Schools define what is not to be taught and what is not to be learned as well as what is taught and learned" (p. 2). As a setting in which cultural transmission takes place, the classroom is a remarkably complex environment. Teachers and students each bring a personal cultural background, one that influences perceptions of self, of other individuals, and of the school itself. Together, teachers and students create a cultural environment of meanings and define their positions within it (Spindler & Spindler, 1994).

In multicultural contexts, the process becomes even more complicated, as children are likely to experience both enculturation and acculturation. Through *enculturation*, children are initiated into their own culture, and develop "a sense of cultural or social identity, a network of values and beliefs, patterned ways of living, and, for the most part, ethnocentrism, or belief in the power and the rightness of native ways" (Damen, 1987, 140). Through *acculturation*, children are also learning to adapt to the dominant culture. With social and psychological integration, they experience the "new ways and systems of beliefs and patterns of an unfamiliar cultural group" (Damen, 1987, 140, 225).

Language is central to both processes and is one of the "most powerful transmitters of culture" (Darder, 1991, 37). Within the larger society, English is unquestionably the dominant language. Within ethnic communities, the native language also plays an important role, for it contains "the codification of lived experiences that provide the avenues for students to express their own realities" (p. 37).

This chapter focuses on important aspects of the cultural context. After completing this chapter, you will be able to

1. develop a basic understanding of the acculturation process
2. describe the personal and private context in which language and culture are acquired
3. interview English language learners
4. explore cultural therapy as a process of developing awareness

Acculturation

For students whose primary language is not English, acquiring a second language usually means adapting to a second culture as well. As individuals learn a second language, they do more than change the way they communicate. They undertake a major reorientation that affects every aspect of their lives. "A person's world view, self-identity, his [her] systems of thinking, acting, feeling, and communicating, are disrupted by a change from one culture to another" (Brown, 1986, 34).

The essence of acculturation is a change in the language learner's perspective of others, as people once viewed as "they" are gradually embraced and encompassed as a part of "we" (Damen, 1987, 220). The process is a complex one, sensitive to the broader social and affective conditions that characterize the context in which language is learned, sensitive also to individual factors that determine how a given learner responds to the realities of adaptation.

As Kleinjans notes, the process of culture learning accompanies language learning, although in many ways it is more complex because of the nature of culture and its many manifestations. In addition, culture learning is likely to cause greater change in the individual. It may force the transcending of native and familiar culture patterns and, in some cases, result in their being discarded. This may produce culture shock, disorientation, and temporary loss of identity. If prolonged, these side-effects can lead to marginality and even alienation (Damen, 1987, 222).

For students whose primary language is not English, acquiring a second language usually means adapting to a second culture as well.

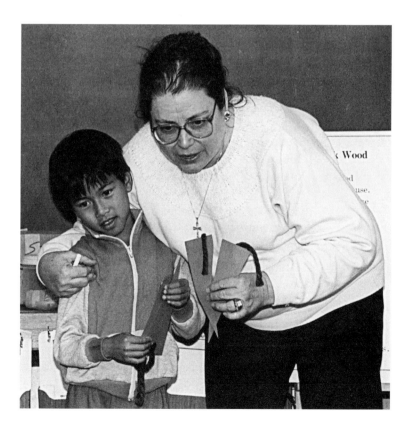

Acton and de Félix (1986) and Brown (1986, 1992) provide a general overview of the process. Initially, the learner enjoys a period of exhilaration and excitement—everything is new, there is a sense of adventure. This feeling is short-lived, however. When the euphoria subsides, the learner experiences *culture shock* as familiar behaviors and communication strategies fail and the new culture seems incomprehensible. The range of feelings encompassed by culture shock includes estrangement, hostility, indecision, frustration, sadness, loneliness, and physical illness. "The person undergoing culture shock views his [her] new world out of resentment, and alternates between being angry at others for not understanding him [her] and being filled with self-pity. . . . [Culture shock emerges] as the individual feels the intrusion of more and more cultural differences into his [her] own image of self and security" (Brown, 1992, 35, 36). Encounters with people in a second culture are intense, as tremendous effort is required to sustain communication (Clarke, cited in Brown, 1986, 37). Wanting to respond appropriately, the learner strives to comprehend the messages that are being conveyed by others. Not surprisingly, "social encounters become inherently threatening, and defense mechanisms are employed to reduce the trauma" (Clarke, cited in Brown, 1986, 37). Brown advises teachers to encourage students to work their way through these feelings, not to deny them. These emotions are a "powerful and personal form of learning" that must be understood and expressed before students can move forward to higher levels (p. 39).

Culture shock is followed by a period in which the learner is able to begin to function within the culture. The level of skills acquired is now adequate to satisfy basic functional needs. However, this, too, is a stressful period for the learner. Problems in adapting to a new culture persist and remain unresolved. The learner faces what has been termed a cultural "critical period," a point at which the individual must synchronize linguistic and cultural development (Brown, 1986, 42). Mastery and fluency can be achieved only after this synchronization occurs. Adults who manage to cope with the new culture without developing concomitant language skills are likely to never achieve mastery. Conversely, those whose linguistic fluency far exceeds their cultural adaptation find it difficult to deal with culture effectively on a psychological level and may not develop appropriate levels of acculturation.

> What I have suggested here might well be termed a culturally based *critical period* that is independent of the age of the learner. A young child, because he [or she] has not built up years and years of a culture-bound world view and view of himself [or herself], has fewer perceptive filters to readjust, and therefore, moves through the stages of acculturation more quickly, and of course acquires the language more quickly. He [she] nevertheless may move through the same four stages, just as an adult does. Cases of unsuccessful child second language learning might possibly be attributable to less than optimal synchronization of stages of acculturation and stages of language mastery. (Brown, 1986, 43)

Acton and de Félix (1986, 21) refer to this as an *acculturation threshold*. As they explain it, the individual grapples with aspects of the new language and culture that are more subtle and difficult than those confronted before. These are the nuances, for example, that determine whether the learner will comprehend the full repertoire of connotations associated with words. Failure to cross this threshold means that the learner will neither achieve linguistic mastery nor fully acculturate. Only when the learner crosses the threshold and is past the critical period can he or she attain a higher degree of acculturation. Most who reach this plateau are described as comparable to educated learners—literate in their own language—who have studied, lived, and worked extensively within the cultural milieu to which they are adapting. A few learners may eventually adapt or even assimilate to such an extent that they deal with the finer aspects of language and culture almost as well as native speakers. These individuals are regarded as the exception, however, rather than the rule.

In conclusion, research on acculturation provides a number of insights of particular interest to teachers. It suggests that (a) acculturation is a process in which individuals proceed through different stages and that (b) there is a critical period in which the learner must synchronize linguistic and cultural development if mastery is to be achieved. Thus, just as second language acquisition proceeds through a series of recognized stages, so, too, does the process of acculturation. In fact, adaptation seems to parallel stages of development in other areas as well (e.g., cognitive and personality) (Acton & de Félix, 1986).

Just as learners differ with respect to the degree of mastery they achieve in a second language, they will also vary in the extent to which they adapt to a new culture (Acton & de Félix, 1986) and in the process of acculturation they experience (García, 1994). García posits that for many children, acculturation is far more than simple substitution. The process involves complex patterns of combination and recombination. "Thus, language minority children who hear some English spoken at home experience a different process of acculturation than children who hear only the home language. These children may all belong to the same ethnic subgroup, but their different acculturation makes them each unique" (p. 60).

García-Castañón (1994) adds another dimension, emphasizing that some ways of acculturating are disparaging to the culture or heritage of origin whereas others are not. Reflecting on his own experience as a Chicano and that of others, he posits that "one could acculturate to the host culture without having to shed one's past cultural bearings. To do the latter was impossible without severe psychological costs" (p. 200). Along similar lines, Trueba (1990, 132–142) describes the process of mainstreaming for Chicanos in terms of culture shock, cultural socialization, and cultural integration. He uses the term "total assimilation" to denote the ability to function within mainstream society with the concomitant loss of ability to function in Chicano settings (p. 139).

Scarcella (1990) brings the focus back to the classroom. Although many language minority students have fully acculturated, others have not. "Teachers should never assume that all students from a particular culture will act in any stereotypical pattern. For instance, a Japanese student who has lived in the United States from birth may have fully acculturated. Like her American peers, this student may interrupt her teacher to ask questions, and she may love McDonald's. Another Japanese student who has lived in the United States all her life may choose to associate only with Japanese and to retain her Japanese identity" (p. 32).

In the final analysis, teachers should remember that acculturation cannot be viewed in isolation from the context in which it takes place (Delgado-Gaitán & Trueba, 1991). Without first understanding the social context in which acculturation occurs, we cannot look at whether or not language minority children learn English and adopt mainstream values as something positive or negative, good or bad. "It is only in the social context that we learn about the knowledge of those in interaction with each other and their goals for what they want to accomplish" (p. 28).

Student Voices

Acculturation describes the process involved in adapting to another culture. However, in describing this process, the emphasis thus far has been on the composite experience of many people. At the individual level, the context in which language and culture are acquired is most private and personal.

What is it like to be in school when English is not your primary language? The life experiences of individual students reflect very private realities, interweaving the dynamics of social, cultural, and psychological factors. Although millions of students in our nation's schools have experienced classrooms in which instruction was in a language different from their own, it is an experience that is not fully understood by many educators. In this section, immigrant students' voices—their own words as reported by the California Tomorrow research project (Olsen, 1988)—are used to help teachers to better understand the private or personal context of this experience.

For immigrant students, the United States represents a new way of life. For many, there are dreams of what the future will bring.

> Before I came to America I had dreams of life here. I thought about tall Anglos, big buildings, and houses with lawns. I was surprised when I arrived to see so many kinds of people—Black people, Asians. I found people from Korea and Cambodia and Mexico. In California I found not just America, I found the world. (p. 10)
>
> Mexican immigrant student

There are also high expectations.

> It is important to my family that I do well. We want our life in this new country to be a good one. I work very hard at school. My father makes me study even when I have no homework. He tells me this is how I can have a better life. America is a wonderful place to have free schools. Sometimes I cry because I am so tired of studying, but I know it is the way. (p. 91)
>
> 10th-grade Vietnamese boy
> (immigrated at age 14)

> I want to be a doctor or an engineer. Nobody from my family has gone to college. They will be very proud, but it is very expensive, I know. My teacher told me there is financial aid, but I didn't tell her we are illegals. I wonder, will they let me go to college? Can I get a scholarship? (p. 93)
>
> 11th-grade Honduran boy
> (immigrated at age 15)

When thinking of the immigrant experience, perhaps the image that comes to mind most often is one of optimism, hard work, and achievement. For many immigrant students, this image is indeed appropriate. But even for those who succeed, life in school can be marked by harsh realities. For students who bring with them a language and culture different from that of the school, becoming oriented to new behaviors, attitudes, and routines can be a challenge in itself. Imagine what the first day of school is like when you speak a different language.

> You don't know anything. You don't even know what to eat when you go to the lunch room. The day I started school all the kids stared at me like I was from a different planet. I wanted to go home with my Dad, but he said I had to stay. I was very shy and scared. I didn't know where to sit or eat or where the bathroom was or how to eat the food. . . . I felt so out of place that I felt sick. (p. 71)
>
> 8th-grade Vietnamese girl
> (immigrated at age 9)

Think of what it's like to not understand.

> I just sat in my classes and didn't understand anything. Sometimes I would try to look like I knew what was going on, sometimes I would just try to think about a happy time when I didn't feel stupid. My teachers never called on me or talked to me. I think they either forgot I was there or else wish I wasn't. I waited and waited, thinking someday I will know English. (p. 62)
>
> 9th-grade Mexican girl
> (immigrated at age 13)

There can be another down side to being an "outsider." Being different is not always given a positive value in our society. According to Olsen (1988), virtually all immigrant students interviewed in the California Tomorrow study reported incidents of prejudice or racism ranging from name-calling to overt hostility and violence.

> Before I came to America I had a beautiful dream about this country. At that time, I didn't know that the first word I learned in this country would be a dirty word. American students always picked on us, frightened us, made fun of us and laughed at our English. They broke our lockers, threw food on us in cafeteria, said dirty words to us, pushed us on the campus.... Many times they pushed me and yell on me. I've been pushed, I had gum thrown on my hair. I've been hit by stones, I've been shot by airgun. I've been insulted by all the dirty words in English. All this really made me frustrated and sad. I often asked myself, "Why do they pick on me?" (p. 34)
>
> Christina Tien, Chinese immigrant student
> Public Testimony, Los Angeles

> The Americans tell us to go back to our own country. I say we don't have a country to go back to. I wish I was born here and nobody would fight me and beat me up. They don't understand. I want to tell them if they had tried to cross the river and were afraid of being caught and killed and lost their sisters, they might feel like me, they might look like me, and they, too, might find themselves in a new country. (p. 35)
>
> 10th-grade Cambodian boy
> (immigrated at age 12)

Differences within ethnic groups between new and more established immigrants further aggravate the situation. In a student's own words:

> There is so much discrimination and hate. Even from other kids from Mexico who have been here longer. They don't treat us like brothers. They hate even more. It makes them feel more like the natives. They want to be American. They don't want to speak Spanish to us, they already know English and how to act. If they're with us, other people will treat them more like wetbacks, so they try to avoid us. (p. 36)
>
> 9th-grade Mexican boy
> (immigrated six months earlier)

Not surprisingly, these negative social and cultural factors take their toll.

> There is lots of teasing me when I don't pronounce right. Whenever I open my mouth I wonder, I shake and worry, will they laugh? They think if we speak Tagalog that we are saying something bad about them, and sometimes they fight us for speaking our language. I am afraid to speak English, I am afraid to even try. And I find myself with fear about speaking Tagalog. (p. 38)
>
> 10th-grade Filipino boy
> (immigrated at age 14)

To be most effective in the classroom, teachers should be familiar with students' cultural and linguistic backgrounds and educational experiences.

To be most effective in the classroom, teachers should be familiar with students' cultural and linguistic backgrounds and educational experiences. Language and culture are inextricably intertwined. As these student voices indicate, each student has a story to tell. When teachers learn about their students' cultures and experiences, when they learn to examine their own culture and become more aware of how cultural assumptions may bias relationships in the classroom, they can enhance students' consciousness of social and cultural factors in ways that empower them in navigating the educational system.

The Immigrant Student Interview Guide presented in Figure 4-1 is a modified version of a guide developed for the California Tomorrow research project (Olsen, 1988) from which the excerpts you have just read were taken. Although developed for use by trained interviewers, the guide identifies important areas that teachers may want to explore as they get to know their students. For teachers unfamiliar with the cultural and linguistic backgrounds of their students, it represents a critical starting point. The questions may also be modified for use in other ways and with other populations (such as native-born language minority students). In the classroom, interview activities can be built around some of the different areas, examining social issues relevant to students' concerns and experiences. (In selecting interviewees, teachers will want to keep in mind that the questions provided here require more advanced levels of language proficiency.)

A word of caution. For some students, an "interview" may recall painful memories of interrogation in their homeland. The general categories are merely a guide suggesting areas that may be explored. If the interview format is uncomfortable for an interviewee, an open-ended chat on one or more of the topics can provide an effective alternative. It should be made clear to everyone agreeing to an interview that they may pass on any and all questions that they prefer not to answer. As a technique used by teachers, interviews provide an effective way of exploring context. As an activity modified for use by students, interviews provide a vehicle for comparing and contrasting ethnic group experiences. The questions can be incorporated as part of oral history projects. For the teacher, the findings can also have implications for instructional programs and support services.

We bring this section to a close with another student's voice in Figure 4-2 (see p. 65). Nancy (Ngoo) Le, a Vietnamese immigrant student, tells the story of how she learned to speak English after coming to the United States. In this award-winning essay, Nancy, then 13 years old, shares her experiences in a most personal way.

Cultural Therapy

For teachers wishing to go beyond interviewing—particularly those with some training in the use of ethnographic techniques—an approach such as cultural therapy may be useful. As described by George and Louise Spindler (1994), *cultural therapy* is a process of bringing one's own culture to a level of awareness that allows for self-examination—a process that promotes understanding "of the ways the culture of the school and classroom, the culture of teaching, peer culture, and personal culture, influence perceptions of self and others, particularly in culturally diverse schools" (p. xii). It is an orientation directed at teachers and, through them, at mainstream and minority students.

Note to the interviewer

Before you begin the interview, introduce yourself and go over each of these points in your own words, stopping to answer any questions if necessary:

1. Identify yourself and your institutional affiliation (e.g., public school, college, or university).
2. Explain that you are especially interested in finding out how schools can help students who are new in this country—what kinds of things are helpful, and what kinds of things don't help. Indicate that this is why you are asking these questions of students.
3. Assure the student(s) that this information will only be used to help teachers better understand what immigrant students experience and need. Explain that names will not be used in reporting information to others. If they are quoted when the information is shared with others, their names will not be used.
4. Secure all appropriate permissions from parents and school *before* conducting any interviews.

Tell the students that they are free to stop you at any time in the interview if they have questions.

Student Interview Guide

Basic background information

Let's begin with some basic information about you.

1. What nationality are you?
2. What is your birth date?
3. When did you enter the United States?
4. What grade are you in now?
5. What school do you go to?

Pre–United States information

Now I'm going to ask you some questions about your life before you came to the United States.

6. In what country were you born?
7. Did you live in a city? town? or in the country?
8. What work did your parents do?
9. How old were you when you left?
10. In your understanding, why did you leave?
11. Did you know when you left that you would be coming to the United States? (If not, at what point did you become aware of your destination?)

The journey

Now tell me about your journey from when you left your home until you arrived in the United States.

12. What family members or friends left with you?
13. How long did it take from when you left your home until you arrived in the United States?
14. Describe the journey to me.
15. Before you got here, what was your view of the United States and of what your life here would be like?

Figure 4-1   Immigrant Student Interview Guide

Source: From *Crossing the schoolhouse border* (pp. 118–121) by L. Olsen, 1988, San Francisco: California Tomorrow. Copyright © 1988 by California Tomorrow. Adapted by permission.

School experience

Let's go back again to your life before arriving in the United States and talk about your schooling then.

16. What language(s) was/were spoken at home before you came to the United States?
17. Did you know how to read and write in your own language before you came here?
18. Did you go to school before you came to the United States? (If no, skip to #20.)
19. How many years were you in school there?
20. Was school in your country different from school in the United States? In what ways?

School experiences in the United States

21. How long after you arrived here in the United States did you enroll in school?
22. What month/year did you start school?
23. Who took you to register for school?
24. What grade were you placed in?
25. In your opinion, did that seem to be the right grade for you? Why or why not?
26. How much English did you know when you first started school here?
27. If you were not fluent in English, who helped you to communicate and understand?
28. Tell me about your first year in school here in the United States. What was it like for you?
29. What subjects did you study in that first year?
30. Did anyone or anything help you get adjusted, feel comfortable, and learn at school during your first two years?
31. What was most difficult for you about school in the first two years?
32. What might have helped you?
33. What was the biggest help to you in learning English?

Current school experiences

34. How do you feel about school now?
35. Are there still times when you do not understand what is being said or done at school because of English language difficulties?
36. What language(s) do you usually speak at home?
37. What language(s) do you usually speak with your friends?
38. Who do you go to for help with your schoolwork when you need it?

Social aspects of school

39. Tell me about the general relations between immigrant students and other students at your school.
40. Are most of your friends also immigrants from your country? Why?
41. Have you had any problems with other students because you are an immigrant?
42. Are there any divisions between recently arrived immigrants from your country and other students from the same country who have been here longer? If yes, describe.
43. Have you gotten into trouble at school?
44. Have you, or someone you know, been treated unfairly by teachers or other students because of language or nationality? If yes, how common do you think this is?

45. In general, do other students seem interested in your experiences and life before coming to the United States?
46. Do you live far enough from your school that you need to take a bus outside of your neighborhood to get to school? If yes, what is it like for you to go to school outside of your neighborhood?

School achievement

47. How well do you do in school?
48. What kind of grades do you get?
49. How many hours of homework do you do on average each school night?
50. What kind of courses do you generally take?
51. Were you ever enrolled in ESL classes? (If no, skip to #56.)
52. Did you feel adequately prepared when you switched from ESL classes to regular classes in English?
53. Have you ever considered dropping out of school? If yes, why?
54. Do you think you will graduate from high school? If no, why not?
55. How much do you worry about how you are doing in school?
56. Have you ever had to repeat a grade or a class? Why?
57. Do you have plans to go on to college?
58. What are the things you think school should teach a young person?
59. What do you think is important to learn in order to be successful in this country?
60. Do you feel you are learning what you need to know?
61. How has being an immigrant made your experiences at school different from other students who were born here?
62. What are your hopes for the future?
63. What are your plans for after high school?
64. Have your parents ever been to your school? If yes, why?
65. Does your school have classes that teach you about your native country and culture?
66. Have you ever been involved in any of your classes as an educational resource to teach other students about your culture or about the immigration experience?
67. What do you feel you have to teach to U.S. students because of your experiences from another culture and as an immigrant?
68. How do you think most people in the United States view immigrants?

The immigrant experience

As someone born in another country and culture, and now living in the United States, you are in a very unique position. You belong, in a sense, to two cultures. We are interested in what this means to you.

69. Are there ways you behave now and things you believe that are very different from the traditional ways in your country?
70. Are there things you do or new beliefs you have that upset your parents because they are different from traditional ways?
71. What, if anything, from your heritage and background do you want to pass along to your children?
72. Do you think about returning some day to your native country?

Thank you.

Figure 4-1 *continued*

On the way home, I looked out the window from the car, and saw cars running so fast, and so many tall buildings. Everything was so different. Then when I got home, I saw everything was new, and the TV was different, too. I couldn't understand a word they said, and I kept changing the channel, but I still didn't know what they were saying, so I had to turn it off.

Then in October, 1991, I went to school. I still remember that the secretary of the school said that my name was really hard for the kids to call me, so she changed my name to Nancy. I wanted to know what the secretary's name was, but at that time I didn't know how to speak English, so I couldn't remember her name.

I was in Miss Yoon's class, and I was in third grade. Every kid in school knew how to speak English except me. I felt lonely, like a bird that had no place to go and had no friend.

I remember some of the kids were teasing me and played tricks on me, but some of them were really nice, like Michelle Escobar. She helped me in English. She explained to me what I was supposed to do for my homework and my work in school.

Then it was her mom that really helped me. She told me to cut any pictures that I liked in magazines out and glue them on to cards, and she wrote the words on the cards for me to read. I also listened to a tape that Miss Yoon had. She told me to repeat everything the tape said. Day by day I did the same thing. Then one day I knew that I could understand what the other kids said, and I could say a little bit to them. There was a teacher, her name was Mrs. Goostree. She was my ESL teacher. She taught me how to read a book and write. She helped me for two years, and I can't thank her enough for what she taught me.

Then in fourth grade, I had a friend. Her name was Jane Sun, she was an ESL student, too, but she was better than I was in speaking English. She helped me a lot, too. Then about a month later, all the kids treated me nice and helped me in English, too.

Then came fifth grade, I was in Mrs. Walz's class. We had to write a page summary of a book. I didn't really know what to write, because some parts of the book I couldn't understand, but my friends helped me. They explained to me what the story was about, so I could write. I remember one time I had to stay in the class to help Mrs. Walz put stuff on the bulletin board, because I was afraid that if I went out to play at recess, no one would really understand what I was saying. But then in January, 1994, I decided that I wanted to play with them. I went out there, and it wasn't so hard to play with them. Instead they were really nice. They explained to me how we played the games and we had fun.

I like sixth grade the most. Mrs. Patin is really nice. She helps me in social studies, and science. She also gave me an idea on how to write a story.

Jennifer Lee is my best friend. She helps me with some of the homework, and I help her.

Now I really feel that I belong in this country. I hope that some day, I can be a doctor, so I can pay my parents and all the people who helped me back.

At last, I would like to thank everybody who helped me.

Thank you.

Figure 4-2 Excerpt from "How I Learned to Speak English"

Source: From "How I Learned to Speak English" by Nancy Le, 1995, *CATESOL News, 27*(1), p. 13. Copyright © 1995 by California Teachers of English to Speakers of Other Languages. Reprinted by permission.

Cultural therapy provides a pathway to cultural awareness. The need for this kind of understanding can perhaps be best understood in light of the following observations (Spindler & Spindler, 1994):

- Children from different sociocultural backgrounds attend schools that are "predicated on mainstream, largely middle-class, and largely white Anglo-Saxon North European Protestant cultural assumptions." (p. 23)
- "There are very few consciously racist teachers but there are many teachers, perhaps even all teachers, who have very strong biases that are quite immovable because they are integrated with their own sense of identity and self." (p. 23)

Cultural therapy is a complex (in some ways ambiguous) process through which individuals (a) make "explicit the nature of conflict in cultural terms" and the involvement of self within the conflict and (b) examine competencies instrumental in the school situation separate from the cultural contexts in which they are embedded (Spindler & Spindler, 1994, 30). Ethnographic techniques such as observation, interviewing, and participation are used to address educational concerns at the individual, group, classroom, or school level. For example, Phelan and Davidson (1994) describe the results of a group process used in an investigation involving 12 adolescents from culturally diverse backgrounds. Schram (1994) works collaboratively with a beginning teacher—herself a language minority—in a "lower track" classroom. His account describes how the behaviors of students reflect and enhance their cultural perspectives, how the teacher's cultural assumptions influence her interaction with students, and how enhancing the teacher's awareness of cultural assumptions translates into responsive educational practice. In a different setting, García-Castañón (1994) applies similar principles to the paraprofessional training of Hmong refugee students in a community college program for mental health nursing assistants.

There is one caveat: Cultural therapy is a process; it is neither a recipe nor a panacea. The process demands commitment, preparation, time, and effort. In return, it holds the promise that "when teachers better understand themselves as teachers, they will teach others better, especially those unlike themselves in ethnicity, social class, and culture" (Spindler & Spindler, 1994, back cover).

————— Summary

According to Spindler and Spindler, "American culture seems extremely complex because it has incorporated populations with different cultures and varying social strata from all over the world. On the other hand, an important aspect of American culture has been to create uniformity, conformity and synchrony" (Delgado-Gaitán & Trueba, 1991, 17). Immigrant, refugee, or native born, language minority students are not only engaged in learning language, they are engaged in the process of adapting to a new culture as well. Ideally, the process of acculturation is an additive one. However, a combination of factors in the home, school, and community can make it a difficult one.

By listening to student voices (and parent voices as well), teachers can develop cross-cultural understandings that empower them to act with competence. The use of ethnographic techniques in processes such as cultural therapy can help teachers to create classroom environments more responsive to the cultural, linguistic, and social needs of their students. "Academic success requires, then, that both teachers and children build learning environments in which success is possible for both" (Trueba, Jacobs, & Kirton, 1990, 135).

References

Acton, W. R, & de Félix, J. W. (1986). Acculturation and mind. In J. M. Valdés (Ed.), *Culture bound* (pp. 20–32). New York: Cambridge University Press.

Brown, H. D. (1986). Learning a second culture. In J. M. Valdes (Ed.), *Culture bound* (pp. 33–48). New York: Cambridge University Press.

Brown, H. D. (1992). Sociocultural factors in teaching language minority students. In P. A. Richard-Amato & M. A. Snow (Eds.), *The multicultural classroom: Readings for content-area teachers* (pp. 73–92). White Plains, NY: Longman.

Damen, L. (1987). *Culture learning.* Reading, MA: Addison-Wesley.

Darder, A. (1991). *Culture and power in the classroom: A critical foundation for bicultural education.* New York: Bergin & Garvey.

Delgado-Gaitán, C., & Trueba, H. T. (1991). *Crossing cultural borders: Education for immigrant families in America.* London: Falmer Press.

García, E. (1994). *Understanding and meeting the challenge of student cultural diversity.* Boston: Houghton Mifflin.

García-Castañón, J. (1994). Training Hmong refugee students. In G. D. Spindler & L. Spindler (Eds.), *Pathways to cultural awareness: Cultural therapy with teachers and students* (pp. 197–219). Thousand Oaks, CA: Corwin Press.

Le, N. (1995). How I learned to speak English. *CATESOL News, 27*(1), 13.

Olsen, L. (1988). *Crossing the schoolhouse border* (California Tomorrow Policy Research Report). San Francisco: California Tomorrow.

Phelan, P., & Davidson, A. L. (1994). Looking across borders: Students' investigations of family, peer, and school worlds as cultural therapy. In G. D. Spindler & L. Spindler (Eds.), *Pathways to cultural awareness: Cultural therapy with teachers and students* (pp. 35–59). Thousand Oaks, CA: Corwin Press.

Scarcella, R. C. (1990). *Teaching language minority students in the multicultural classroom.* Englewood Cliffs, NJ: Prentice-Hall.

Schram, T. (1994). Players along the margin. In G. D. Spindler & L. Spindler (Eds.), *Pathways to cultural awareness: Cultural therapy with teachers and students* (pp. 61–91). Thousand Oaks, CA: Corwin Press.

Spindler, G. D., & Spindler, L. (1994). What is cultural therapy? In G. D. Spindler & L. Spindler (Eds.), *Pathways to cultural awareness: Cultural therapy with teachers and students* (pp. 1–33). Thousand Oaks, CA: Corwin Press.

Spindler, G. D., & Spindler, L. (Eds.) (1994). *Pathways to cultural awareness: Cultural therapy with teachers and students.* Thousand Oaks, CA: Corwin Press.

Trueba, H. T. (1990). Mainstream and minority cultures: A Chicano perspective. In G. D. Spindler & L. Spindler, *The American cultural dialogue and its transmission* (pp. 122–143). London: Falmer Press.

Trueba, H. T., Jacobs, L., & Kirton, E. (1990). *Cultural conflict and adaptation: The case of Hmong children in American society.* London: Falmer Press.

5

Language Processes

Language is the memory of the human race.

William Smith

From a global perspective, bilingualism is commonplace. Many well-known persons in politics, philosophy, religion, fine arts, science, literature, music, and other fields are or were bilingual. Consider the following (Grosjean, 1982):

Mahatma Gandhi (Gujarathi, Hindi, English); Menachem Begin (Polish, Hebrew, English); King Hussein (Arabic, English); Julius Nyerere (Swahili, English); Martin Luther (German, Latin); Jesus Christ (Aramaic, Hebrew, Latin?, Greek?); Desiderius Erasmus (Dutch, Latin, French, Italian, English); Albert Schweitzer (Alsatian, German, French); Pablo Picasso (Spanish, French); Marie Curie (Polish, French); Roman Jakobson (Russian, French, English, German, Czech); Samuel Beckett (English, French); Rabindranath Tagore (Bengali, English); George Frederick Handel (German, English); Frederic Chopin (French, Polish); and Arthur Rubenstein (Polish, German, French, English). (p. 285)

The truth is that many of the most intelligent, gifted, creative, and talented people in the world are bilingual. In fact, research suggests that speaking another language may have a positive effect on cognitive abilities (Cummins, 1989). Furthermore, from a global perspective, a very significant proportion of the people who speak English—probably the majority—do so as a second language. Although English is the second most used language in the world, surpassed only by Chinese languages (with over 1 billion speakers!), it is the native language of only about 15 percent of the world's population (Meléndez, 1989). Another estimate suggests that English is spoken as a native language by about 325 million people and as a second language by upwards of 1 billion (Crystal, cited in Larsen-Freeman & Long, 1991, 1).

The human capacity for language is amazing. The more researchers learn about the processes involved, the greater their appreciation of the complex interrelationship that exists between language and culture. Although much remains to be investigated, knowledge of the processes involved enables researchers to describe what generally happens when people become proficient in more than one language. This knowledge also provides insights as to why the experiences of individual learners will vary, as some progress more quickly than others and achieve different levels of competence. For teachers, an understanding of these processes and the factors involved serves as the basis for facilitating second language development, promoting academic achievement, and providing a supportive environment for acculturation.

After completing this chapter, you will be able to

1. examine the basic components of language proficiency
2. draw insights from second language acquisition theories and processes
3. recognize the implications of theory and research on classroom practice
4. identify three principles for program development derived from second language research

Language Proficiency

Language proficiency encompasses what individuals *know* about a language system and what they can *do* with the language skills that they have. With the acquisition of language, individuals develop an understanding of the way language systems operate. For example, even though they may not be able to explain why, native speakers of English *know* that they would not say, "He no(t) can go" (Celce-Murcia & Larsen-Freeman, 1983, 97), "The car of my friend is new" (p. 127), or "It is able to study that I am in the kitchen" (p. 407). When individuals use a language, their performance is a reflection of how well they can apply the knowledge they have to achieve a specific task in a particular setting.

Educators can think of language proficiency as falling along a continuum. At one end, an individual has no ability to use the language at all. He or she cannot even satisfy basic survival needs. At the other end, the individual possesses skills comparable to those of a native speaker.

Nonproficient   Fully proficient

Non-native speaker   Native speaker

It may also help to think of language proficiency by picturing the image of a dual iceberg (Cummins, 1996). As illustrated in Figure 5-1, what individuals know

Language proficiency encompasses what learners know about a language system and what they can do with the language skills they have.

Figure 5-1 The dual-iceberg representation of bilingual proficiency

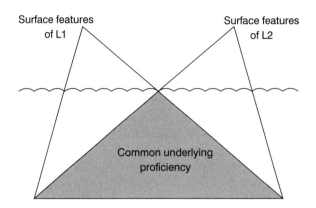

Source: From "Primary Language Instruction and the Education of Language Minority Students" by J. Cummins, 1996, *Schooling and Language Minority Students: A Theoretical Framework,* 2nd ed. (p. 18). Los Angeles: Evaluation, Dissemination and Assessment Center, School of Education, California State University, Los Angeles. Copyright © 1996 by Charles F. Leyba. Reprinted by permission.

is in their minds and remains hidden below the water line. Only what they do with language through actual performance can be observed by others. On the iceberg, performance is the part that is visible above the surface. The portion that is hidden beneath the water line is the underlying proficiency common to all of the languages an individual acquires.

Think of how a second language learner in a classroom setting might respond when the teacher says, "Can you open the window?" If the student answers yes instead of getting up to open the window, he or she would have failed to understand that this was a command rather than a question. Take a moment to reflect. How did *you* know that this was a command and not a question? Sinclair and Coulthard (1975, 30–33) explain that native speakers' knowledge of their language and the classroom situation enables them to recognize this as a command and not a question. To interpret an interrogative as a command requires three conditions. First, the interrogative must contain a modal (such as *can, could, will,* or *would*). In the example, "Can you open the window," it was *can.* Second, the interrogative must be directed to the person who is also the subject (*you,* the student, in the example). Finally, the action described must be physically possible at the time. We assume that the student is physically able to close a classroom window. (Notice how we also assume that the teacher has the authority to mandate the action.) This synthesis sounds complicated, but native speakers do it all the time without even thinking. This is part of the underlying knowledge of a language that provides the basis for performance.

What does it take to become a competent user of another language? For teachers promoting second language development, this is an important question. Effective communication is more than listening, speaking, reading, and writing skills. In fact, language is more than the sum of its parts (Enright & McCloskey, 1988, 28). Communicative competence—our ability to communicate with others— encompasses grammatical, sociolinguistic, discourse, and strategic knowledge and skills (Canale & Swain, cited in Hadley, 1993, 5–7).

Most teachers would readily identify the need for *grammatical competence.* That students need to master grammar, vocabulary, and syntax comes as no revelation. By age five, children master most of the rules governing the underlying sentence structures of their primary language (Larsen-Freeman & Long, 1991). They achieve command of their native language "regardless of intelligence, social class, or any of those environmental factors thought to play a role in other aspects of development" (p. 114). Given its pattern of development in children, grammatical competence is clearly an essential aspect of proficiency.

Most teachers know much less about the three other components that are essential if second language learners are to develop full proficiency. *Sociolinguistic competence* is one of these areas. To promote language acquisition, teachers must consider the social contexts in which learners are to use language as well as the purposes for which they need language. Communication does not take place in a vacuum. When people communicate, they consider many aspects relevant to the social situation in which they find themselves. For example, individuals are sensitive to such elements as speaker (who is involved), role (their position), topic (what is being discussed), purpose (the reason for communicating), and setting (place).

Language also must be appropriate to the function for which it is used. As a child, I once greeted a doctor I had never met before with a line straight out of a Bugs Bunny cartoon—"Eh, what's up, Doc!" She was neither impressed nor amused. The "problem" was not grammatical; it was sociolinguistic. Given my age and our "formal" relationship as doctor and patient, it was clearly an inappropriate greeting.

We adjust our language as we go from one situation to another. Consider the kinds of adjustments you would make in shifting from making plans for the weekend with family and friends to interviewing for a new job or accepting a prestigious award at a formal banquet. For native speakers of English, taking the factors identified earlier into account is automatic. However, for English language learners, these considerations represent another set of rules to be deciphered and internalized.

To be competent, second language learners must also be able to deal with language at the suprasentential level, that is, they must learn "to combine ideas to achieve cohesion in form and coherence in thought" (Hadley, 1993, 6). This is the domain of *discourse*. The following two examples are illustrative (Kramsch, 1981, 2). Although both are examples of coherent discourse, only the first would be considered a cohesive text:

1. A: Can you go to Frankfurt tomorrow?
   B: No, I can't.

2. A: Can you go to Frankfurt tomorrow?
   B: Lufthansa pilots are on strike.

Clearly, it is not enough for students to acquire only the rules of grammatical usage. Proficiency also demands adherence to the often unwritten rules of use that govern spoken and written discourse.

Strategic competence is another important dimension of language proficiency. Children use contextual clues, they imitate, and even generate their own set of rules for interacting. Children employ many of the same strategies they relied upon in developing their first language. Older learners add to this repertoire, making up new words, translating or substituting, and sometimes avoiding subjects or ideas that are difficult to express. It is natural for second language learners to develop strategies for communication. Before teachers try to facilitate the second language development process, it is to their advantage to understand what learners will typically do on their own.

Fillmore (cited in Lindfors, 1987) and Lindfors (1987) describe some of the strategies that children often use. At the survival stage, children rely on nonlinguistic knowledge to decipher the meaning of language. They draw on what they know of the physical and social context and assume that what people say is directly related to an immediate situation or experience. Children appear to understand the predictable language that accompanies daily routines because they learn to rely on the contextual cues inherent in these situations. They learn to make "good" guesses before the actual meaning of the words is clear.

Observation suggests that children develop a set of operating principles. These can be thought of as one's own set of rules to interact by. Fillmore reported on some of the cognitive and social operating principles used by the children in a study she conducted (Fillmore, cited in Lindfors, 1987). These include the following:

Cognitive strategies

1. "Assume that what people are saying is directly relevant to the situation at hand, or to what they or you are experiencing" (p. 461). Contextual clues in predictable routines enable children to respond appropriately before they understand the language associated with the routine.

2. "Get some expressions you understand, and start talking" (p. 461). Formulaic speech enables children with very limited second language skills to begin interacting with others.

3. "Look for recurring parts in the formulas you know" (p. 461). Children will repeat and recycle words and phrases they hear. They will extract elements from the formulas and gradually use these in new and creative ways.

4. "Make the most of what you've got" (p. 461). Children will overextend the meaning of words and overuse the expressions they know to maximize whatever English they do know.

5. "Work on big things; save the details for later" (p. 461).

Social strategies

1. "Join a group and act as if you understand what's going on, even if you don't" (p. 462).

2. "Give the impression—with a few well-chosen words—that you can speak the language" (p. 462).

3. "Count on your friends for help" (p. 462).

If teachers are sometimes fooled into thinking that children understand English and are choosing not to speak, it may be due in part to misinterpreting the social strategies that the children are using. To be included in activities, children will act as if they understand. They will imitate and use the words they know to make others think that they understand, even when they don't.

In her observations of children, Fillmore also found that as the concerns of second language learners evolved over time, so did the strategies they used to communicate. Initially, the children were most concerned with establishing social relationships with speakers of the new language. Becoming involved in activities characterized by interaction meant greater reliance on verbal formulas, key words, and nonverbal communication. The next stage was marked by efforts to communicate content. As the desire to convey a message became more important than socializing, the children were more creative with their language. They produced new sentences and used vocabulary they had not used before. It was only after these two stages that the children became concerned with speaking correctly.

When older learners—adolescents and adults—find that they lack the words they need to convey meaning in real-life situations, they also rely on communication strategies. Among the strategies most frequently mentioned are those identified in Tarone's (1980) typology of communication strategies. Recognizing the strategies presented in Figure 5-2 can help teachers to better understand how students compensate when they are placed in situations that demand language exceeding their level of proficiency.

In the final analysis, when teachers think of language proficiency in relation to instruction, they must go beyond consideration of mere grammatical competence. The other dimensions of competence described here—sociolinguistic, discourse, and strategic—are no less important in determining the ultimate level of proficiency that learners will attain. As Higgs and Clifford (1982) suggest, language proficiency is relative:

> The question that needs to be asked is not merely "Was the student able to communicate?" but "*What* was he [or she] able to communicate, and *how well*?" The *what* requires consideration of both the topic or context of the communication and of the language function that must be performed in that context. The *how well* entails judgments of linguistic accuracy and cultural authenticity." (p. 60)

The remainder of this chapter focuses attention on processes that influence how students develop the ability to communicate and how well they do so.

Second-Language Acquisition

Understanding the processes involved in acquiring a second language is as essential to effective teaching as anything else that teachers may study. Elementary school teacher Moyra Contreras (quoted in Olsen & Mullen, 1990) puts it this way:

> This issue has impacted me so personally. When I first came here I wasn't allowed to speak Spanish at school. Later I refused to speak Spanish out of shame. And when I became unable to speak Spanish, I had to go back to reclaim it. Each of these stages had a big impact on me and my self-esteem and my development. I knew from my own experiences that language development depends upon the messages and support in your environment, and your interactions with the world around you. It's not just a matter of linear natural development; it's affected by a lot of things. I wanted to understand it better. And as a teacher it seemed more and more important for me to understand it. As I began to study the theory of second language acquisition and language development it made so much sense to me. (p. 64)

Paraphrase

Approximation	Use of a single target language vocabulary item or structure, which the learner knows is not correct, but which shares enough semantic features in common with the desired item to satisfy the speaker (e.g., "pipe" for "waterpipe").
Word coinage	The learner makes up a new word in order to communicate a desired concept (e.g., "airball" for "balloon").
Circumlocution	The learner describes the characteristics or elements of the object or action instead of using the appropriate target language structure ("She is, uh, smoking something. I don't know what's its name. That's uh, Persian, and we use in Turkey, a lot of").

Transfer

Literal translation	The learner translates word for word from the native language (e.g., "He invites him to drink" for "They toast one another").
Language switch	The learner uses the native language term without bothering to translate (e.g., "balon" for "balloon" or "tirtil" for "caterpillar").
Appeal for assistance	The learner asks for the correct term or structure (e.g., "What is this?")
Mime	The learner uses nonverbal strategies in place of a meaning structure (e.g., clapping one's hands to illustrate applause).

Avoidance

Topic avoidance	Occurs when the learner simply does not talk about concepts for which the vocabulary or other meaning structure is not known.
Message abandonment	Occurs when the learner begins to talk about a concept but is unable to continue due to lack of meaning structure, and stops in mid-utterance.

Figure 5-2   Communication strategies
Source: From "Communication Strategies, Foreigner Talk, and Repair in Interlanguage" by E. Tarone, 1980, *Language Learning, 30*(2), p. 429.

Educators have certain assumptions and attitudes regarding the processes involved in their own acquisition of one or more languages. These assumptions and attitudes may or may not be consistent with what theory and research suggest is really happening (see Figure 5-3). However, in the absence of more "scientific" information, teachers often act on the basis of their intuitive notions of how language is acquired and how it should be developed and taught. The sections that follow highlight some of the insights emerging from the study of second language acquisition processes that inform more effective classroom practice.

Let's begin by looking at your current beliefs about second language acquisition and learning. This survey is designed to help you better understand your own assumptions and attitudes. Below are a set of statements that may or may not be supported by theory and research. After reading each statement, indicate the extent to which you agree or disagree.

Respond as follows:

SA	A	NA	D	SD
Strongly agree	Agree	Neither agree nor disagree	Disagree	Strongly disagree

1.	Theory is "irrelevant" to teaching language.	SA	A	NA	D	SD
2.	There is a relationship between the second language learner's perception of the learning environment and how well the learner does.	SA	A	NA	D	SD
3.	Language learning is a conscious and subconscious process.	SA	A	NA	D	SD
4.	Learners can communicate even with an imperfect knowledge of the language system.	SA	A	NA	D	SD
5.	No two individuals acquire language in exactly the same manner.	SA	A	NA	D	SD
6.	Cognitive differences between young children and adults are reflected in strategies adopted in language learning.	SA	A	NA	D	SD
7.	Student errors in language learning are usually the result of intelligence.	SA	A	NA	D	SD
8.	Most student errors are sporadic and haphazard; they do not usually follow systematic patterns.	SA	A	NA	D	SD

Now compare your responses with those of others and discuss why you responded to each statement as you did. Repeat the procedure after reading this chapter. Did you change any of your responses? If so, which ones? Why did you change your thinking?

Figure 5-3   What do you think?

Source: Scovel (1988, 170–173, 177, 179, 185); Littlewood (1984, 90–92, 95–96); Snow with Shapira (1985, 10–11); Hatch, Gough, and Peck (1985, 55). If you would like to compare your responses with those of the researchers, refer to the key located at the end of the chapter.

Theoretical Perspectives

Familiarity with the basics of second language acquisition theory and research can help teachers to better understand the strengths, abilities, and needs of language minority students. Estimates are that researchers have proposed at least 40 different second language acquisition "theories" (Larsen-Freeman & Long, 1991, 227). Generally speaking, explanations of the processes involved vary according to the factors that researchers regard as most critical in the acquisition process. Larsen-

Freeman and Long describe the theories as falling along a continuum from those most concerned with innate capabilities and endowments to those that look beyond the individual to emphasize contextual factors within the environment.

Nativist——— Interactionist ——— Environmentalist

Where a group of theories falls on the continuum is determined by how innate endowments, learned abilities, and environmental factors are viewed. If the primary focus is on innate mechanisms and knowledge, theories are regarded as *nativist* (e.g., Chomsky & Krashen). Theories that emphasize experience and environmental contributions are *environmental* (e.g., Schumann). Those that are most concerned with the relationship between nature and nurture are defined as *interactionist* (e.g., Givon, Pienemann). Every theory has its advocates and critics; all have limitations.

The Nativist View   From the nativist perspective, second language acquisition is explained in terms of innate biological endowments (Larsen-Freeman & Long, 1991). Many nativist theories are predicated on Chomsky's notion that "humans are innately (i.e., genetically) endowed with universal language-specific knowledge" (p. 228). This "universal grammar"—as Chomsky calls it—assumes the existence of an innate biological capacity for language acquisition. Without such a capacity, it would not be possible to account for how quickly people acquire language and how consistent language learning is for individuals of widely differing abilities.

Chomsky's ideas have influenced many nativist theories, Krashen's monitor theory perhaps the most notable among them. There are five basic hypotheses encompassed in this theory (Krashen, 1981, 1983, 1985a, 1996). The first is the *acquisition-learning hypothesis*. In this hypothesis, Krashen claims that acquisition and learning are independent processes in second language development. He defines *acquisition* as the subconscious process utilized in first language acquisition. *Learning*, on the other hand, is a conscious process characterized by explicit knowledge of language (grammar and rules), formal instruction, and error correction. Krashen believes that it is acquisition, not learning, that promotes fluency in a second language.

The *natural order hypothesis* posits that grammatical structures are acquired in a predictable order, some structures early, others later in the process. Krashen also finds that the developmental sequence in the first language is similar, though not identical, to the order of acquisition in the second language for children as well as adults. This order appears to be independent of the order in which grammatical structures may be taught.

In the *monitor hypothesis*, Krashen addresses the relationship between acquisition and learning in language production. By asserting that conscious learning does not significantly contribute to fluency, he limits the role of the learning system to that of a monitor or editor. The role of learning is circumscribed by the conditions for its use. These include the time in which to apply what one knows, the need to focus on grammatical accuracy (i.e., correctness of form), and a knowledge of the rules to be applied.

The focal point of the monitor theory is the *input hypothesis*. Krashen claims that individuals acquire language by understanding messages that meet the criteria of "comprehensible input." "We move from *i*, our current level, to *i + 1*, the next level along the natural order, by understanding input containing *i + 1*" (1985a, 2). With language in context and a focus on meaning, learners comprehend messages slightly beyond their current level of competence and acquire structure in the process. Speech emerges as a result of acquisition, and accuracy develops as the learner is exposed to more comprehensible input. For Krashen, "input is the essential environmental ingredient" for second language acquisition (1985a, 2). If the learner receives enough comprehensible input, grammatical structures will be provided consistently and automatically without formal instruction.

Finally, the *affective filter hypothesis* completes the theory. Krashen contends that whereas comprehensible input is essential in acquisition, it is not the only requirement. Affective factors mitigate the acquirer's subconscious openness to input. A negative combination of factors creates a "mental block" that inhibits full utilization of comprehensible input. Krashen finds anxiety, motivation, and self-confidence especially critical. Not surprisingly, he argues that high self-confidence and motivation combined with low anxiety predict better second language acquisition than low self-confidence, lack of motivation, and high anxiety.

Krashen (1985a) has summarized these five hypotheses as follows:

> People acquire second languages only if they obtain comprehensible input and if their affective filters are low enough to allow the input "in." When the filter is "down" and appropriate comprehensible input is presented (and comprehended), acquisition is inevitable. It is, in fact, unavoidable and cannot be prevented—the language "mental organ" will function just as automatically as any other organ." (p. 4)

He also claims that the theory "makes definite predictions for second and foreign language teaching" (1985b, 61). On the basis of his theory, Krashen predicts that effective second language teaching programs (a) provide ample access to interesting and relevant comprehensible input, (b) do not require students to speak before they are ready, (c) demonstrate tolerance of errors during early production, and (d) put grammar in its proper place.

Despite the theory's serious limitations (see Barasch & James, 1994; Hadley, 1993; Larsen-Freeman & Long, 1991), it remains one of the most influential in educational circles. In highlighting applications of the theory to classroom instruction, Larsen-Freeman and Long (1991) write:

> Common to all these applications are advocacy of: (1) a focus on meaning, not form[1] by teacher and students at all times (communication which will ensure the provision of CI [comprehensible input]; (2) proscription of structural grading and error correction (either of which would lead to a focus on language as object); and (3) creation of a positive affective classroom climate in order to "lower the filter." (p. 244)

For many practitioners, the applications described by Krashen and Terrell in *The Natural Approach* (1983) have produced effective results in the classroom. For researchers, many of the theoretical questions and issues they address are yet to be resolved.

---

[1]*Form* refers to grammar, syntax, etc.

The Environmentalist View   Environmentalist theories of second language acquisition emphasize nurture or experience over innate endowment (Larsen-Freeman & Long, 1991). Some environmentalist theories use cognitive processes to explain acquisition (e.g., behaviorist) while others rely on variables outside the learner (e.g., acculturation model). Of the theories in this group, the claims in Schumann's acculturation model are among the best known and most important for educators.

Schumann's claims emerged from his efforts to explain an adult language learner's relative lack of success acquiring English as a second language in a non-instructional setting (Larsen-Freeman & Long, 1991; Schumann, 1978a, 1978b). After other factors were eliminated, Schumann's explanation centered on group and individual factors related to social and psychological distance from speakers of the target language. Hence, his emphasis on acculturation: "the social and psychological integration of the learner with the target language group" (Schumann, 1978b, 29).

At the group level, Schumann (1978a, 1978b) identified eight factors that influence naturalistic second language acquisition when two groups in contact speak different languages. These notions draw on work done on bilingualism, second language acquisition, sociolinguistics, and ethnic relations. "They represent societal factors that either promote or inhibit social solidarity between two groups and thus affect the way a second language learning group acquires the language of a particular target language group" (1978a, 77). In other words, the social factors serve as indicators of the distance between these two language communities, reflecting the frequency and nature of contacts between language groups—factors that favor or inhibit second language acquisition. "These factors operate on a group level to mediate contact between the target language and second language communities; they are expressions of collective relationships" (McGroarty, 1988, 319). The eight factors identified by Schumann (Larsen-Freeman & Long, 1991, 252–253; Schumann, 1978a, 77–80; 1978b, 29–31) are paraphrased as follows:

1. *social dominance*—whether the language groups have equal social status or are in a status relationship in which one is politically, culturally, technically, or economically dominant and the other subordinate

2. *integration pattern*—whether those acquiring the new language display tendencies toward assimilation, acculturation, or cultural preservation

3. *enclosure*—whether those acquiring a language belong to a group that has social institutions (e.g., churches, schools, professional or trade organizations, clubs, etc.) providing group identity and support for its members

4. *cohesiveness*—whether those acquiring a new language are members of an ethnic or cultural group characterized as cohesive

5. *size*—whether the size of the ethnic or cultural group tends to encourage more frequent contacts within or outside the group

6. *cultural congruence*—whether perceptions as to similarities and differences between the language groups facilitate or inhibit contact

7. *attitude*—whether attitudes toward members of the other group are positive, neutral or negative; and

8. *intended length of residence*—whether the language learner expects to remain in the target language environment for a long, short, or undefined period of time.

At the individual level, Schumann claims that four affective factors—*language shock, culture shock, motivation*, and *ego permeability*—are particularly critical in determining psychological distance. "The affective factors determine how close or far from speakers of the target language potential learners perceive themselves to be and, thus, how much effort they are likely to expend in acquiring the second language well" (McGroarty, 1988, 324). An individual may find himself or herself in a more or less favorable language learning situation. It is at this point that the "*psychological* distance or proximity between the learner and the TL group . . . accounts for successful versus unsuccessful second language acquisition" (Schumann, 1978a, 86).

Language and culture shock encompass the complex emotional reactions (e.g., anxiety, fear, frustration, inadequacy, disorientation) that individuals experience using a new language or interacting in a new culture (Schumann, 1978b, 31–34). Motivation refers to the orientation that gives language learners their sense of purpose—whether the impetus for language learning comes primarily from a desire to become more involved with people from another culture or from more pragmatic objectives related to academic, professional, or occupational goals. The level of psychological solidarity that a learner achieves is commensurate with these goals. Ego-permeability is described with words like empathy, openness, receptivity, and inhibition. The term *language ego*, borrowed from Guiora, conveys a sense of the boundaries individuals create around themselves—boundaries that are more or less permeable or receptive to a new language "identity" (Schumann, 1978).

As Larsen-Freeman and Long (1991) observe, the acculturation model does not explain how social and psychological factors actually influence the individual's internalization of language or how they affect acquisition rates and outcomes. Despite these and other limitations, however, Schumann may have identified "several of the contextual factors relevant in predicting group-level success in acculturating to a new society" (pp. 265–266).

The Interactionist View   Interactionist theories are more powerful than their nativist and environmental counterparts (Larsen-Freeman & Long, 1991, 266). Drawing on both innate endowments and environmental factors, interactionist theories typically utilize more factors and processes to explain the complexities of acquisition. They also represent a wide variety of perspectives, from cognitive psychology and psycholinguistics to sociolinguistics and social theory. From an instructional standpoint, the multidimensional model is one of the most relevant to emerge from work in this area.

The ZISA (Zweitspracherwerb Italienischer, Spanischer und Portugiesischer Arbeiter) group's multidimensional model began with research on adult native speakers of Spanish, Italian, and Portuguese learning German as a second language (Larsen-Freeman & Long, 1991). It was an attempt "to tie contextual factors, including a range of social and psychological variables, to internal psycholinguistic processes, in the form of simplification and processing strategies" (p. 283). By taking a two-dimensional approach, the model addresses those aspects of second language acquisition that are developmental (the sequences that all learners follow) as well as variational (the individual differences observed within defined stages of development).

On the developmental side, the multidimensional model posits universal constraints that control developmental sequences in the second language. The model claims that the ability to process language is constrained by a set of speech-processing strategies that operate at various stages in the developmental sequence. Initially, the learner sequences words and phrases according to meaning and information. In subsequent stages, the learner recognizes that elements belong to different categories and produces structures applying this knowledge. Eventually, the learner develops the ability to move elements in more complex hierarchical structures.

Because the strategies impose constraints on what the learner is able to process, development is viewed as a process of shedding strategies and their corresponding constraints. This is the basis for Pienemann's claim that "the strategies constrain what is comprehensible, and so *learnable* at any time, and hence, what is *teachable*, implying that attempts to teach structures will be futile if they involve permutations and analysis beyond a learner's current processing level" (Larsen-Freeman & Long, 1991, 272). Since each stage in the developmental sequence builds on the processing strategies developed earlier, instruction does not enable learners to skip stages. "The Teachability Hypothesis (Pienemann, 1984) predicts that the *teachability* of an item, and indeed the effects of any external factors, such as natural exposure to a target structure, will always be constrained by its *learnability*. . . . Items will only be successfully taught when learners are psycholinguistically 'ready' to learn them" (p. 280).

On the variational dimension, the model differentiates between two types of learner orientation (Larsen-Freeman & Long, 1991, 280–282). Learners demonstrating a more "standard" orientation seem to delay the use of linguistic items until they can be produced in ways that better approximate standard usage. By contrast, learners with a more "simplifying" orientation appear to favor the use of less accurate or more deviant forms in order to achieve more effective communication sooner.

Larsen-Freeman and Long (1991) observe that "whereas the effects of instruction are subject to processing constraints where developmental features are concerned, this is not the case with variational features" (p. 282). Once the learner has begun to produce variational features, instruction can make a considerable difference in the development of accuracy. This has considerable implications, especially with respect to methodology and assessment. Knowledge of developmental and variational features may eventually enable teachers to classify errors and determine which are and are not responsive to treatment (Larsen-Freeman & Long, 1991, 287).

Implications

Research conducted from each of these theoretical perspectives has contributed to our understanding of second language acquisition in important ways. From this research, insights that are of particular interest to teachers have emerged. Given the shortcomings inherent in all second language acquisition theories and the significant gaps that still exist in our knowledge of the processes involved, teachers are cautioned regarding the application of theory to practice (e.g., Larsen-Freeman & Long, 1991; Littlewood, 1984).

> What we can find in this research, however, is a source of insights and ideas about learning which we can add to our present understanding and experience, to help us in our constant search for better ways of teaching. In some cases, these insights and ideas may suggest new orientations and methods. In other cases, they may reinforce developments which have already begun to take place. Always, of course, the final criterion for accepting any pedagogical idea is not whether it is valid from a theoretical perspective, but whether it produces more effective practice. (Littlewood, 1984, 90)

In summarizing some of the insights revealed from the research on second language acquisition, Littlewood (1984) identifies the following ideas as particularly important for teachers to consider.

Concept 1   *Language learning is a conscious and subconscious process* (pp. 90–92). Littlewood asserts that "perhaps the most important fact that is highlighted by second language research is that progress does not only occur when people make conscious efforts to learn. Progress also occurs as a result of spontaneous, subconscious mechanisms, which are activated when learners are involved in communication with the second language" (pp. 90–91). This means that teachers need to develop a new paradigm for the activities they use to promote language development. Traditional activities that focus on language learning only at the conscious level are not enough. Learners need activities that reach the subconscious, with an emphasis on the communication of meanings and ample opportunities for creative construction.

Concept 2   *Language learning can take place—particularly during the initial stages of acquisition—without oral and written production* (pp. 92–94). Productive practice may be less central to early phases of the basic learning process than once believed. That is, learners appear to be able to operate internal processing mechanisms and engage in creative construction without producing language initially. "The very fact that learners can produce spontaneous utterances which reflect their own created systems is itself evidence that creative construction precedes production" (p. 93). Hence, allowing for a silent period in which learners are exposed to comprehensible input without being required to produce oral language is consistent with naturalistic acquisition.

Concept 3   *Language development adheres to natural acquisition sequences* (pp. 94–95). Natural sequences imply a process of gradually developing accuracy, as learners progress from one linguistic element to another in stages. Learners are ready to acquire a language item A (for example, the use of *-s* to mark plural nouns in English) before they are ready to acquire item B (such as the use of *-s* to mark third-person verbs). As they master specific structural operations (for example, yes/no interrogatives or negatives), learners proceed through natural learning sequences. Eventually, learners move from one stage to the next (p. 94).

The teaching implications are significant. Implied in the notion of natural sequence is Pienemann's idea that "learners will only benefit from appropriately timed instruction" (Larsen-Freeman & Long, 1991, 284). Where students are in the natural sequence will determine which structures are appropriate and which are inappropriate at a given time. This also changes perceptions of errors as part of the acquisition process.

Concept 4   *Learners can communicate even with an imperfect knowledge of the language system* (pp. 95–96). Littlewood advises teachers to reconceptualize their view of language development, "not in terms of individual items which should be mastered to perfection, but in terms of a system which is elaborated globally and increases gradually in communicative potential" (p. 96). Learners can do a great deal with language, even though they operate with a reduced system. To maximize this potential, students can be encouraged to develop confidence in their limited language systems and to exploit the language they have for purposeful communication. Learners can use communication strategies to compensate for gaps in their knowledge of the second language. For their part, teachers can emphasize effectiveness of communication over accuracy in assessing student performance.

Three Guiding Principles

Cummins (1989, 29–32, 40–50; 1996) draws on psychoeducational research as well as second language acquisition theory and research to develop a set of principles that teachers can use to guide program development. The first—the conversational/academic language proficiency principle—draws attention to the significant distinctions between social and academic language skills. The second—the linguistic interdependence principle—examines the relationship between the first and second language. The third—the additive bilingualism enrichment principle—focuses on the importance of the primary language in developing second language proficiency. Each of these principles is highlighted in the sections that follow.

The Conversational/Academic Language Proficiency Principle

The conversational/academic language proficiency principle explains a phenomenon that teachers have often observed but not fully understood. Many teachers are puzzled by the fact that second language learners may perform in social situations as if they were native speakers and yet fail to achieve academically. What teachers overlook is the fact that there are significant differences between the language skills used for communication and those utilized for academic purposes.

Conversational and academic language skills fall along a continuum denoting language functions that are acquired over time (Cummins, 1989, 1996). Students will first develop basic interpersonal communicative skills (originally referred to as BICS). In the social arena, language is characterized by its use in interpersonal interaction. Meaning is negotiated between participants and conveyed through language with a relatively high reliance on context. Feedback is provided naturally. Interpretation is amply supported by situational and nonverbal clues. "In face-to-face conversation the meaning is supported by a range of contextual cues (e.g., the concrete situation, gestures, intonation, facial expression, etc.)" (1989, 27). Children in the process of learning language associated with classroom routines, for example, can follow the actions of other children and interpret teacher gestures and facial expressions. Consider the contextual clues that support understanding when a teacher asks children to line up for lunch or recess. On the playground, imagine how much a child can glean from watching other children play and then joining in the activity (Hernández, 1989).

Cognitive and academic tasks require language skills known as cognitive-academic language proficiency (originally referred to as CALP) (Cummins, 1996). In this realm, language, particularly in written form, is primary; little information, if any, is provided by other sources. Reading selections from literature, social studies, or science texts demands language skills significantly different from those used in interpersonal communication. Meaning is inherent almost exclusively in the written text itself, and the task of deriving meaning is essential if higher-level thinking skills are to be brought into play. "A central aspect of what I have termed 'academic' language proficiency is the ability to make complex meanings explicit in either oral or written modalities by means of *language itself* rather than by means of paralinguistic cues (e.g., gestures, intonation, etc.)" (1989, 30). Thus, limitations in language skills are far more likely to affect how students perform on academic tasks than to interfere with their participation in social situations in which meaning is negotiated and supported contextually and tasks are generally less intellectually demanding.

How long, then, does it take for second language learners to develop a full range of language and literacy skills in English? Although there is no way to predict the length of time an individual will need to acquire proficiency in English, accumulating evidence indicates that, for most students, it may be considerably longer than teachers would expect. Cummins (1981) reports that immigrant students arriving in Canada after age six require approximately two years to develop certain aspects of age-appropriate English communicative skills and five to seven years to develop age-appropriate academic skills in English. In a study of 2,000 English language learners, Collier (1989) found that at least 4 to 7 years were required for students to reach grade level norms for different English academic skills. Children with no schooling in their primary language may require more time, even as long as 7 to 10 years (pp. 526–527). For those who wonder why it takes such a relatively long period of time to achieve full proficiency, the answer is simple. "Native English speakers continue to make significant progress in English academic skills (e.g., vocabulary knowledge, reading and writing skills, etc.) year after year. They do not stand still waiting for the minority student to catch up. In conversational skills, on the other hand, after the first six years of life, changes tend to be more subtle" (Cummins, 1989, 27). Clearly, the expectation that second language learners can acquire native-like proficiency in English in a matter of months or even a year or two is unrealistic. Schools need to recognize this reality in providing programs for English language learners.

Cognitive and academic tasks require different language skills than does communication.

The distinction between conversational and academic language proficiency is a critical one for teachers (Cummins, 1984, 1989). In essence, the acquisition of conversational language skills is no guarantee that students have achieved a comparable command of academic language. Failure to recognize this fact has often resulted in misconceptions regarding the abilities of second language learners. It has also contributed to the assumption that learners have cognitive deficits rather than academic-cognitive language skills that are not yet fully developed. Based on examination of 400 referral forms and psychological assessments on second language learners, Cummins (1996) found that such misconceptions were commonplace. Many of those assessing students concluded that because they "are fluent in English, their poor academic performance and/or test scores cannot be attributed to lack of proficiency in English. Therefore, these students must either have deficient cognitive abilities or be poorly motivated (p. 9). In addition, this "surface fluency" also results in the premature exiting of students from bilingual education programs (Cummins, 1989, 1996). The perception that students are fully proficient in English disguises gaps in academic English development. As a result, primary language support is not continued when students enter regular classrooms, and performance often falls below grade level.

The Linguistic Interdependence Principle

Research indicates that proficiency in one's first language provides the foundation for acquisition of the second (Cummins, 1989, 1996). Looking at the primary language, we see that language acquisition in the first language is a longer process than once believed, extending well beyond age 5 (Larsen-Freeman & Long, 1991). Although much of an individual's primary language is developed in the first 5 years, there is strong evidence that more complex syntax is not acquired until children are considerably older. For example, Larsen-Freeman and Long (1991) cite studies indicating that some WH-questions (those beginning with who, what, where, etc.) are not fully controlled until age 10. Other elements of grammar are not mastered until about age 16. This means that language minority children will continue to be engaged in first language acquisition even as they acquire English as a second language.

Research also indicates that first and second language development are interdependent (Cummins, 1989, 1996; McGroarty, 1988). Cummins has stated this interdependence principle in more formal terms as follows: "To the extent that instruction in Lx is effective in promoting proficiency in Lx, transfer of this proficiency to Ly will occur provided there is adequate exposure to Ly (either in school or environment) and adequate motivation to learn Ly" (1996, 19). This principle is supported by a number of studies conducted in different social and cultural contexts reporting a positive relationship between the first and second language. Cummins cites investigations by Kemp, Ramírez, Hakuta and Díaz, Geva and Ryan, Carlisle, and McLaughlin, to name a few. More informally, the same principle has been expressed as follows:

> Having a strong foundation in the native language makes learning a second language both easier and faster. . . . Moreover, there is general agreement that knowledge transfers readily from one language to another, so that students do not have to relearn in a second language what they have already learned in a first. In fact, it is clear that the ability to transfer to English what is learned in the native language applies not only to content-area subjects like science and math, but also to skills in reading and writing—even when the orthographic system is quite different from the Roman alphabet" (Association for Supervision and Curriculum Development, cited in Cummins, 1989, 45).

On an intuitive level, it seems obvious that a high level of competence in the primary language would expand the cognitive and linguistic resources available to the individual in another language. Anecdotal accounts have long recognized the importance of primary language skills in educational achievement. Cárdenas's (1986) personal observations illustrate the connection between proficiency in a first and second language.

> It is interesting to note that, almost without exception, those of us who learned the English language grew up in homes with a strong language capability. Although this capability was usually in a language other than English, the level of language ability within our families was high during our developmental years. This is as true for language-minority persons of my generation who grew up to become legislators, mayors, educators, and successful business people as it is today for the Korean or Vietnamese children who are graduating as valedictorians. The common denominator invariably is extensive competence in the use of some language. (p. 360)

The Additive Bilingualism Enrichment Principle

The additive bilingualism enrichment principle is related to the linguistic interdependence principle. Based upon research on the academic, linguistic, and cogni-

tive effects of bilingualism, Cummins (1989) posits that "the development of additive bilingual and biliteracy skills entails no negative consequences for children's
academic, linguistic, or intellectual development. On the contrary, although not
conclusive, the evidence points in the direction of subtle metalinguistic, academic
and intellectual benefits for bilingual children" (p. 44). The level of proficiency
achieved by an individual in two languages influences academic and intellectual
development as follows:

> Specifically, there may be a threshold level of proficiency in both languages which stu-
> dents must attain in order to avoid any negative academic consequences and a sec-
> ond, higher, threshold necessary to reap the linguistic and possibly intellectual bene-
> fits of bilingualism and biliteracy. (p. 42)

With additive bilingualism, bilinguals with high levels of proficiency in both
languages may enjoy academic, cognitive, and linguistic advantages over individuals proficient in only one. When second language acquisition is an additive process
and both languages are fully developed, Cummins argues that there is evidence to
support the position that cognitive effects are positive. This is evidenced by the
proficient bilinguals who Cárdenas describes. (For a methodological critique of
research on the cognitive consequences of bilingualism, see Reynolds, 1991.)

The scenario in which an individual is highly proficient in his or her native
language but is limited in a second is very common. For example, many people
have taken Spanish, French, Russian, Chinese, or German in school. As a result,
they are proficient in English and have a smattering of skills in another language.
This level of bilingualism probably has no significant effect on English proficiency. Falling short of the upper threshold by achieving less than relatively high
levels of proficiency in both languages, such individuals would not accrue the full
benefits of bilingualism.

However, ultimate attainment in both languages may suffer when the
process of becoming bilingual is a subtractive one. If the second language supplants the first before a critical level of proficiency has been reached, the consequences may be serious. For example, "the research suggests that achievement in
English literacy skills is strongly related to the extent of development of L1 literacy skills" (Cummins, 1981, 44). As a result, Cummins strongly urges teachers and
administrators to provide children in bilingual programs with enough time "to
develop 'threshold' levels of biliteracy" (p. 44). Clearly, there is reason for concern
when the new language supplants the primary language rather than serving to
enhance a child's developing linguistic base.

For regular classroom teachers, the relationship between the child's two language systems has important implications (Hernández, 1989). In the past, teachers
have often discouraged the use of ethnic languages in the classroom, on school
grounds, and even at home. There are legal mandates requiring the use of English
as the medium of instruction in many states (Kloss, 1977, 98–99). Students have been
reprimanded (slapped across the palm of the hand with a ruler or sent to serve
detention) for using their primary language to interact with other students. Popular
myths about language have held that the home language should not be maintained

if English is to be learned quickly and well, that individuals have a limited capacity for language, and that the first language must make way for the second.

Although the situation in each school, home, and community is different, mounting evidence indicates that teachers are best advised to adopt a position supportive of primary language development. This is particularly critical until such time as English language skills are sufficiently developed to fully support academic and cognitive development. Even when they themselves are not bilingual, however, teachers are encouraged to promote continued development and maintenance of the primary language at school and in the home. In many regular classrooms, this is done with instructional aides, parents, and community volunteers, in special after-school classes, and through activities integrated as part of the curriculum (e.g., oral history projects, surveys, free reading).

Summary

Language proficiency encompasses grammatical, sociolinguistic, discourse, and strategic competence. To be proficient in a second language, learners must internalize the underlying structures of the new language, adjust their language to make it appropriate socially and culturally in different situations, and master the dynamics of interaction. They must also develop strategic competence by learning to use verbal and nonverbal techniques to compensate for limitations in proficiency.

The process of second language acquisition is as complex as it is fascinating. Researchers look at the processes involved from divergent perspectives. The nativists emphasize innate biological endowments and abilities while the environmentalists look more toward environment and experience. Interactionists attempt to integrate nature and nurture, balancing innate endowments with environmental factors.

Whereas many questions remain to be answered, research does have implications for instruction. Second language development follows natural acquisition sequences. What can be taught and learned at a given time is determined by the learner's psycholinguistic readiness to learn. Language learning is conscious and subconscious, and to be effective, instruction must address both dimensions. Last but not least, learners can communicate effectively even with less than total command of a new language system.

Research from linguistics, psychology, education, and other fields should be used to inform program development for language minority students. Applying insights from the principles of conversational/academic language proficiency, linguistic interdependence, and additive bilingual enrichment, teachers can distinguish between academic and conversational proficiency and recognize the interdependence of first and second language development.

Key to Figure 5–3

The following key will allow you to compare your responses to the numbered items in Figure 5–3 with those drawn from researchers.

Item 1	SD/D	Scovel (1988, 170–173)
Item 2	SA/A	Brown, cited in Snow with Shapira (1985, 10)
Item 3	SA/A	Littlewood (1984, 90–92)
Item 4	SA/A	Littlewood (1984, 95–96)
Item 5	SA/A	Hatch, Gough, and Peck (1985, 55)
Item 6	SA/A	Scovel (1988, 185)
Item 7	SA/A	Scovel (1988, 177)
Item 8	SD/D	Scovel (1988, 179)

References

Barasch, R. M., & James, C. V. (Eds.). (1994). *Beyond the monitor model*. Boston: Heinle & Heinle.

Cárdenas, J. A. (1986). The role of native-language instruction in bilingual education. *Phi Delta Kappan, 67*(5), 359–363.

Celce-Murcia, M., & Larsen-Freeman, D. (1983). *The grammar book*. Rowley, MA: Newbury House.

Collier, V. P. (1989). How long? A synthesis of research on academic achievement in a second language. *TESOL Quarterly, 23*(3), 509–531.

Cummins, J. (1981). The role of primary language development in promoting educational success for language minority students. In Office of Bilingual Bicultural Education, *Schooling and language minority students: A theoretical framework* (pp. 3–49). Los Angeles: Evaluation, Dissemination and Assessment Center, California State University, Los Angeles.

Cummins, J. (1984). *Bilingualism and special education: Issues in assessment and pedagogy*. San Diego: College-Hill Press.

Cummins, J. (1989). *Empowering minority students*. Sacramento: California Association for Bilingual Education.

Cummins, J. (1996). Primary language instruction and the education of language minority students. *Schooling and language minority students: A theoretical framework* (2nd ed.) (pp. 3–46). Los Angeles: Evaluation, Dissemination and Assessment Center, School of Education, California State University, Los Angeles.

Enright, D. S., & McCloskey, M. L. (1988). *Integrating English: Developing English and literacy in the multilingual classroom*. Reading, MA: Addison-Wesley.

Grosjean, F. (1982). *Life with two languages*. Cambridge: Harvard University Press.

Hadley, A. O. (1993). *Teaching language in context* (2nd ed.). Boston: Heinle & Heinle.

Hatch, E., Gough, J. W., & Peck, S. (1985). What case studies reveal about system, sequence, and variation in second language acquisition. In M. Celce-Murcia (Ed.), *Beyond basics* (pp. 37–59). Rowley, MA: Newbury House.

Hernández, H. (1989). *Multicultural education: A teacher's guide to content and process*. Upper Saddle River, NJ: Merrill/Prentice Hall.

Higgs, T. V., & Clifford, R. (1982). The push toward communication. In T. V. Higgs (Ed.), *Curriculum, competence and the foreign language teacher* (pp. 57–79). Skokie, IL: National Textbook.

Kloss, H. (1977). *The American bilingual tradition*. Rowley, MA: Newbury House.

Kramsch, C. J. (1981). Language in education: Theory and practice: Vol. 37. *Discourse analysis and second language teaching*. Washington, D. C.: Center for Applied Linguistics.

Krashen, S. D. (1981). *Second language acquisition and second language learning*. Oxford: Pergamon Press.

Krashen, S. D. (1985a). *The input hypothesis: Issues and implications*. New York: Longman.

Krashen, S. D. (1985b). Applications of psycholinguistic research to the classroom. In C. J.
  James (Ed.), *Practical applications of research in foreign language teaching* (pp. 51–66). Lincolnwood, IL: National Textbook.

Krashen, S. D. (1996). Bilingual education and second language acquisition theory. *Schooling
  and language minority students: A theoretical framework* (2nd ed.) (pp. 47–75). Los Angeles:
  Evaluation, Dissemination and Assessment Center, School of Education, California
  State University, Los Angeles.

Krashen, S. D., & Terrell, T. D. (1983). *The natural approach*. Oxford: Pergamon/Alemany.

Larsen-Freeman, D., & Long, M. H. (1991). *An introduction to second language acquisition
  research*. New York: Longman.

Lindfors, J. W. (1987). *Children's language and learning* (2nd ed). Englewood Cliffs, NJ: Prentice-Hall.

Littlewood, W. (1984). *Foreign and second language learning*. New York: Cambridge University
  Press.

McGroarty, M. (1988). Second language acquisition theory relevant to language minorities:
  Cummins, Krashen, and Schumann. In S. L. McKay & S. C. Wong (Eds.), *Language
  diversity: Problem or resource? A social and educational perspective on language minorities in
  the United States* (pp. 295–337). New York: Newbury House.

Meléndez, S. E. (1989, January). A nation of monolinguals, a multilingual world. In
  National Education Association, *Bilingually Speaking* (pp. 70–73).

Olsen, L., & Mullen, N. A. (1990). *Embracing diversity* (California Tomorrow Immigrant Students Project Research Report). San Francisco: California Tomorrow.

Reynolds, A. G. (1991). The cognitive consequences of bilingualism. *ERIC Clearinghouse on
  Languages and Linguistics News Bulletin, 14*(2), pp. 1, 4–5, 8. Center for Applied Linguistics, 1118 22nd Street NW, Washington, DC 20037.

Schumann, J. H. (1978a). *The pidginization process*. Rowley, MA: Newbury House.

Schumann, J. H. (1978b). The acculturation model for second-language acquisition. In R. C.
  Gingras (Ed.), *Second language acquisition and foreign language teaching* (pp. 27–50).
  Washington, DC: Center for Applied Linguistics.

Scovel, T. (1988). Multiple perspectives make singular teaching. In L. M. Beebe (Ed.), *Issues
  in second language acquisition* (pp. 169–190). New York: Newbury House.

Sinclair, J. McH., & Coulthard, R. M. (1975). *Towards an analysis of discourse*. Oxford: Oxford
  University Press.

Snow, M. A., with Shapira, R. G. (1985). The role of social-psychological factors in second
  language learning. In M. Celce-Murcia (Ed.), *Beyond basics* (pp. 3–15). Rowley, MA:
  Newbury House.

Tarone, E. (1980). Communication strategies, foreigner talk, and repair in interlanguage.
  Language Learning, 30(2), 417–431.

6

Classroom Processes

You must work—we must all work—to make this world worthy of its children.

Pablo Casals

From a teaching perspective, "language" should be thought of as a verb—as in *using* language—rather than as a noun—as in *knowledge* of a language (Enright & McCloskey, 1988, 19). There are many ways that teachers and students use language in a classroom setting; communication and instruction are basic. This chapter is an exploration of various facets of second language development in the classroom context. It opens with a look at the often confusing and difficult experiences that mark English language learners' introduction to school. Attention is focused on designing an orientation process that can make the transition into a new school, language, and cultural environment less traumatic for children and older students. The chapter continues with consideration of important cultural, social, and linguistic dimensions of language development in the classroom setting and exploration of selected strategies and techniques that teachers can use in elementary and secondary classrooms.

After completing this chapter, you will be able to

1. provide a basic school orientation for learners from different linguistic and cultural backgrounds
2. explore the sociocultural context of classroom second language development in relation to instructional conversations, small groups, and the dynamics of classroom language use
3. explore language use patterns in the classroom
4. describe the dynamics of classroom discourse

The Orientation Process

Law and Eckes (1990) describe how many teachers feel when they first receive a student who does not speak English into their classroom. In their description, they use words like awkward, apprehensive, intimidated, terrified, and helpless. They describe the "wave of panic" that overcomes teachers facing the prospect of teaching one or more students with whom they are unable to communicate. Teachers find that "nothing erodes . . . confidence faster than an inability to communicate with someone" (p. 7).

Non-English-speaking students—children and adolescents, native born, immigrant, and refugee—often look back on their first day in school as confusing and even traumatic. Everything is different—the language, the teachers, the students, the routines, and the expectations. One student describes how even the simplest of routines can create problems (L. Olsen, 1988):

> I started in 7th grade and had trouble looking for classes. In Mexico we stay in the same place all day. I went to the first class because that is where I was taken. It was over so soon and I didn't know to go to another class, so I went home. I got in trouble.

They should have told me, and had someone walk me to my classes at first. I didn't know! (p. 71)

9th-grade Mexican boy
(immigrated at age 12)

L. Olsen (1988) reports that most school districts provide students with no orientation or support structure upon their arrival. Demystifying routines and expectations is left to chance, as students must rely on their own resources to figure out what is going on. Interaction between teacher and student is difficult; miscommunication is virtually guaranteed.

The school was so big! There were students everywhere all the time—not just in classes. I didn't know how you were supposed to know where to go when. There was no one who could speak Mien and explain to me. My uncle told me if I needed any help to go to the Dean. My teacher asked me something and I didn't understand her. So I just said "Dean, Dean" because I needed help. That is how I got my American name. She was asking me "What is your name?" and I kept saying "Dean." Now everybody calls me Dean. Now it is funny, but it is also sad. My name comes from not knowing what was going on. (pp. 72–73)

12th-grade Lao Mien boy
(immigrated at age 14)

How teachers respond when students are first introduced leaves a lasting impression. Learning the student's name and making an effort to say it correctly is an important first step. Law and Eckes (1990, 8) are on target when they advise teachers not to anglicize or change a student's name just because they find it difficult to pronounce. A student's name is an integral part of his or her identity; efforts to "change" it may convey the message that the child and his or her language and culture are not accepted. Teachers with students of all ages—children, adolescents, and adults—are encouraged to learn to pronounce correctly the names of students from different language backgrounds.

Peregoy and Boyle (1993, 4–5) suggest that teachers follow a three-step process when new students arrive. First, teachers need pertinent information about the child, including the country of origin, length of residency in the United States (for non-native-born), home language(s), who the child is living with and where, whether the child is an immigrant, refugee, or native born, and so on. Second, teachers need to gather information regarding the child's educational background. This includes information as to where the child was enrolled in school, how much schooling he or she has had, whether and to what extent it has been interrupted, the language or languages used, grade level or equivalent, level of literacy in the primary language, and so on. The final suggestion is that teachers acquire basic information regarding the child's culture. This includes the cultural group characteristics such as those identified by Saville-Troike (1978): information regarding family, roles, interpersonal relationships, religion, food, dress and personal appearance, traditions, notions of time and space, expectations, and aspirations. Teachers will need to exercise their professional judgment and proceed

People
- Names of key people, especially the teacher
- A "buddy" who speaks the same language and is able to help the new student become familiar with the school and classroom (For students from certain cultures, class or gender differences may affect the choice of a buddy.)

Schedule
- Daily
- Time of arrival and dismissal
- Lengths and times for recesses or breaks
- Lunch periods
- Bus schedules
- Academic calendar
- Dates when school is not in session (e.g., holidays, staff development or inservice days, vacation)
- Ways of indicating time (e.g., use of bells, buzzers, whistles)

Facilities
- Location of classrooms, offices, cafeteria, rest rooms (identify which is appropriate), lockers, etc.
- Designated areas (e.g., bus stops; area where family members or friends drop off and pick up children; area on the playground where the class lines up to go back to class; for elementary children, designated play areas for different age groups; for secondary, detention area)
- Areas that are off-limits (e.g., at certain times of the day, high school student parking lots; or to students in certain grades, preschool, kindergarten, primary, or intermediate play areas)

Figure 6-1   Orientation to the school and classroom
Source: Law and Eckes (1990, 10–13)

with appropriate sensitivity as they gather information. While instructionally appropriate under normal conditions, some questions may seem threatening in certain situations (e.g., with undocumented immigrants).

The suggestions presented in Figure 6-1 will help teachers to design and implement an orientation process for students in their own schools. Information in the areas identified is likely to benefit all new students. However, support is even more critical for students whose native language is not English. If the teacher does not anticipate learners' needs, their confusion and anxiety are likely to be greater and to persist longer.

This overview is just a starting point. Niepoth's (1992) research at the secondary level suggests that orientation processes should be a schoolwide commitment. For example, other students at the school—those who arrived unable to speak English

Procedures

In the classroom:

- Going into the classroom and leaving it
- Lining up
- Turn taking (when students need to raise their hands, when they may leave their seats, whether they must stand when speaking [this is the custom in many countries])
- Talking and working cooperatively (when students are encouraged to work cooperatively, when talking is encouraged or permitted, when cooperation or collaboration is considered cheating)

In school:

- Paying for lunch, field trips, etc.
- Using lockers
- Going to the restroom
- Traffic patterns in the hallway

Policies

- Dealing with absences (e.g., permission, written excuse)
- Handling tardies and other infractions
- Staying after school or serving detention
- Requiring attendance of students
- Making a phone call home

Emergencies

- Significance of special sirens or horns
- Contact persons (parents, family, neighbors) if the student becomes ill or is injured while at school
- Restrictions regarding medical conditions or first aid
- Instructions on how child is to get home if he or she misses a ride or bus (parents may instruct the child not to walk home alone)

and who are now developing proficiency—can be tapped for their insights as to what is most critical to include as part of the orientation and integration process.

The study took place in a small, rural intermediate school that had recently experienced an increase in the number of students for whom English is not a primary language. The teachers involved had no specialized preparation for working with English language learners. Teachers and students were asked to address the following questions (Niepoth, 1992):

1. What can the administration and staff of the school do to create an environment that makes students feel welcome and facilitates their acquisition of English at school?

2. What can the teacher do to best teach students who are in the process of learning English as their second language while taking subjects taught in English?

3. What can other students do to assist students who are learning English?

4. What can new students who are learning English do to facilitate their own language and academic language learning? (pp. 7–8)

Whereas each school site is unique and must look for its own set of answers to these and other questions, the experience of this one school demonstrates the value of bringing teachers and students together to generate practical ideas for meeting long- and short-term needs. The recommendations they generated illustrate the possibilities for change that can emerge through such a collaborative process (Niepoth, 1992, 131–133). For example, students recommended that English language learners integrate into the classroom community through groupwork and participation in class activities. It is important for students to have opportunities to ask questions and to get the help they need by working in groups. Teachers were cautioned to avoid room arrangements that relegate second language learners to the periphery. They were asked to make English language development a part of every class, to teach vocabulary and provide contextual clues that help students make meaningful connections. When using textbooks, teachers were encouraged to read aloud and assist students in finding their place. It was suggested that assignments be appropriate to the students' level of language proficiency and that parents be kept informed.

Recommendations also addressed what students could do to help themselves and to support each other (Niepoth, 1992, 133–135). Newcomers whose primary language is not English were encouraged to participate in class activities and to respond as appropriate to their level of language proficiency (e.g., using one-word answers at the beginning). Seeking out friends and peers for assistance and getting involved in outside activities were other suggestions. It was deemed important that students maintain their primary language and use it in preparing for class whenever possible. Students in the school were advised to learn a few words in the primary language of the newcomers and to make an effort to communicate with those who are learning English. In class, they were encouraged to make it a point to use key words related to the topic discussed during groupwork.

Recommendations for administration and staff were insightful. Support personnel were encouraged to

- develop an orientation program to familiarize new students with rules, facilities, etc. (e.g., translate the student handbook into other languages)
- provide information on new students (and, if possible, from the student) to help teachers and staff begin to know the student as an individual
- make instructional and library materials available in the primary language
- provide translations of instructions for daily assignments and information sent home to parents
- develop an appropriate school grading policy for English language learners
- provide computer programs designed to facilitate development of communication skills
- provide bilingual dictionaries
- develop a program to provide tutoring (Niepoth, 1992, 131–132)

Since the context of each school and community is different, the recommendations will also vary. The set of recommendations that emerged from the Niepoth study represent a starting point for teachers and students at the school.

Many of the ideas do not require additional resources; those that do will be prioritized along with other needs. The point to be made is that teachers and students working together and with administration and staff can best define the specific strategies that will be most effective in meeting the needs of the new students in their communities whose primary language is not English.

From Theory to Practice

The contributions of researchers attempting to understand and explain conditions that influence the education of culturally diverse populations have been described as falling along a theoretical continuum from "cultural match/mismatch" to "general principles" (García, 1995, 382). At one end are educators who adopt the cultural significance position that student success is contingent upon identifying critical differences that exist across and within ethnic groups and incorporating these as an integral part of schooling practices. At the other end, there are those who adopt the instructional perspective that the best way to promote academic achievement is through appropriate implementation of the general principles of effective teaching and learning that have been demonstrated to work with all students, whatever their backgrounds. Other positions emphasizing societal conditions inside and outside of school fall at different points along this continuum (pp. 381–382).

As García observes, these are not mutually exclusive approaches. Rather, they are complementary and necessary elements within a more comprehensive view of the educational process—a conceptual framework that embraces "an understanding of the relationship between home and school, the psycho-socio-cultural incongruities between the two, and the resulting effects on learning and achievement" (Tharp & Gallimore, cited in García, 1995, 382). In its own way, each position contributes to a better understanding of effective schooling as a whole.

This conceptualization provides the basis for a more responsive pedagogy for linguistically and culturally diverse populations (García, 1995, 382). Such pedagogy is sensitive to cultural differences, appropriate to psychological, economic, and social realities, and characterized by the best educational practices. It is based on the understanding that

- children acquire language and culture within their homes and communities
- by the time children come to school, they possess some understanding of language and how it is used
- involvement in socially meaningful activities is conducive to development of higher level cognitive and communicative skills
- language and academic development are interactive processes involving linguistic, sociocultural, and cognitive knowledge and experiences
- socioculturally *and* linguistically meaningful contexts enhance learning (p. 382)

For teachers, this pedagogy has important implications. Teachers cannot realize these concepts without changing the way they teach. As they look for instructional practices that reflect these understandings, they will adopt approaches and strategies that (a) view the classroom as a community of learners within which speakers, readers, and writers collaborate in giving meaning to academic experience; (b) respect and integrate learners' culture, language, values, and experiences; (c) demand active student involvement in the learning process; (d) use learners' immediate experiences in ways that extend their knowledge beyond the limits of those experiences; and (e) capitalize on first and second language capabilities (García, 1995, 383). "For those embracing this new concept of responsive pedagogy, new educational horizons for themselves and their students are not only possible but inevitable" (p. 383).

This brief introduction to a more responsive pedagogy sets the stage for the discussion of classroom processes that follows.

Social and Interactional Processes

In combination with other perspectives on teaching, the ideas of L. S. Vygotsky are contributing to a more unified theory of education in general and to an increasingly social interactionist view of language issues in particular. Observe the centrality of language in this emerging view of schooling from Tharp and Gallimore (cited in Gallimore & Tharp, 1990):

> The purpose of schooling is teaching students to be literate in the most general sense of the word—capable of reading, writing, speaking, computing, reasoning, and manipulating visual as well as verbal symbols and concepts. Literacy is achieved through the creation of opportunities for students to be assisted in the use of word meanings, conceptual structures, and discourse itself—so that signs and symbols take on new and shared meanings as they are hallowed by use during joint productive activity, taken underground, and stripped down to the lightning of thought. (p. 200)

This perspective on schooling focuses greater attention on the role of language within the social contexts in which teachers and students actively interact and influence each other. Within this framework, language is viewed as "a socioculturally mediated product" (Minami & Ovando, 1995, 431).

Instructional Dialogue

In his writings, Vygotsky emphasizes "the unique form of cooperation between the child and the adult that is the central element of the educational process" (cited in Moll, 1990, 2). This culturally ideal relationship between adult and child can be observed in one of Vygotsky's key theoretical constructs—the zone of proximal development (ZPD) (Minami & Ovando, 1995, 431). It may help to think of this construct as the zone of "next" or "potential" development. In essence, real teaching takes place within a zone in which the level of difficulty of a task or activity is challenging to the learner, but developmentally appropriate. Initially, the child can perform only with assistance and guidance provided by a teacher, adult, or more competent peer. Eventually, the child develops competence and is able to perform independently. A new definition of teaching emerges. "Teaching consists of assisting performance through the zone of proximal development. Thus teaching can be said to occur at that point in the zone where performance can be achieved with assistance" (Tharp & Gallimore, cited in Gallimore & Tharp, 1990, 200).

The most productive social contexts for teaching and learning operate within this zone. According to Vygotsky, good teaching awakens and stimulates those functions that are reaching maturity within the ZPD (Gallimore & Tharp, 1990, 177). The task of schooling, then, is the creation of activity settings in which teachers adopt the role of assisting students in the ZPD. "We may characterize the task of schooling as creating and supporting instructional conversations" (Gallimore & Tharp, 1990, 197).

Language is central to such a task. It is paramount in the internalization of concepts as well as in the development of discourse meaning and higher cognitive processes that take place in instructional conversations:

> *To converse* is to assume that the learner may have something to say beyond the "answers" already known by the teacher. To grasp a child's communicative intent requires careful listening, a willingness to guess about the meaning of the intended conversation, and responsive adjustments to assist the child's efforts. Instructional conversation in the school setting requires that "teachers" engage "learners" in discourse. (Gallimore & Tharp, 1990, 197)

This explains why Tharp and Gallimore assert that "to most truly teach, one must converse; to truly converse is to teach" (cited in Gallimore & Tharp, 1990).

Inspired by Vygotsky's ZPD, Enright and McCloskey (1988) strongly encourage teachers to engage in "real" dialogue with second language learners. What they describe is a special kind of instructional conversation, one in which teachers and children engage in social negotiations about meanings and appropriate each other's understandings (White, 1989, xii). For second language learners, part of this process may involve creating a scaffold to provide social and linguistic support. Scaffolding techniques are useful in that they enable students to extend what they can do with the language they have and to expand their language capabilities. Eventually, the use of a scaffold becomes unnecessary. Scaffolds are used within the zone, but should not be confused as being synonymous with the zone itself (White, 1989).

Several scaffolding characteristics are effectively illustrated in the transcribed dialogue between a student and a teacher presented here (Enright & McCloskey, 1988, 150–160). Take note of how the teacher's input is meaningful and useful, how it is adapted to the student's language and language abilities, and how it is strategically provided so as to be comprehensible and helpful. Bakir, the Lebanese student in this dialogue, is nine years old and a beginning English language learner with 60 to 80 words in his English vocabulary. He has been living in the United States for less than a month. The visiting teacher is watching the class while Bakir's teacher is getting some materials that he needs to borrow. Bakir is

Teachers are encouraged to engage in "real" dialogue with English language learners.

part of a group of six students engaged in chopping vegetables for a class snack. He initiates the interaction.

Bakir:	(Smiles and waves.)
Teacher:	Hey, Bakir, how are you doing? You look busy!
Bakir:	Fine! (He gestures amusedly to the vegetables.)
Teacher:	What are you doing? What are you guys making?
Bakir:	Kah-kah-kah-rotes. (Carrots.) We . . . kah-rotes.
Teacher:	You sure do! You do have carrots. Wow! What are you doing with those carrots?
Bakir:	We, uh-h . . . we . . . (he makes chopping motions with the knife) . . . kah-rotes.
Teacher:	Oh yeah, I see. You're *chopping* those carrots. I should have known. You've got some *big* carrots! And you're chopping them.
Bakir:	Yes! (He pauses to think. His grin slowly widens.) Big kah-rotes . . . (he makes chopping motions) . . . little kah-rotes! Fine!
Teacher:	(Laughing.) You got *that* right! You're chopping those big carrots into little carrots. You're quite a chopper. You're quite a cook!
Bakir:	(Puzzled.) Cook?
Teacher:	Yes, you know, uh, someone who makes the food. Like Mrs. Sprague at lunch. *She* chops! She chops too! She's the *cook*!
Bakir:	Oh! Oh yes. Oh yes, lunch. (Slyly.) But I no . . . (shakes head, negatively).
Teacher:	You're not what?

Bakir:	I no kah-rote!
Teacher:	(Scoffingly.) No, you're not a carrot. You're a *cook*! Like Mrs. Sprague!
Bakir:	(Grins widely, stands up very straight, and makes body rigid with arms held to his sides.) I a kah-rote!
Teacher:	(Dubiously.) What?
Bakir:	(With emphasis.) I a *kah-rote!*
Teacher:	(Amazed.) You *are* a carrot? OK, then I'll chop you! (He makes pretend chopping motions, tickling Bakir as he does so.) Chop! Chop! Chop that carrot! Chop, chop, chop.
Bakir:	(Collapses, giggling.) No! No chop! No kah-rote! I no kah-rote! No chop! I cook! I a cook! I a cook! (Enright & McCloskey, 1988, 150, 152)

As you read, did you notice how the dialogue scaffolds supported Bakir's effort to communicate? Did you observe how the teacher

- collaborated with Bakir to create a conversation that was authentic and meaningful?
- enabled Bakir to concentrate on language and conversation by assuming much of the responsibility for their discourse?
- accepted Bakir's verbal and nonverbal efforts to communicate?
- supplied new vocabulary and syntax when needed?
- provided many models of correct pronunciation for the main topic (e.g., "carrots")?
- adjusted his discourse to Bakir's level by repeating, rephrasing, and providing contextual clues?
- adjusted his discourse to Bakir's level by embedding vocabulary that is new for the child in language and meanings that they both share?
- created a positive and supportive social atmosphere?
- expressed genuine interest and delight in what Bakir had to say and incorporated the child's language directly into his own responses?
- conveyed confidence in Bakir's ability to extend his language abilities? (Enright & McCloskey, 1988, 154–157)

As you read, did you notice how Bakir contributed to the dialogue as well? Did you observe how Bakir

- collaborated with the teacher to create a conversation?
- took advantage of the teacher's adaptations by focusing on what the teacher said and how he said it?
- assumed his share of responsibility for maintaining the conversation?
- made original and creative use of language? (Enright & McCloskey, 1988, 155, 158)

The conversation between Bakir and the visiting teacher is equally powerful when viewed from another perspective. Wells (1986) has studied how teachers and parents can maximize children's potential as meaning makers and creators of knowledge. He has observed that when participants in conversation come from different cultural backgrounds or have different levels of cognitive and linguistic maturity, the likelihood of misunderstandings is always present and significant. This puts greater responsibility on teachers and parents to take an active role in initiating and maintaining conversations and in ensuring that the meanings constructed by children do not diverge considerably from their own. Like Vygotsky, Wells recognizes the importance of collaborative conversation as "an effective medium for learning and teaching" (p. 218). To facilitate conversations in which minds make contact, he suggests that teachers and parents follow this basic set of principles (p. 218):

- Treat what children say as important and worthy of attention.
- Make every effort to understand what children say and to grasp what they mean.
- Respond on the basis of their meaning.
- Make your response appropriate to their level of understanding.

Looking back at the dialogue, it is striking to see how closely the visiting teacher adhered to these principles in conversing with Bakir. In the final analysis, providing English language learners with genuine input and real dialogue will do more than facilitate English language development. "It will facilitate the development of their minds!" (Enright & McCloskey, 1988, 159).

Small-Group Dynamics

How conducive the classroom is as a social setting for cognitive and language development is determined by many factors, one of which is organizational structure. "How classrooms are organized for instruction can influence the ways in which teachers and students communicate with one another; how language is used in the instructional program can have a major effect on the learning of the language skills needed for school" (Wong Fillmore & Valadez, 1986, 670). Maximizing the use of activities for purposes of content and language learning, however, requires a considerable degree of thought and planning. Positive outcomes do not occur automatically. Activities that take place in small-group settings appear to be especially critical, for there is ample evidence indicating that small-group learning benefits students of all ages across subject areas and on a variety of tasks (Cohen, 1994a, 1994b).

Although small groups are not a panacea, Cohen (1994a) finds that they are a particularly useful tool "for specific kinds of teaching goals and especially relevant for classrooms with a wide mix of academic and English language skills" (p. 1). Influenced by Dewey and Vygotsky, some researchers stress the importance of small-group processes in providing the level of instructional conversation required for conceptual learning and higher order thinking (Cohen, 1994b, 3).

Other researchers are more interested in small-group dynamics from the standpoint of cooperative learning, equity, prosocial behavior, personal development, and related issues (p. 3). It is worth noting that research findings on small groups (that is, cooperative learning) in linguistically diverse settings are consistent with those in settings with speakers of the same language (McGroarty, 1989, 128).

From the perspective of second language development, there are important added benefits. For example, McGroarty suggests that small groups provide natural language practice characterized by input that is abundant and complex as well as a variety of opportunities for language use through efforts to communicate and negotiate meaning. She notes that in bilingual settings, students are also able to use and develop primary language resources while they make progress in English. Along similar lines, R. Olsen and Kagan (1992) cite the myriad of alternatives available for structuring student interaction—alternatives that allow for increased active communication, increased complexity of communication, and increased comprehension.

Second language development is further stimulated through the integration of language and content instruction and use of instructional materials that rely on multiple channels and a broad range of strategies to promote both language and concept learning (McGroarty, 1989). R. Olsen and Kagan (1992) take this one step further. They assert that because teachers are able to use the same organizational framework to address both academic and linguistic needs, the "effect of combining language learning with content learning may be multiplicative rather than simply additive" (p. 7).

Small groups also contribute to social language development (Coelho, 1992; R. Olsen & Kagan, 1992). The social skills required for effective participation in small groups seem to parallel important language functions that English language learners need to acquire anyway. There is a place in cooperative learning for explicit training in language functions such as paraphrasing, clarifying, reporting facts, summarizing group progress, expressing agreement and disagreement, and so on (R. Olsen & Kagan, 1992, 7). Most teachers assume that their students already know how to use these language functions (Coelho, 1992). Unfortunately, this does not apply to English language learners or to many native speakers:

> Conversational skills such as effective turn-taking, disagreeing, and paraphrasing employ a set of linguistic strategies to convey the intentions of participants in the group process. Ability to recognize and use these strategies can provide students with the tools for interacting effectively with peers and adults in a variety of relationships. . . . If we want to empower students so that they can interact effectively with peers, teachers, and employers, we have to make sure they do have access to this repertoire of language. (p. 42)

Specific strategies for teaching these skills are presented later in this chapter.

In an extensive review of research on productive small groups, Cohen (1994b) reveals important insights into the processes involved in group learning. For example, for students to participate in the social construction of knowledge, they need both cognitive and social skills. Effective interaction requires cognitive skills such as defining problems, generating hypotheses, and presenting evidence, and

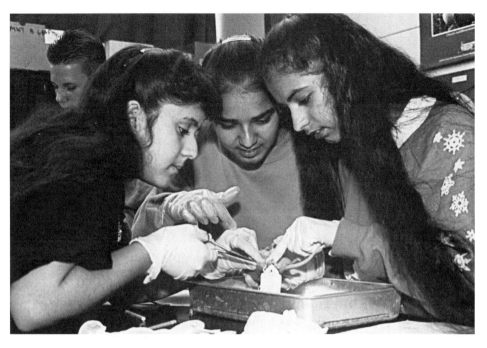

Effective interaction requires both cognitive and social skills.

social skills such as managing conflict, using divergent points of view, and providing mutual support. Students are likely to function at the most concrete level unless taught otherwise. "If teachers want high-level operation, particularly verbal, the students will require specific development of skills for discourse, either in advance of cooperative learning or through direct assistance when groups are in operation" (Cohen, 1994b, 7). The same holds true for interpersonal skills.

Cohen's analysis also indicates that there is no one optimum type of interaction; what is most effective differs according to the task and instructional objective (p. 4). When the teaching objective calls for a low-level outcome, interaction focused upon getting information and generating correct answers is at least as adequate as and sometimes superior to more elaborate and less restricted interaction. However, when the objective requires higher order thinking, then tasks and instructions that constrain dialogue appear to be less productive than those promoting interaction, mutual exchange, and elaborated discourse (pp. 19–20). In addition, for small groups to be productive in grappling with problems that are "ill-structured" (e.g., open-ended, discovery), interaction should also require reciprocal interdependence among its members (i.e., a pooling of resources such as knowledge, abilities, and skills).

Another critical aspect of groupwork is ensuring equity in interaction (Cohen 1994a, 1994b). Systematic inequalities in participation among members of cooperative groups can be attributed to a number of status characteristics. These include, but are not limited to, academic status (perceived ability), peer status (e.g., perceived attractiveness, popularity), and social status (e.g., gender, race, ethnicity, language). Status characteristics can negatively influence interaction and learning outcomes. Within small groups, students who are perceived as having higher status are more active and influential than those perceived as having lower status. When this occurs, lower status students do not have full access to group resources nor are they able to contribute and participate fully. Although research suggests that these are frequent patterns, on a given day, a particular group working on a specific task may not reflect domination by high-status children. This depends in part on the nature of a given task and whether students participate early in the discussion. Cohen (1994a) emphasizes that unequal interaction is of concern to teachers because participation is linked to learning outcomes. Those with greater access to interaction learn more; those who do not participate due to low status learn less. In addition to questions of basic equity, the dominance of high-status students affects productivity by preventing the best ideas within a group to be shared or, if shared, to be heard. Speaking directly to teachers, Cohen advises that "when ability in one area is used as an index of general intelligence and classroom competence, you are dealing with a status problem" (p. 38).

To address these inequalities, Cohen proposes the use of appropriate status treatments. Powerful and positive changes in expectations can be achieved by establishing cooperative norms, using a multiple ability strategy, and assigning competence to low-status students. First, by requiring that every student participate and take on a specific role in groupwork, the use of cooperative norms can help teachers to increase participation rates for both high- and low-status students. Second, using the multiple ability strategy, teachers can alter the basic expectation that a few students are competent in everything they do while others have little or no competence in anything they do. To do this, teachers must emphasize the existence of diverse intelligences and abilities, specify those relevant to particular activities, and help students to recognize and draw upon the multiple abilities represented within their own group. To this end, students are reminded that "none of us has all these abilities; [e]ach one of us has some of these abilities" (1994a, 128). Finally, assigning competence to low-status students enables teachers to make positive use of their evaluative power to influence student expectations. This is done by observing low-status students and taking note of specific and relevant intellectual contributions to the group. These relevant and specific evaluations are then publicly recognized, with appropriate cultural sensitivity, before the student's classmates. Done correctly, this can help to modify student's self-perceptions as well as the expectations of other students.

Where to start? Teachers interested in making small groups an integral part of their classrooms will discover a richness of resources in this area. These provide teachers at all levels with the theoretical foundation, models, curriculum materials, and a wealth of strategies and activities for small groups. Among the readings of special interest to teachers in multilingual settings are Cohen's introduction to complex instruction, *Designing Groupwork* (1994a); Kagan's comprehensive and practical handbook, *Cooperative Learning Resources for Teachers* (Kagan, 1989); and Kessler's edited volume on *Cooperative Language Learning* (Kessler, 1992). Teachers of multilevel high school classes specifically targeting use of cooperative jigsaw groups may want to consider *All Sides of the Issue* (Coelho, Winer, & J. Olsen, 1989). For cooperative learning activities related to mathematics and language arts, McGroarty (1992) recommends *Cooperative Learning and Mathematics: A Multi-structural Approach* (Andrini, 1989) and *Cooperative Learning and Language Arts: A Multi-structural Approach* (Stone, 1989).

Management

Second language development is a social process par excellence. Schools and classrooms are social settings for language learning in which outcomes vary significantly (Wong Fillmore & Valadez, 1986, 668–670). As an example, the proportion of English language learners in a classroom has implications for language learning. Language minority students appear to achieve better when they are neither the vast majority nor a small minority in the classroom; linguistically balanced classrooms are the ideal (p. 668). Language learning is also influenced by the concentration of students from the same language background. Students in multilingual schools appear to perform better than those in schools with a single predominating language (pp. 668–669).

Yet another factor to be considered is the range of proficiency levels within a classroom. It is difficult for teachers to manage classroom situations where language proficiency levels vary greatly (Fillmore, 1982):

> Teachers find it considerably more difficult to tailor instructional language to the needs of language learners in classrooms where there are both language learners and fluent speakers of the target language. . . . It is hard to make the adjustments the language learners need for figuring out what is being said in the presence of others who find such efforts unnecessary and boring. The tendency for most teachers in a mixed language situation is to talk to the students who understand best rather than in a way that can be understood by everyone. Often, the easiest solution is to aim at a point somewhere in the middle of the various abilities, and hope for the best. Indeed, this is what we have frequently observed during group instruction in mixed classes. Such language is modified somewhat, but not enough to allow children who do not know the language well to figure out what is being said. The consequence is that the English used instructionally is not very useful to learners as input data. (p. 293)

Although there are no easy answers, Enright and McCloskey (1988, 133–150) do offer teachers some practical advice. First, they suggest adapting both "teacher talk" and "interactional talk" (p. 133). Teachers can use a variety of language in whole-class activities for mixed-level groups. This helps to maximize comprehension, relevancy, and interest for students at each of the different levels. Second, they advocate organizing full-group activities that are not teacher centered, such as games and group discussions. Finally, they recommend using small-group and individualized activities to establish genuine dialogue with students—more personal interaction that is focused on authentic tasks.

Because classroom language is an important source of input for language minority students, teachers must make every effort to create instructional environments in which the language of communication and instruction also promotes language development effectively. "How teachers organize students for instruction can affect the amount and quality of exposure learners will have to the new language" (Fillmore, 1982, 285). In multilingual classrooms, learners and speakers should have many reasons to interact with each other and appropriate activities for doing so. Applying ideas such as those presented in this section can help teachers to maximize the positive potential of interaction for all learners and to create classroom environments that help language learners to achieve native-like proficiency over time.

The Language of the Classroom

Researchers investigating how language is used in home and school contexts have identified school discourse patterns that are different from those typically used within certain minority group families and communities (Mehan, Lintz, Okamoto, & Wills, 1995, 130). Illustrative of this line of research are studies involving children from Native American (Philips, 1982), Hawaiian (Au & Jordan, 1981), Hmong (Findlay, 1994, 1995), and black and white working-class (Heath, 1983) backgrounds. Concerned that discontinuities may have negative implications (e.g., lower academic achievement, higher drop-out rates) for the students involved, many educators recommend that teachers become proactive in enhancing the compatibility of home-school discourse. "When the discourse structure of the classroom corresponds to the discourse pattern of the low-income home, students' academic performance improves" (Mehan et al., 1995, 130).

Heath's (1983, 1992, 1995, 1996) investigations as to how children from different language and ethnic groups learn to use language within their homes, schools, and communities are among the most salient for teachers of language minority students. Two particularly significant conclusions have emerged from her efforts to study language learning as cultural learning and to explain the impact of sociocultural differences on the classroom. First, children's ability to use the language they know may be more critical to their academic success than their knowledge of a particular language. Second, by providing a full range of activities for using both oral and written language, teachers can foster children's academic and vocational success, whatever their primary language.

One important aspect of Heath's work is that it makes explicit some of the underlying assumptions made when children enter school. "Not only is there the general expectation that all children will learn to speak English but also the assumption that they have internalized *before* they start school the norms of language used in academic life" (1992, 105–106). These are very specific norms related to language use. For example, children are expected to provide labels and descriptions for objects, events, and so on, and to retell past events or information in a predictable sequence and format. They must be able to follow oral and written directions and engage in social interactions as part of a group. Formal schooling also demands that children know how to use language to deal with information—to obtain and clarify, to create and integrate. The implications are profound.

Those students who achieve academic success either bring to school all of these language uses, and the cultural norms that lie behind them, or they learn quickly to intuit the rules of these language uses for both speaking and writing. Those who ultimately succeed in the highest academic lanes acquire or bring with them the facility for using oral and written language for multiple purposes and in varying styles. (1992, 107)

It is the teacher's task to facilitate expansion of language use by incorporating a wide range of language forms in classroom lessons. Curriculum in elementary and secondary schools is predicated on the assumption that "both the range of occasions for these language uses and their sequencing, in oral and written forms, represent a 'normal' pattern of development for all children" (Heath, 1992, 107). What this assumption fails to take into account is the fact that the school's expectations about "when, where, and how children learn language" may not be shared by all groups (e.g., working-class English-speaking groups and language minorities) (p. 107). Whereas the possible range of language forms available to speakers of any language is large, each cultural group appears to have preferred forms that recur in set patterns. Furthermore, although there is considerable continuity between home and school settings across cultural groups, there are also areas in which they have been found to differ, due in part to factors in language socialization and even aspects of the native language itself.

Genres

It is imperative for students from all cultural and class backgrounds to have consistent, reinforced access to multiple uses of language—including those valued by the school—in the primary language or English. Teachers must not only be aware of how students use specific forms of language, they must be prepared to provide opportunities for students to practice and use a variety of language forms, as appropriate, in all subject areas and at all levels (Heath, 1996). To assist teachers with this task, Heath (1996, 168–170) identifies several school language patterns that are particularly dominant:

- Naming items; asking for items; identifying attributes
  Examples: "What's this?"; "Who's that?"
- Explaining the meanings of words, pictures, combinations of events, and children's own behaviors; making inferences from written texts (The explanations provided typically require stating what something means, what the intent is, what will happen, how it is to be interpreted.)
  Examples: Asking the meaning of passages; inferring what an author means in a written text
- Providing summaries of known material orally and in writing (The retelling normally involves displaying knowledge that is familiar to both teacher and child.)
  Example: Test questions that depend upon recounting a reading passage
- Providing an account of new information or an interpretation of information (The information that is conveyed is not familiar to the listener.)
  Examples: Show-and-tell; creative writing
- Explaining or narrating the sequence of steps to be taken to accomplish a current task or future goal

Examples: An essay outline; a plan for a group project

- Providing fictional accounts of animate beings or creatures

    Examples: Basal texts; literary texts (Adapted from the summary of Heath [1986] in Hernández, 1989, 100–101)

According to Heath (1996, 171), children's access to these and other school-valued forms of language at home and the extent to which their use involves written texts determines, to a considerable degree, success in school and beyond.

One important implication of Heath's work is the impetus that it provides for teachers to incorporate forms of language used in students' homes and communities as a part of classroom activities. Use of the "talk story" with Hawaiian children, for example, is just one example of how this approach can enhance achievement in reading (Au, 1993). Ample illustrations of the process of cultural bridging are provided in Heath's (1983) study of children's language development in both black and white working-class Piedmont communities in the Carolinas. Teachers can expand the narrow parameters of language use in schools to incorporate the wider variety required for effective participation in communities beyond the school. One final example is Gallas's (1992) exploration of the "languages" of learning in her own multilingual classroom. Elementary teachers will particularly enjoy and benefit from her observations and insights into children's use of a broad range of narrative functions, from sharing time to children's stories about science and art.

Sociocultural Influences

Sociocultural influences are manifest in many ways. Children learn how to perceive and interpret feedback consistent with cultural values inculcated within their homes and communities (Scarcella, 1990). For example, cultures associate different expectations with praise and compliments. Students from some Asian groups are likely to question the sincerity of verbal praise that is given too frequently. For those Asian children brought up to regard humility as a virtue, happy faces, stickers, and stamps may even produce feelings of discomfort. By contrast, communication patterns within many Latino communities would lead to the expectation of more frequent praise, more personal attention, and even a hug or a pat on the back (132–135).

Other areas such as error correction, requests for clarification, and spotlighting are affected as well (Scarcella, 1990, 135–137). Classroom practices in France, Japan, China, and Russia place greater emphasis on error correction than what is customary in the United States. Within other cultures, however, children's language mistakes are not of particular concern (e.g., Chipeweyan). For the student to take the initiative in requesting clarification from the teacher when he or she does not understand something is not common practice within all educational systems. For some Latino students, it may seem impolite to do so; for many Asian students, it may appear aggressive or disrespectful; and for some Native American students, requests for assistance may be conveyed silently, by looking up from a task. Students accustomed to relatively formal and structured environments (e.g., India, Saudi Arabia, Russia) may find the idea of interrupting activities (e.g., lectures, reading-aloud sessions) a novel experience. Although it is common practice in many classrooms to single out students and ask that they perform publicly before the class, spotlighting is not consistent with cultural expectations for all students (e.g., among Native Americans such as the Choctaw and Warm Springs people and among Asians such as the Japanese).

There are numerous illustrations of the potential for misunderstandings when the expectations of teachers and students are not the same:

> Choctaw (Native American) students don't display as much excitement as middle-American students, but that doesn't mean that they are not interested or that they dislike you (Richmond 1987). Latino students may avoid looking at you when you speak, but their lack of eye contact may indicate respect and is not intended to display dislike, defiance or disinterest. Head nods may signal that Asian students are politely listening, not necessarily *understanding* what you are saying. The Asian student's smile may simply mean that the student is politely attending to your speech, not that he agrees with you, finds your lessons amusing, or comprehends what you are saying (Tran 1984). (Scarcella, 1992, 131–132)

It is imperative that teachers in multilingual classrooms provide students with feedback that is culturally appropriate and effective (Scarcella, 1990). Teachers need to learn how to "read" their students and how their students "read" them. "Direct eye contact with a student may be positive, but it may be interpreted as aggressive or humiliating; smiling may be positive, but it may be derisive; touching may be positive, but it may be embarrassing or repugnant" (Saville-Troike, cited in Scarcella, 1990, 133). Although there is no definitive set of guidelines for teachers to follow, there are practical strategies that can provide direction and assistance. Some suggestions are highlighted in Figure 6-2.

Mastering Classroom Discourse

The interaction that typically takes place within a classroom is different from that in other settings—different in ways that are of importance in language development. Rivers (1987) describes students as becoming proficient by using language through interaction. For English language learners, interaction is essential to survival in the new language and culture, for it demands that students "use all they possess of the language—all they have learned or casually absorbed—in real-life exchanges where expressing their real meaning is important to them" (Rivers, 1987, 4). Learners engage in a creative process, making sense of the messages they hear and then conveying their own meaning to someone else.

Language is learned and used in groups (Kramsch, 1987, 17). It is this interactive use of language that enables the collective group of students in a class to achieve a social identity. As Vygotsky observes, language is "a highly personal and at the same time a profoundly social human process" (Vygotsky, 1978, 126).

Classroom interaction differs from normal conversation. An analysis by Kramsch (1981) provides some interesting and useful insights from the perspec-

Interpreting feedback
- Make students aware of the types of feedback you use (e.g., marking papers) and your interpretation of their feedback behaviors.
- Identify your students' preferences related to feedback and try to adapt your feedback to make provision for the different patterns of your students.
- Ensure that all students have an opportunity to respond to questions, be it individually or in small groups, in lieu of participation in large-group situations. Avoid assuming that students will volunteer to answer.
- Be consistent in providing feedback. Provide some opportunities for systematic turn taking.

Complimenting and criticizing
- Be conscious of how you compliment students. Students are more likely to appreciate praise that is sincere and specific rather than generic and vague.
- Avoid using strategies likely to embarrass or frustrate students, particularly the practice of singling out students to perform correctly in front of the class (e.g., spotlighting).

Requesting clarification
- Avoid assuming that students will ask you questions when they do not understand a lesson. Use different strategies to check for understanding.

Questioning and answering
- When the questioning strategies used at home and school differ, be explicit about the kinds of questions you are using in the classroom and your expectations regarding student responses.
- When students do not understand, make it clear that they are encouraged to ask questions and that you welcome requests for clarification, simplification, and repetition.
- Model ways in which your students should get your attention or interrupt when they do not understand (e.g., "What?", "Excuse me. I'm not sure I understand.")
- Emphasize questioning in a nonthreatening manner. Remember that open-ended questions such as Why? and How? are more verbally demanding than yes/no questions (Did John ride his bike to school?), or-choice questions (Did John ride his bike or skateboard to school?), and what questions (What did John ride home?).
- When working individually with students whose proficiency in English is very limited, accept responses in their primary language if you have proficiency in that language.
- Avoid forcing students to participate. Allow them the right to pass.

Wait time
- Allow sufficient wait time for students to respond. English language learners need additional time.
- Ask students about how much wait time they need.

Figure 6-2   Practical strategies for providing effective feedback
Source: Scarcella (1990, 141–143)

tive of language teaching. Traditional classroom interaction is clearly marked by differences in status and authority between participants. Teachers dominate classroom interaction, exercising a full range of language functions, while restricting students in their use of language. In classrooms characterized by a disproportionate amount of teacher talk, students respond to questions more often than they ask them.

Kramsch describes how teachers exert control. In traditional classrooms, teachers select the topics to be discussed as well as the tasks to be completed. They determine who will speak and when. They regulate interaction through the questions they ask, often using display questions for which they already know the answer. The basic pattern of classroom recitation reveals that teachers initiate interactive exchanges with students and then bring closure to these exchanges by reacting to and evaluating the responses that students are asked to provide. This pattern is a very distinctive feature of classroom discourse. (If teachers routinely provided such a systematic barrage of "unsolicited" feedback in interaction with people outside the classroom, they certainly would find themselves with few friends.) Whereas normal conversation is more personal, the classroom provides a very public forum for most interaction between participants.

By contrast, normal conversation offers participants a much broader range of options than those normally afforded students in the classroom setting. Kramsch indicates that the distribution of turns between speakers is not predetermined. It is negotiated, back and forth, between individuals. Speakers also share control of the topic, deciding when to clarify meaning, extend or avoid discussion, change topics, and repair breakdowns in communication. Participants take turns asking questions and responding. They react by showing surprise or interest, by expressing agreement or disagreement. Normal conversations are unrehearsed and unpredictable. Speakers interrupt each other, shift topics, call on other speakers, and ask "real" questions.

It should be clear by now that the classroom—as typically structured—is not the ideal setting in which to develop communicative skills in a second language. The classroom is characterized by a number of discourse patterns that are not typical of natural language use in the students' first or second languages. Because of these differences, traditional discourse patterns in classroom settings do not provide the variety of interactive opportunities that second language learners need. Speaking directly to language teachers, Rivers (1987) states that "real interaction in the classroom requires the teacher to step out of the limelight, to cede a full role to the student in developing and carrying through activities, to accept all kinds of opinions, and be tolerant of errors the student makes while attempting to communicate" (p. 9).

This is especially critical for students whose primary exposure to English comes in the school setting. As Oller has observed, "the difficulty is not to teach second languages, but to teach them in classrooms" (cited in Kramsch, 1981, 14). To develop conversational fluency, students must learn to "speak like the teacher" (p. 17). Students need opportunities to create their own questions and to answer these themselves. In order to create their own understandings, students must interact with other students. They must be allowed to expand their interactive role in the classroom in ways that are appropriate and conducive to language learning.

This is not to say that language teachers should abandon all of the patterns of interaction that they currently use in the classroom in order to incorporate all the features of "natural" discourse. "Relinquishing the control of the interaction entirely to the students is both deceiving and threatening to all parties involved" (Kramsch, 1987, 28). Rather, the goal is to reexamine existing patterns to expand the opportunities available so that learners can "become the active architects of interpersonal and intercultural understanding" (p. 28).

What kinds of skills do students need to develop in order to "speak like the teacher"? There is a range of skills required for effective interaction. At the elementary level, it is critical that students master the variety of genres described by Heath and the languages of learning captured by Gallas. For students at the secondary level, teachers can be more explicit in teaching some of the rules of the game. Strategies such as those described by Kramsch (1987) (e.g., indirectness, turn taking, topic management, and repair tasks) are useful. In addition to helping students develop the language skills they need, these techniques also complement strategies emphasized in different models of cooperative learning and groupwork. Keeping in mind that adolescents often have what seems to be a language all their own, the examples provided may be adapted in keeping with current usage.

Strategies of indirectness.   Saving face, Kramsch observes, is a real concern for language learners (pp. 20–21). This is understandable given the very public nature of classroom discourse and the somewhat limited options students have for avoiding the risks and consequences inherent in interaction. Saving face is described as a dichotomy that involves both saving one's own face and that of others. It is natural for individuals to not want to lose face when they use language in ways that are neither correct nor appropriate. It is also natural for language learners to seek the appreciation and acknowledgment of others while experiencing a need to be free from unwanted interference when difficulties in communication arise.

For students to take an active part in classroom interaction, they must learn discourse strategies that include turn taking and topic management.

Kramsch (1981, 1987) describes how language learners can use strategies of indirectness to save face in classroom situations. When speaking, for example, students at the secondary level can learn to stall for time and hedge by using elements like *well, you know, I mean, actually,* and so on. Students can acknowledge their limitations and request assistance by asking questions such as *How do you say———? What did you say? Excuse me? Would you repeat that please?* Statements like *I don't know how to say———* are also useful. To participate in group conversations even when they have nothing to add, students can learn to paraphrase, comment, or expand upon what others have said. Along similar lines, to save the face of others, Kramsch suggests that students use markers to preface or mitigate what is said (e.g., *Could you please———? Would you mind repeating———?*). They can also learn to restate or paraphrase what has been said (e.g., *You mean to say ———?; So———; In other words———; If I understand you correctly———*) or to provide feedback (e.g., *Yes, yeah, you're right, okay*).

Turn taking. Teaching students to take turns is not as easy as it appears (Kramsch, 1987, 22). Many skills are involved, not all of which are readily transferred from the primary language. The process encompasses listening to the message, comprehending what is said, and interpreting the meaning, then formulating a response, finding a break in the speaker's turn, and taking the floor at an appropriate point. When working in groups, students can routinely incorporate strategies such as those recommended by Kramsch. For example, all students working in groups can be more tolerant of silence and allow English language learners the extra time they need to respond. Second language learners can rehearse what they need to do as group members. For example, they can practice how to take the floor when they have something to say, using expressions like *I have a question; Wait a minute; I'd like to add or make a point; I feel or believe———.* They also can practice taking longer turns by expanding their contributions to discussions or by directing comments to other students.

Topic management. Teachers normally control the topic of classroom discussion. Kramsch describes topic management as falling on a continuum. At one end, interaction follows a predictable ritual as teachers use display questions to solicit predetermined information from the students. At the other end, interaction resembles more natural discourse, as information gaps exist and questions are used to elicit and negotiate information that is new to all participants. Kramsch observes that "if students are to take an active part in interactions, they must be shown how to control the way topics are established, built, and sustained, and how to participate in the teaching and learning of lessons" (1987, 23). Teachers can enhance students' involvement in topic management by minimizing use of display questions (displays of student knowledge) and maximizing use of real questions (genuine requests for information). Teachers can also work with students to jointly construct the topics to be discussed. As with younger learners, teachers should try to treat contributions to discussions as relevant, recognizing that what is said may be very relevant from the student's perspective.

Repair tasks. Repair tasks are defined in terms of linguistic errors, procedural problems, and other forms of miscommunication (Kramsch, 1987, 23). In most classrooms, these fall within the purview of the teacher, who would typically highlight learners' errors and engage in error correction (directly or indirectly). As teachers adopt the position that errors are a natural part of second language acquisition and learn to employ more natural patterns of interaction in the classroom, they also learn to be facilitators. They allow students to choose linguistic structures, and accept alternative forms when students avoid the grammatical elements that they have not yet mastered. Teachers rely less on evaluative feedback (e.g., *very good, fine, that's right*) while providing more natural feedback (e.g., *I agree, I feel the same way, I think so too*). They avoid overpraising students, and quote what students say, taking care not to assume credit for student ideas. As explained earlier, when dealing with error correction covertly, teachers focus on meaning rather than form.

Summary

Classroom settings are very complex language environments. Almost inevitably, everything that teachers and students do with language and through language seems to affect second language development either directly or indirectly. As a result, teachers intent on actively promoting language development will find it useful to look at communication and interaction in new and different ways. A good place to begin is with the arrival of English language learners to a new school and classroom. Most schools have been remiss in providing an orientation for English language learners upon their arrival. While it is important to make all new students feel welcome, it is especially critical for newcomers who are not familiar with the language and culture of the school. When communication is difficult and no processes are in place to provide basic information and support, misunderstandings—and the unnecessary confusion, fear, and anxiety that they produce—are virtually guaranteed. Schools can do more to anticipate student needs by providing information for newcomers and asking for relevant information about them whenever possible. Teachers, students, administrators, and staff need to be involved in identifying the needs and strategies that are most critical to their school site. Development of a process or procedure for student orientation and integration can make the transition a more positive experience for teachers and students alike.

It is also important to look at the richness and complexity of the classroom as a sociocultural setting in which language and academic development take place. The importance of "talking to learn" is clearly evident in instructional conversations and small groups. Influenced by Vygotsky's notions about the centrality of collaboration between children and adults in the learning process, increased attention has been drawn to instructional discourse and the social context of learning. Providing opportunities for real dialogue between teachers and students is critical. No less important are opportunities for students to work in small groups that provide the kind of interaction required for higher levels of cognitive and language development.

Awareness of patterns of language use within the classroom as a whole is another part of the bigger picture. Children reflect their cultural, social, and linguistic backgrounds in what they do with language. In school, the prevailing forms of language use reflect only some of the possibilities. Children need access to multiple uses of language—those valued by the school as well as those used within the home and community that can be made part of the classroom repertoire. Since children also reflect their cultural, social, and linguistic backgrounds in how they perceive and interpret feedback from teachers, teachers may want to consider what they do with language when engaged in interpreting feedback, complimenting and criticizing, and so on.

Finally, from a discourse perspective, the nature of interaction between teacher and students is unique. Differences in status and authority result in teacher-dominant patterns of language use. If second language learners are to develop a full spectrum of language proficiency, teachers will want to provide opportunities for them to "speak like the teacher" (Kramsch, 1981, 17). Doing so will require specific strategies for indirectness and skills in turn taking, topic management, and handling repair tasks.

References

Andrini, B. (1989). *Cooperative learning and mathematics: A multi-structural approach*. San Juan Capistrano, CA: Resources for Teachers.

Au, K. H. (1993). *Literacy instruction in multicultural settings*. Fort Worth, TX: Harcourt Brace Jovanovich College Publishers.

Au, K. H-P., & Jordan, C. (1981). Teaching reading to Hawaiian children: Finding a culturally appropriate solution. In H. T. Trueba, G. P. Guthrie, & K. H-P. Au (Eds.), *Culture and the bilingual classroom* (pp. 139–152). Rowley, MA: Newbury House.

Coelho, E. (1992). Cooperative learning: Foundation for a communicative curriculum. In C. Kessler (Ed.), *Cooperative language learning* (pp. 31–49). Englewood Cliffs, NJ: Prentice-Hall.

Coelho, E., Winer, L., & Olsen, J. W-B. (1989). *All sides of the issue*. Hayward, CA: Alemany Press.

Cohen, E. G. (1994a). *Designing groupwork* (2nd ed.). New York: Teachers College Press, Columbia University.

Cohen, E. G. (1994b). Restructuring the classroom: Conditions for productive small groups. *Review of Educational Research, 64*(1), 1–35.

Enright, D. S., and McCloskey, M. L. (1988). *Integrating English: Developing English language and literacy in the multilingual classroom*. Reading, MA: Addison-Wesley.

Fillmore, L. W. (1982). Instructional language as linguistic input: Second-language learning in classrooms. In L. C. Wilkinson (Ed.), *Communicating in the classroom* (pp. 283–296). New York: Academic Press.

Findlay, M. S. (1994). Structure and process in speech subcommunities of Hmong students at a Northern California high school. *Linguistics and Education, 6*(3), 249–264.

Findlay, M. S. (1995). Who has the right answer? Differential cultural emphasis in question/answer structures and the case of Hmong students at a Northern California high school. *Issues in Applied Linguistics, 6*(1), 1–16.

Gallas, K. (1992). *The languages of learning: How children talk, write, dance, draw, and sing their understanding of the world*. New York: Teachers College Press, Columbia University.

Gallimore, R., & Tharp, R. (1990). Teaching mind in society: Teaching, schooling and literate discourse. In Luis C. Moll (Ed.), *Vygotsky and education: Instructional implications and applications of sociohistorical psychology* (pp. 175–205). New York: Cambridge University Press.

García, E. E. (1995). Educating Mexican American students: Past treatment and recent developments in theory, research, policy, and practice. In J. A. Banks & C. A. Banks (Eds.), *Handbook of research on multicultural education* (pp. 327–387). New York: Macmillan.

Heath, S. B. (1983). *Ways with words.* New York: Cambridge University Press.

Heath, S. B. (1992). Sociocultural contexts of language development: Implications for the classroom. In P. A. Richard-Amato & M. A. Snow (Eds.), *The multicultural classroom: Readings for content-area teachers* (pp. 102–125). White Plains, NY: Longman.

Heath, S. B. (1995). Ethnography in communities: Learning the everyday life of America's subordinated youth. In J. A. Banks & C. A. Banks (Eds.), *Handbook of research on multicultural education* (pp. 114–128). New York: Macmillan.

Heath, S. B. (1996). Sociocultural contexts of language development. *Beyond language: Social and cultural factors in schooling language minority students* (pp. 143–186). Los Angeles: Evaluation, Dissemination and Assessment Center, School of Education, California State University, Los Angeles.

Hernández, H. (1989). *Multicultural education: A teacher's guide to content and process.* Upper Saddle River, NJ: Merrill/Prentice Hall.

Kagan, S. (1989). *Cooperative learning resources for teachers.* San Juan Capistrano, CA: Resources for Teachers.

Kessler, C. (1992). *Cooperative language learning.* Englewood Cliffs, NJ: Prentice-Hall.

Kramsch, C. J. (1981). *Language in Education: Vol. 37. Discourse analysis and second language teaching.* Washington, DC: Center for Applied Linguistics.

Kramsch, C. (1987). Interactive discourse in small and large groups. In W. Rivers (Ed.), *Interactive language teaching* (pp. 17-30). New York: Cambridge University Press.

Law, B. & Eckes, M. (1990). *The more-than-just-surviving handbook: ESL for every classroom teacher.* Winnipeg, MB: Peguis Publishers.

McGroarty, M. (1989). The benefits of cooperative learning arrangements in second language instruction. *NABE Journal, 13*(2), 127–143.

McGroarty, M. (1992). Cooperative learning: The benefits for content-area teaching. In P. A. Richard-Amato & M. A. Snow (Eds.), *The multicultural classroom: Readings for content-area teachers* (pp. 58–69). White Plains, NY: Longman.

Mehan, H., Lintz, A., Okamoto, D., & Wills, J. S. (1995). Ethnographic studies of multicultural education in classrooms and schools. In J. A. Banks & C. A. Banks (Eds.), *Handbook of research on multicultural education* (pp. 129–144). New York: Macmillan.

Minami, M., & Ovando, C. (1995). Language issues in multicultural contexts. In J. Banks & C. A. Banks (Eds.), *Handbook of research on multicultural education* (pp. 427–444). New York: Macmillan.

Moll, L. C. (1990). Introduction. In L. C. Moll (Ed.), *Vygotsky and education: Instructional implications and applications of sociohistorical psychology* (pp. 1-27). New York: Cambridge University Press.

Niepoth, M. (1992). *The use of participatory study methods to plan educational experiences for students learning English as a second language.* Unpublished doctoral dissertation, University of San Francisco.

Olsen, L. (1988). *Crossing the schoolhouse border* (A California Tomorrow Policy Research Report). San Francisco: California Tomorrow.

Olsen, R. E. W-B., & Kagan, S. (1992). About cooperative learning. In C. Kessler (Ed.), *Cooperative language learning* (pp. 1–30). Englewood Cliffs, NJ: Prentice-Hall.

Peregoy, S. F., & Boyle, O. F. (1993). *Reading, writing, and learning in ESL.* White Plains, NY: Addison Wesley Longman.

Philips, S. U. (1982). *The invisible culture: Communication in classroom and community on the Warm Springs Indian Reservation.* New York: Longman.

Rivers, W. (1987). Interaction as the key to teaching language for communication. In W. Rivers (Ed.), *Interactive language teaching* (pp. 3–16). New York: Cambridge University Press.

Saville-Troike, M. (1978). *A guide to culture in the classroom.* Rosslyn, VA: National Clearinghouse for Bilingual Education.

Scarcella, R. (1990). *Teaching language minority students in the multicultural classroom.* Englewood Cliffs, NJ: Prentice-Hall.

Scarcella, R. (1992). Providing culturally sensitive feedback. In P. A. Richard-Amato & M. A. Snow (Eds.), *The multicultural classroom: Readings for content-area teachers* (pp. 126-141). White Plains, NY: Longman.

Stone, J. (1989). *Cooperative learning and language arts: A multi-structural approach.* San Juan Capistrano, CA: Resources for Teachers.

Vygotsky, L. S. (1978). *Mind in society.* M. Cole, V. John-Steiner, S. Scribner, and E. Souberman (Eds.). Cambridge, MA: Harvard University Press.

Wells, G. (1986). *The meaning makers.* Portsmouth, NH: Heinemann.

White, S. H. (1989). Foreword. In D. Newman, P. Griffin, & M. Cole (Eds.), *The construction zone: Working for cognitive change in school* (pp. ix–xiv). New York: Cambridge University Press.

Wong Fillmore, L., & Valadez, C. (1986). Teaching bilingual learners. In M. C. Wittrock (Ed.), *Handbook of research on teaching* (3rd ed., pp. 648–685). New York: Macmillan.

P A R T

4 Content

7

Language and Literacy Development: Foundations

In my view, the teacher is the difference between whether some pupils will become fully literate or all will.

Ken Goodman

Spoken and written language can be viewed as part of the same spectrum of communicative and interactive language use—parallel language processes in which oral language occurs in speech events and written language in literacy events (K. Goodman, 1986, 21–22). Both processes share many similar characteristics, as language is used to convey purposes, intentions, and social relationships. Both speakers and writers must deal with context in relation to setting, cultural and social norms, and the emotional state of participants. Many culturally patterned communicative activities—from learning to read and write and performing professional and occupational tasks to conducting family and community activities—routinely demand use of both speech and writing. The overlap between the functions and features of speech and writing is more significant and extends across a greater range of cultural practices than previously thought (Reder, 1994, 38).

In this chapter, the exploration of language and literacy proceeds along this language continuum. After completing this chapter, you will be able to

1. consider function and accuracy, comprehension, cultural background, and cognitive strengths in language and literacy development
2. examine basic issues in literacy instruction
3. explore aspects of reading and writing as reciprocal processes
4. promote critical literacy

Considerations in Developing Language and Literacy Skills

In this section, attention is drawn to five important considerations related to the development of language and literacy skills. These are language functions, accuracy, comprehension, cultural background, and cognitive strengths.

Language Functions

Whether in oral or written form, language serves different functions. It is used to inform, to entertain, to express a point of view, and on occasion, to argue or complain. Language functions encompass the tasks or purposes for which language is used. Urzúa (1988) describes functional language as talking purposefully, that is, speaking with a purpose. We know that meaning is central to language development. Purpose is no less important.

In communication, form and function are closely interrelated (Lindfors, 1987, 323–324; Urzúa, 1988, 4–5). Our sounds, words, and structures and the written symbols used to represent them are *forms*. When we look at what a person is saying—"I'm sorry" or "I wasn't listening"—we deal with form. When we think in terms of the action being represented—observing that the person is apologizing or explaining—we think in terms of function. Thus, forms are used to express *functions*. Lindfors (1987, 324–325) illustrates the distinction between form and function as follows: Form is what an individual is saying; function is what an individual is doing in the communication by saying it (p. 324).

SITUATION	FORM	FUNCTION
A father and his ten-year old daughter are standing beside a dog that looks hungry.	Father says, "Betsy, have you fed Bruno yet?"	Father is <u>requesting</u>.
One adult to another.	Adult says, "C'mon over for dinner around 7:00."	The adult is <u>inviting</u>.

As children, we come to school knowing that language is "purpose-full" (Urzúa, 1988). We also arrive knowing how to use language "purpose-full-y," that is, for different purposes. Language development builds on the ever-enlarging circle of experiences and interactions that children have as they grow: "Human beings expand their language forms when they see purpose and meaning in a communication situation" (p. 5). Home and community are only part of a child's linguistic world. The school further enlarges the child's language environment, providing new experiences and interactions for the development of language. These provide new purposes for communication and situations in which familiar purposes are refined and extended (Lindfors, 1987, 154–155).

Teachers have traditionally emphasized form over function. Form and function, however, are closely intertwined. Urzúa (1988) talks about children's development of functional language. There is variation in the extent to which individuals develop functional use of language, and we seem to prefer the functions that "match" our personality (p. 13). The sections that follow provide a closer look at three basic functions examined by Urzúa: self-expressing, informing, and persuading.

Self-expressing *Self-expressing* language emphasizes aspects of the person speaking, such as feelings and personality (Urzúa, 1988, 13). Its purpose, according to Urzúa, is to express emotions and individuality. Research in this area reveals some interesting insights. The first emotion—whatever the culture, gender, or home environment—is excitement. By age six months, this emotion is differentiated into distress and delight. Differentiation continues, and by the time a child is two years old, he or she is able to express 12 or more emotions (Bridges, cited in Urzúa, 1988, 15). As children develop language, some learn to use more expressive vocabulary than others.

Cultural differences also enter into the picture because feelings are expressed and handled differently across cultures (Urzúa, 1988, 16–17). Teachers of second language learners must recognize that although feelings are expressed differently, they develop along similar lines. Older children are better able to internalize their feelings than younger children. As a result of socialization, boys and girls learn to respond differently. Teachers will also want to be cognizant of how the child's native culture influences the way that emotions are expressed.

Self-expressing, informing, and persuading are very basic language functions.

> In general, expect children to recognize those feelings that have more overt behavioral manifestations: happiness, sadness, anger, fear. . . . Expression of more abstract emotions—pride, remorse, elation, etc.—will, undoubtedly, come much later, in both the first and second language. The key to learning emotional responses is context, and the feedback from the environment concerning the appropriateness of the emotions expressed. (pp. 16–17)

As they react to what children do, teachers can become adept at modeling the use of expressive language in their own speech (e.g., *You're proud of ———. I'm glad.*) (p. 21). They can also highlight the presence of expressive language in story books through repetition (e.g., *Oh, the lion is there. The elephant is afraid of the lion. He's afraid.*) (p. 22).

Urzúa offers several activities that provide practice with self-expressing. In pairs, children can photograph emotions by taking pictures of people, places, things, and events that evoke emotional feelings, such as anger, frustration, joy, and delight. A survey can be used to poll people regarding what makes them feel happy or sad (angry, etc.) and what they do when they feel that way. Later this can be reported through drawings or in writing. Using stories that children know, role play can be a vehicle for exploring how different characters feel at various points of a story. Feelings can also be expressed through movement, using body language to show fear or anger, for example, or using mime to respond to music or sounds. One teacher suspended sets of words from the ceiling that were generated by the children. These words related to different kinds of feelings and were then used in the children's stories.

Informing   *Informing* is language used to represent "a reality the speaker understands" (Urzúa, 1988, 3). This is one ability that children do not develop early (pp. 27–28). Younger children include more irrelevant details in their accounts than older children. Not surprisingly, informing language is used more in middle and junior high school than in the primary grades. It is not until the ninth grade that children are able to give each other feedback concerning speaker effectiveness, for sensitivity to audience—the ability to take another person's point of view—develops as children grow older. We learn to recognize what information (e.g., identifying the people we mention, explaining the relevancy of actions and events) the listener needs in order for our message to be understood.

When interacting with children, teachers can make the most of naturally occurring repetitions by expanding on what children say. They can also ask questions about the information children share in ways that signal the message was heard and understood. If a child is using gestures to convey meaning (pointing to objects or pictures, for example), the teacher can supply the missing word. He or she should then check for understanding, without asking the child to repeat what was said (pp. 29–31).

There are a variety of activities teachers can use to provide practice with informing. Interviews and sharing activities are popular activities that involve informing. A short walk around the neighborhood provides ample opportunities for description and reporting (e.g., number and color of houses, pets and animals, and age of people encountered). Observing insects and snails enables students to draw and tell about how these creatures behave. Urzúa suggests dipping pill bugs very lightly in a solution of food coloring and watching the trail left behind. (I used to do the same with garden snails.) Pair activities in which cards or exercises are designed in such a way as to provide each partner with different information have applicability across content areas. Cantoni-Harvey (1987) uses this approach on a magic quilt math activity at the primary level. Palmer, Rodgers, and Olsen (1985) use it as the basis for a range of activities and exercises, from pronunciation and picture description to developing meaningful dialogs. Pictures can be used to require students to describe physical features and characteristics, to express semantic relationships (e.g., location, agent, instrument, etc.), and to describe spatial relationships (pp. 3–4).

Persuading   As language users, we are constantly confronted by situations that involve *persuading* (Urzúa, 1988). We engage in attempts to persuade others. Our efforts may run the gamut from hinting and inviting to directing and commanding. We are also on the receiving end of others' efforts to persuade us, be it family, peers, or the media. Persuading is pervasive. In tracing the development of persuading, Urzúa suggests that it begins at birth with our first cry. A preschooler's succinct statement of need (*I want———. Can I have———?*) is expanded at age eight or nine by such additions as an offer to exchange for what is needed (*I've been a good boy/girl. Can I have———?*) (p. 38). Parents will appreciate knowing that the shift from repetition to cajoling reflects cognitive development. Justification for requests comes later, and there are fewer direct requests as children grow older.

Urzúa reports information that is of special interest to teachers. For students through the fifth grade, response to a message is based more on the source of the message (the *who*) than on the message itself (the *what*) (p. 38). Awareness of the techniques of persuasion and the ability to evaluate them generally develops when students are in the eighth grade. By the ninth grade, students are able to focus attention on the message conveyed and to consider the source. For second language learners in the primary grades, social aspects of persuading are particularly important in helping children develop sensitivity to the social context, specifically the listener and the potential reactions of others to their persuasive efforts.

Younger learners enjoy guessing games (e.g., estimating the number of beans or kernels of corn in a jar) (Urzúa, 1988). The class can work cooperatively for a "prize" if all of the students in the class agree on a number that is within a certain range of the correct answer. Planning a trip or class fund-raising activity can provide the context for persuading when groups favoring different options are invited to present a convincing case for their choice.

Finally, it is important to remember that language functions operate within a cultural context. Specific functions are not the same across cultures. There are cultural "rules" and traditions that govern how functions are used. For example, different traditions are associated with greeting a visitor to one's home, and the parameters of requesting and apologizing differ across cultures. In many Hmong and Mien communities, insulting is reported to be virtually unknown among children raised within traditional households. One teacher noted that whenever she observes these children exchanging "insults" with other children on the playground, she recognizes it as a sign of acculturation. Although current studies of language functions across cultures provide valuable insights, they do not yet offer a complete picture of how the variety of language functions used in English are realized in other languages and cultures (and vice versa). As a result, teachers need to be keen observers, alert to differences and similarities in how language functions are used by their students in the classroom and in other settings. Figure 7-1 (see pp. 130–131) provides a list of selected language functions appropriate for developing language activities for use with English language learners.

Accuracy

Research suggests that learners of a second language construct a systematic, rule-governed language system of their own that is distinct from both the native language and the one being acquired (Larsen-Freeman & Long, 1991). Larsen-Freeman and Long suggest that the only way to explain how certain constructions are acquired in the first or second language is to posit constraints on initial hypothesizing—constraints that are eventually modified as individuals encounter more input. Over time, initial hypotheses are refined to account for ever-greater complexity along a developmental continuum.

An individual's *interlanguage* is an evolving linguistic system based on the input to which the learner has been exposed (pp. 60–61). Interlanguage is dynamic, as developmental sequences and accuracy follow predictable stages marking the learner's progress toward native-like proficiency. The stages reflected in interlanguage are common to all learners of the same language. However, there is considerable variability across individuals. These differences are accounted for by variations in learning experience and the influence of the primary language. For example, Krashen (1981, 59–62) proposes a highly reliable "natural order" of grammatical morphemes in English second language acquisition—an order that is neither "rigidly" invariant nor random in any way.

Errors are indicators of the progress learners are making toward competence in a second language. Viewed within the context of the highly variable and systematic interlanguage that language learners develop, they are "mirrors to the mind." Errors can be likened to visible signposts on the road to proficiency—signs that teachers can learn to read. Research tells us that teachers are selective in choosing the treatment given learner errors (Chaudron, 1988). Classroom observations reveal that teachers neither ignore nor correct all of the errors that second language learners produce. They make choices. Overall, they seem most likely to treat those errors that interfere with communication or relate directly to the pedagogical focus of a lesson (p. 136).

In treating learner errors, teachers face a dilemma. On the one hand, students must strive for accuracy in order to achieve full proficiency in the second language. On the other, there is considerable debate as to how accuracy can best be achieved and what kind of role error correction plays in the process. According to Chaudron (1988), "the greatest error teachers make may be the assumption that what occurs as 'correction' in classroom interaction automatically leads to learning on the part of the student" (pp. 152–153). This is reminiscent of Pienemann's teachability hypothesis and the notion that the *teachability* of an item is constrained by its *learnability*, as learners can only be taught what they are psycholinguistically "ready" to learn (cited in Larsen-Freeman & Long, 1991, 280).

Although empirical studies are still needed to assess the effectiveness of correcting specific types of errors, researchers agree that there is probably some validity to treating certain types of errors (particularly with adolescent learners). Among these are errors of comprehensibility and frequency (Chaudron, 1988; Walz, 1982). Errors involving comprehensibility impair communication and cause misunderstandings. These are treated by focusing on meaning rather than form. For example, if a student engaged in a science lesson assigns an incorrect label to an organ that is part of the digestive system, correction would focus on the association between the label and the organ it represents. Attention to meaning would take precedence over grammar or pronunciation.

The second type are those errors that seem to stand out because of their frequency in speech or writing. These are systematic errors—errors that are repeated often—rather than those occurring at random or as a function of performance. "Grammatical errors which occur repeatedly and consistently may simply indicate that a student is not quite ready to be using specific structures. Grammatical structures which are used inconsistently, sometimes correctly and sometimes incorrectly, may indicate that the student is in the process of acquiring these structures" (Scarcella, 1990, 62). As Pienemann observes, however, not all systematic errors can be remediated.

Getting and sharing information
- Identifying objects, persons, and processes
- Stating facts
- Seeking information
- Stating hypotheses and reporting generalizations
- Summarizing
- Explaining how something works

Conveying attitudes and positions
- Expressing/inquiring about agreement/disagreement, understanding/misunderstanding, certainty/uncertainty, obligation/nonobligation, belief/opinion, intentions, need)
- Admitting, affirming, or denying
- Extending/inquiring about an invitation or offer
- Offering to do something
- Stating/inquiring about intentions
- Expressing warning
- Remembering (recalling, reminding)/forgetting
- Granting/withholding permission
- Requesting/denying permission
- Confirming, evaluating, predicting, or rejecting
- Describing, comparing, or narrating
- Giving examples/citing exceptions
- Classifying, categorizing, or listing
- Proposing solutions
- Making excuses/promises
- Declaring/stating
- Protesting/objecting/resisting
- Interviewing/questioning

Expressing emotions
- Expressing/inquiring about pleasure/displeasure (likes/dislikes, satisfaction/dissatisfaction, importance/unimportance, surprise, complaint)
- Expressing disappointment (gratitude, sympathy, patience/impatience, interest/boredom, happiness, enthusiasm, friendliness/hostility, trust/suspicion, admiration, respect/disrespect, insults, criticism, blame, love/hate)
- Expressing/asking about fear/worry

Figure 7-1   List of selected language functions
Source: Omaggio (1986, 444–449)

Teachers need to take individual student concerns into account (Walz, 1982, 11–12). Learner sensitivity to correction varies, and correction benefits older learners more than children. While some students may solicit corrections, others will be inhibited if overcorrected. As a result, teachers must consider how individual students respond. Do they want to be corrected? To what extent will the learner profit from feedback? Will correction create anxiety and inhibit production? Teachers

- Stating/asking about preference (hope)
- Stating want/desire
- Making a wish
- Giving reasons for an action/nonaction

Expressing moral attitudes
- Apologizing/granting forgiveness
- Expressing appreciation (embarrassment, regret, amazement, relief, resignation, pride, humility, modesty, honor/dishonor, approval/disapproval
- Stating indignation/reproach
- Expressing/asking about indifference
- Expressing moral/religious beliefs

Socializing
- Greeting and addressing (formally and informally)
- Introducing oneself/others and responding to an introduction
- Taking leave/departing/planning to meet again
- Ending a conversation
- Extending wishes
- Being hospitable
- Presenting/receiving gifts
- Asking for/offering help
- Telling jokes/anecdotes/teasing
- Expressing thanks (compliments, congratulations, praise, flattery, concern, compassion)
- Acknowledging polite comment
- Telling secrets
- Recounting personal experience

Telephone behavior
- Answering/making a telephone call
- Responding to answer/questions
- Requesting to speak to someone/responding to request to speak to someone
- Stating "wrong number"
- Putting caller on hold
- Stating reason for call
- Returning a telephone call
- Ending a telephone conversation

and researchers do agree on one point: When corrections are made, the techniques used should be positive and not embarrass the learner (p. 16).

To this end, Walz suggests a hierarchy for error correction. First, whenever possible, learners should correct their own errors (pp. 17–18). Studies indicate that advanced and intermediate language learners are capable of correcting a significant proportion of their own errors. Second, peer correction can be an effective approach if handled with care and sensitivity. However, the potential that peer correction has for greater student involvement and enhanced motivation can be undermined if learners perceive that it is used to compare or favor students. As a last resort, Walz recommends teacher correction, with covert or indirect correction (e.g., providing a correct model embedded within a response or a reaction to what the student said). This is preferred over overt or direct correction (e.g., drawing attention to the error and asking the student to repeat the correct form).

In assessing the implications of research on factors affecting students' grammatical development in a second language, Scarcella (1990) concludes that

> what we do know is that if students are not psychologically *ready* to acquire a grammatical structure, it will be impossible to teach them the structure. All this means is that it is probably best to keep comprehensive grammar explanations to a minimum, and to avoid over-emphasis of form and error. Grammar explanations may help adolescent and adult students when presented by teachers who are sensitive to the particular needs of their students. . . . Optimally, such explanations can serve to motivate students who desire grammar rules, improve their ability to monitor their output, and expedite the acquisition of certain grammatical structures. Yet, perhaps even more important than giving such grammar explanations, it is critical that teachers emphasize the importance of good grammar. The psychological impact of stressing the importance of grammatical accuracy may be of critical importance in acquiring a second language. (pp. 62–63)

In the final analysis, researchers are generally in agreement that teachers will want to focus first and foremost on the meaning of what students say. "Whatever they say, and however they say it, we need to recognize, understand, appreciate, and nurture their attempts to communicate by responding to the message" (Law & Eckes, 1990, 138). With adolescents in particular, accuracy is appropriately addressed in precommunicative activities that provide guided practice with new grammatical elements and structures—activities that serve as precursors to communicative tasks designed to promote fluency. It is also addressed as part of the editing stage in the writing process or when students have a grammatical structure correct, but their pronunciation makes it difficult for them to be understood (Law & Eckes, 1990).

Whereas the way in which individuals process print is essentially the same in reading and writing English as a first or second language, there are critical differences as well (Peregoy & Boyle, 1993, 64, 112). The sections that follow address three areas in which these differences are critical to literacy instruction: comprehension, cultural background, and cognitive strengths.

Comprehension

Comprehension is constrained by powerful social and cultural factors that determine the meaning that readers assign to texts and mitigate their understanding. "We understand texts because they are part of a discourse community with which we have things in common, *in addition to the language*" (Williams & Snipper, 1990, 21). Reading links readers to particular communities (e.g., art, cooking, sports, history) and these, in turn, mediate comprehension by delimiting the interpretations and meanings available to the reader. Texts are incomprehensible to readers outside the discourse community, because they do not share the same representations of reality (Williams & Snipper, 1990).

Comprehension is highly socialized (Williams & Snipper, 1990). In school, students learn which of the meanings they construct are acceptable and which are not. The implications for teachers and students are significant. In multilingual classrooms, socialized comprehension takes place through reading activities. The teacher's selection of texts and activities influences how "young people define who they are and how they fit into a variety of communities" (p. 23). By selecting reading texts and activities that encourage cultural literacy, teachers can reinforce cultural identity and promote identification with the home language and community. They can also introduce students to mainstream culture and promote identification with its institutions.

Teachers may not realize that comprehension involves such a wide range of social and cultural factors. The following is an example from Williams and Snipper (1990) that many English language learners can relate to.

> A middle school text about an adolescent testing the limits of her personal freedom with her parents . . . may be largely incomprehensible to students from cultures that place more value on respecting parents and less on individuality—not because they fail to understand the words or even the sentences, but because they fail to grasp the cultural value Americans place on individuality. And it is this social factor that shapes the meaning of the text. (p. 22)

On a personal note, while I do not recall having experienced difficulty understanding American and English literature, what I read in high school and even college did not reflect many aspects of the language or culture that I knew at home. Only when I read literature in my first language did I find characters who shared not only the language, but also the values and traditions that my family did. This experience is consistent with Williams and Snipper's (1990, 22) observation that older learners are more likely to experience conflict than those who are younger. It also appears to be the case when students are required to deal with texts that expect them to identify with mainstream values and accept the writer's representations of reality as their own. As they get older, English language learners become increasingly aware of the juxtaposition created by assimilationist pressures on the one hand and obstacles to full inclusion on the other. They also become more cognizant of the reality that stronger ties with the mainstream culture may eventually weaken those with the home and ethnic community.

Hadley (1993, 131) observes that the comprehension process in a second language involves three types of background knowledge. These are (1) linguistic knowledge (the learner's knowledge of the language code itself), (2) world knowledge (the learner's experiential and conceptual information base), and (3) knowledge of discourse structure (the learner's insight as to how different spoken and written texts are organized). Hadley hypothesizes that the activation of knowledge beyond the linguistic level is most critical for learners at the initial stages of proficiency. Research even suggests that background knowledge is a more significant factor in comprehension than knowledge of vocabulary: "The effects of vocabulary difficulty on reading comprehension are not as clear as the effects of background knowledge" (Johnson, cited in Hadley, 149).

Sánchez (1989) explains the relationship of prior knowledge and academic achievement as follows:

> This seems to be the single most important indicator of academic success for language minority students. Concept development and comprehension both depend and build upon a student's prior knowledge: what s/he already knows, understands, believes about the world and how it operates. Determining the extent and nature of a student's prior knowledge is essential for a teacher because if a student does not possess the appropriate prior knowledge required for a particular lesson or activity, s/he will not be able to succeed at that lesson or activity. Once we know *what* our students already know, then we can determine if a gap exists between what they know and what they need to know to undertake a specific task. If such a gap does exist, teachers must fill that gap, provide the requisite prior knowledge so that both the teachers and students can then build on that critical foundation. A note of caution: prior knowledge is dependent on a variety of socioeconomic, cultural, and linguistic factors. (pp. 17–18)

From a teaching perspective, the best activities for promoting language acquisition and learning—those that provide the most meaningful learning experiences—require that the learner activate all three types of knowledge. Hence, teachers will find that they must not only determine the nature of the prior knowledge that students bring to a learning task, but they must provide the foundation required when the necessary knowledge base has not yet been developed. To quote Smith (1983), "Unless the various aspects of language, and our efforts to teach them, are integrated in the learner's understanding, then there will be no useful learning in any case" (p. 71).

For students with *appropriate levels of proficiency*, Sánchez (1989) questions the value of simplifying the complex syntactic and lexical forms that students will need to master if the addition of contextual clues can provide comprehensible access to the content. She recommends that teachers contextualize language using informal definitions, apposition, repetition, paraphrase, examples, origin, synonyms and antonyms, and comparison and contrast.

It is also important to keep in mind differences between comprehension in the first language and the second. Omaggio (1986) suggests that in the native language, listeners and readers operate at an automatic or intuitive level that enables them to rely on the "sum total of their experience and of their language and thought development" (p. 98). This puts English language learners at a disadvantage when it comes to reading (pp. 98–99). First, their knowledge of the second language and culture is not comparable to that of a native speaker. This makes it more difficult for them to recall, predict, and relate contextual cues. Second, early in the acquisition process, a learner's memory span in the second language is shorter than in his or her native language because the process is more complicated. Not only is the material new; the process used to extract sense from the text may require changes. For example, readers who never learned to fully exploit the use of contextual cues in their native language will need to develop new and different strategies for utilizing such cues in the second language (see Chapter 2). As Carrell's research suggests, when language *and* form *and* content are familiar and expected, reading is relatively easy, but when one or the other or all are unfamiliar, efficiency, effectiveness, and success for the writer or the reader can be problematic. In an ESL class, the differences in cultural knowledge can be dramatic; students without appropriate linguistic, content, and/or formal schemata encounter difficulty in relating discrete words and ideas to their own background knowledge. (cited in Reid, 1993, 41)

Cultural Background

Teachers need to recognize that culture plays a critical role in the constructive processes involved in composing meaning from text. What students know influences what and how they learn.

> The implicit cultural content knowledge presupposed by a text interacts with the reader's own cultural background knowledge of the content to make texts whose content is based on one's own culture easier to read and understand than syntactically and rhetorically equivalent texts based on a less familiar, more distant culture. (Carrell, cited in Reid, 1993, 40)

As Carrell's work reveals, schemata are culturally specific (Reid, 1993, 40). The effects of cultural schemata or frameworks of knowledge are seen in the following two examples. In a study of adults living in a university community, participants were asked to read two letters describing two weddings: one in India, the other in the United States (Steffensen, Joag-dev, & Anderson, cited in Au, 1993). Half of the adults were from India, the other half from the United States. Not surprisingly, the adults remembered more information and made more culturally appropriate inferences when they read the letter describing the wedding in their own country. In reading the description of the wedding in the other country, their interpretations were more likely to be deemed as inappropriate by a native of the other culture. American readers saw only a single event, failing to recognize that two events—a feast and a reception—followed the wedding in India. In interpreting the American wedding, one Indian reader did not recognize the family tradition represented by the bride wearing her grandmother's wedding dress, describing the gown simply as "too old and out of fashion" (p. 22). This reader's cultural schemata dictated that a stylish new sari would be a more appropriate indication of the economic status of the bride's family, as consistent with the custom in Indian weddings familiar to her.

Along similar lines, Au (1993) demonstrates how interpretation of passages can differ along ethnic lines, with the failure of those outside the African American community to recognize an instance of sounding—"a form of ritual insult and verbal play practiced mainly by teenage boys in many African American communities" (p. 23)—described in a reading passage (Reynolds, Taylor, Steffensen, Shirey, & Anderson, cited in Au, 1993). Teachers as well as students fail to acknowledge literacy patterns and traditions different from their own (Gilmore, cited in Au, 1993; Heath, 1983). The practical implications are clear. For many students, school literacy practices represent socialization into a different culture. The key, according to Au, is to provide literacy instruction that reaffirms students' own cultural identities and actively involves learners in the process of making meaning (pp. 29–30). In the final analysis, "'making meaning' varies from reader to reader" as each brings to the task a most unique and complex set of experiences, expectations, prejudices, and desires (Reid, 1993, 40).

Cognitive Strengths

Capitalizing on an English language learner's cognitive strengths is central to literacy. Strategies that tap existing knowledge more effectively contribute to literacy development. Pehrsson and Robinson (1985) believe that many children require assistance in organizing prior and present knowledge as they engage in reading and writing tasks: "Such help is especially needed when the school curriculum imposes content and tasks on pupils on which they have little background" (1985, vii). The teacher is then left to provide both direction and structure.

The use of organizers can facilitate this task considerably. *Clustering*, for example, is "a visual structuring of concepts, events, and feelings," an "open-ended [and] nonlinear form of sorting ideas" (Pierce, 1987, 22). Using one word as the focal point for brainstorming, students generate ideas, images, and feelings that provide the basis for their writing. "Clustering makes silent, invisible mental processes visible and manipulable; hence, teachable and utilizable" (Rico, 1987, 17). Fifth grader Jefferson Newman used clustering to generate a descriptive

Capitalizing on an English language learner's cognitive strengths is central to literacy.

piece of writing on circles (Reeves, 1987). What caught his teacher's attention is how the cluster described in Figure 7-2 reflected the student's thought processes. She observed how ideas seemed to move from the concrete to the abstract, from literal to symbolic. Reeves (1987) describes how the language of Jefferson's writing became rhythmical, almost circular she says, its very form reflecting content.

> The circle is round and smooth. Coins like dimes and fifty cent pieces are in circles. A circle takes the formation of your knee cap. It is the form of Saturn's rings. The circle is the shape of a medallion glittering in the sun. A circle is like the rings of a bracelet. People get married and have a circle placed on their finger, a wedding ring. A circle shows the significance of how God is infinite. A circle takes the brightness of the full moon. I wear a button almost every day, a circle button. It reminds me of a classroom clock—ticktock, ticktock, ticking time slowly away. A circle is the egg that rests on your table. A circle is the base on which your hair rests. It is the turning of the doorknob, the orbiting of the planets, the parachute springing out as the person leaps out of the airplane. It is the thumbprint of a human being twisted and turned, making the whirls in your thumb. It is the wheel on a bicycle spinning round and round. A circle is a fascinating two-dimensional object. (p. 23)

According to Pehrsson and Robinson, *semantic organizers* provide a natural extension for children's thought and language, making it easier for learners to organize ideas as they engage in tasks involving reading and writing. Although designed with elementary, middle school, and junior high students in mind, the approach works effectively with high school students as well. It has been used successfully in ESL/ELD (English language development) programs and in bilingual settings. For Pehrsson and Robinson, proximity is the key to communication and literacy (p. 3). Proximity involves the bridging of knowledge and background information between reader and writer or between writer and reader. Proximity is contingent upon cultural, cognitive, linguistic, and affective factors. The better the match

Figure 7-2 Clustering
Source: From "Clustering on Circles" by E. W. Reeves in *Practical Ideas for Teaching Writing as a Process* (p. 23) edited by C. B. Olson, 1987, California Department of Education Publications, 515 L Street #250, Sacramento, CA 95814. Copyright © 1987 by California Department of Education. Reprinted by permission.

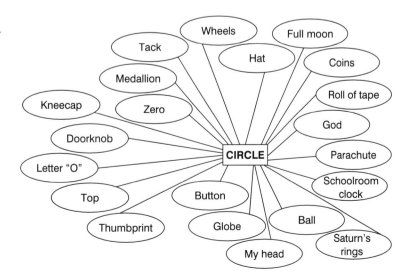

- *culturally* between the second language learner's perceptions, interpretations, and understandings and those of individuals within the culture
- *cognitively* between the way learners think and the way that knowledge is organized
- *linguistically* between the vocabulary and structures used and those meaningful to the reader or writer and
- *affectively* between the learner's interest and involvement and the reading or writing task

the greater the likelihood that communication will be successful (pp. 3–5).

As used by Pehrsson and Robinson, semantic organizers enable students to match what they know, what they think, what is meaningful and interesting with the organization of knowledge for reading and writing. Their approach is consistent with what reading as well as writing researchers have been advocating for years: that "instruction must be more concerned with meaning and less with skills" (Leki, 1993, 19). Descriptions of five of the basic types of organizers identified by Pehrsson and Robinson (1985) follow. Each type of organizer serves a different purpose.

1. *Realia organizers.* Preschool and kindergarten children begin with realia organizers in which the focus is on an activity, and children are asked to identify which of the five real "objects" attached is not associated with the activity (Figure 7-3).

2. *Verb organizers.* Verb organizers emphasize semantic relationships between verbs and nouns, provide repetition of basic sentence structures, and facilitate basic paragraph development. In verb organizers, an action verb is in the central position and three of the four pictures or cards around the verb feature nouns of people, animals, or things that perform the action (Figure 7-4).

3. *Noun organizers.* Noun organizers are characterized by a noun in the key position, that is, surrounded by verbs and verb phrases. Noun organizers help children to summarize, generalize, compare, and contrast. Because nouns typically represent the main topic in paragraphs, noun organizers enable students to begin to generate a greater variety of sentence structures in paragraph writing (Figures 7-5 and 7-6, pp. 142–145).

4. *Concept organizers.* Concept organizers are so versatile and adaptable that they can be used by students from first grade through college. Concept organizers are familiar to most teachers because they are typically used in brainstorming exercises in which attention is drawn to a central concept and key words and ideas form a "web" of related thoughts. Because they are less controlled than verb and noun organizers, concept organizers allow for more creative language and thought. Their organizational power makes them useful for writing activities such as biographies and autobiographies, summarizing, news reporting, extending paragraph writing, comparing and contrasting, research, labeling, generalizing, and writing poetry (Figure 7-7, pp. 146–147).

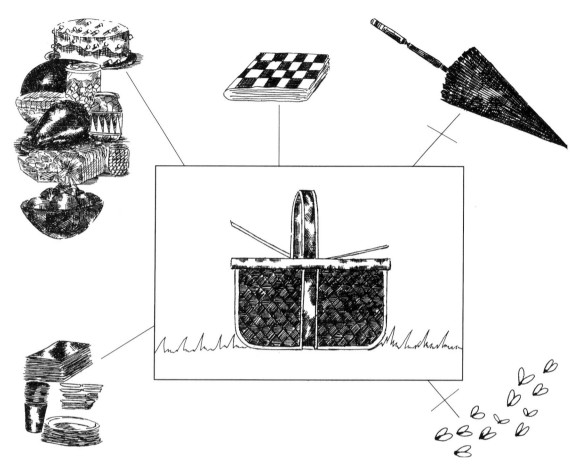

Figure 7-3 Realia organizer
Source: Adapted with permission of F. Hernández.

5. *Episodic organizers.* Episodic organizers lend themselves to content area tasks in which students deal with relationships (e.g., cause and effect, problem and solution) and sequence (e.g., predicting outcomes, narrating a sequence of events). They are used to express order and chronological relationships—the sequence of events that takes place over time. For English language learners, this type of organizer is particularly useful in developing longer and more complicated discourse (Figure 7-8, pp. 148–149).

Sometimes organizers appear under different names. For example, when they are used in the context of reading instruction, they may be referred to as story mapping or cognitive mapping (Peregoy & Boyle, 1993, 131–135). As mapping strategies, they serve as scaffolds that help beginning and intermediate readers to comprehend and remember simple stories and more complex text.

Literacy Issues

Many issues—social, political, cultural, and linguistic—inherent in teaching students from diverse backgrounds are deeply and inescapably embedded within language and literacy instruction. Literacy is a social and political construct. It is "the ability to think and reason within a particular society" (Langer, cited in Cum-

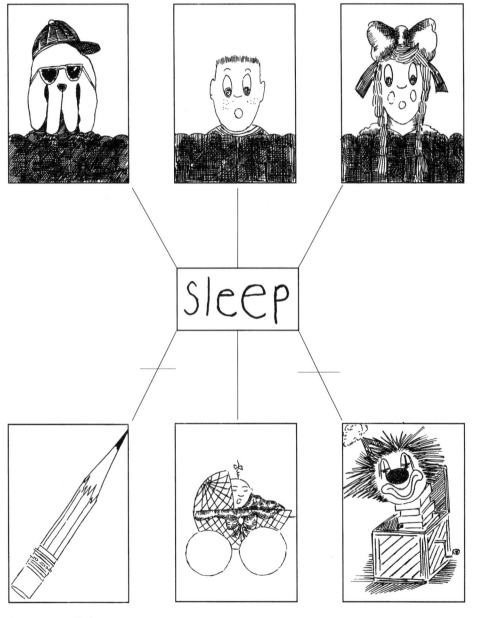

Figure 7-4 Verb organizer
Source: F. Hernández.

Kourtney R Knox

Babies   Doggies

Sleep.   — Girls

pencils

Toys   Boys

sleep

Girls, sleep.   Boys   Babies sleep.   Doggies sleep
Pencils don't   sleep.   sleep. Toys don't   sleep.

Figure 7-4, *continued*

mins, 1994, 306). From a cultural standpoint, literacy emphasizes the common knowledge and experiences that allow members of a community to meaningfully interpret text within a shared cultural context (Cummins, 1994, 304). Ferdman and Weber (1994) see "*becoming* and *being* literate as processes that are very much culturally framed" (p. 8). Along similar lines, Reder (1994) frames discussion of literacy across languages and cultures in terms of cultural practices. Research on young children's literacy development reveals that children acquire knowledge, skills, and values related to specific literacy practices directly, internalizing the structure of literacy activities in their home and the world around them (pp. 40–41). In different societal contexts, studies in settings such as an Eskimo fishing village, rural communities in South Carolina, Hispanic communities in the western United States, and urban areas in the Northeast draw attention to the importance of the literacy environment itself, and to the values, meanings, and processes that underlie literacy activities specific to each setting.

The ways in which reading and writing are used within specific contexts differ across cultures. Students literate in two languages are likely to find different uses for reading and writing in each language. Ramírez (1994, 94) posits that for members of language minority groups, literacy activities in the first language may be tied to intragroup needs (family, religion, recreation) that serve to maintain identity within the family, ethnic group, and linguistic community. By contrast, the need for literacy in the second language is more likely to involve intergroup uses that revolve around work, education, health care, mass media, government, and social services. These might range from basic survival and academic skills to sustaining personal relationships and personal uses. Even the types of texts and genres associated with literacy activities in each language will vary.

Educators addressing literacy issues in multilingual and multicultural settings are often highly critical of what has been the traditional model of literacy instruc-

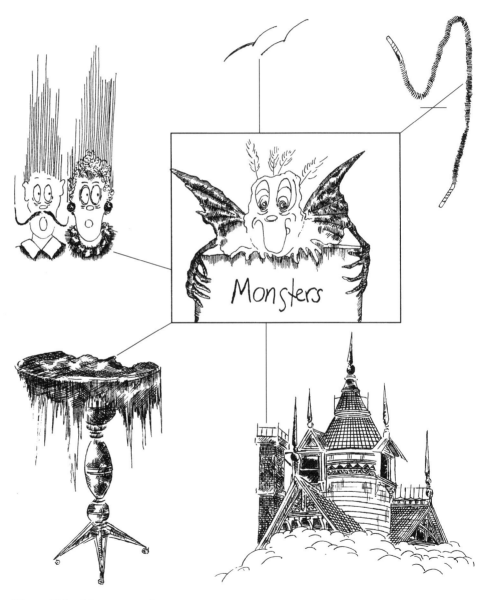

Figure 7-5   Noun organizer
Source: F. Hernández.

Adán Ortega

fly

Scare people — Monsters — Jump rope

tables   *haunted house*

Monsters
Monster fly. Monsters scare people.
Monsters haunt houses. Monsters eat
tables. Monsters don't play jump rope.

Figure 7-5, *continued*

tion. Shannon reports that teacher guide books and basal readers are used by over 90 percent of elementary school teachers for 90 percent of reading instruction: "Teachers teach students what, when, where, how, and why to use the skill listed as next in the basal scope and sequence. . . . Questions asked during practice should be factual, encourage choral response from the group, and be carefully sequenced to lead students successfully to the goal without diversion" (cited in Cummins, 1994, 313). Goodlad (cited in K. Goodman, 1986) finds what he describes as an overwhelming emphasis on textbooks and workbooks, with minimal attention to actual reading and writing: "Excluding 'the common practice of students taking turns reading from a common text,' reading accounts for only 6% of elementary class time and tails off to 3% in junior high school and 2% in senior high" (p. 62).

English language learners fare no better. Gunderson (1991, 8) surveyed elementary teachers on the use of basal readers and the corresponding Directed Reading Activity Approach, and found that approximately 80 to 90 percent of those surveyed reported using this approach to teach reading to ESL students. He draws attention to what happens when teachers impose basal reading on students who do not even "know what's going on. . . . It is unfortunately all too common to see non-English-speaking children in reading groups, usually the lowest, where they are completely lost about what is taking place" (1991, 114). Although "basal

Figure 7-6 Another noun organizer
Source: F. Hernández.

Micaela Rubio

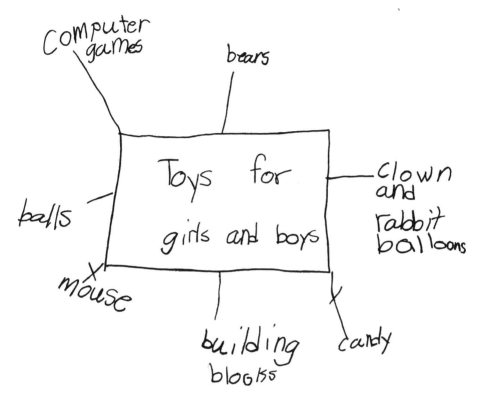

My Huge Toy Box

I have a huge toy box. Six toys
are in my toy box. They are only for girls and
boys. These are the toys in my toy
box. You'll find building blocks, bears, computer games,
clown and rabbit balloons and balls. You won't find
candy or a live mouse in my box!
This box has favorite toys for girls and boys.
I hope it gets filled with more toys soon.

Figure 7-6, *continued*

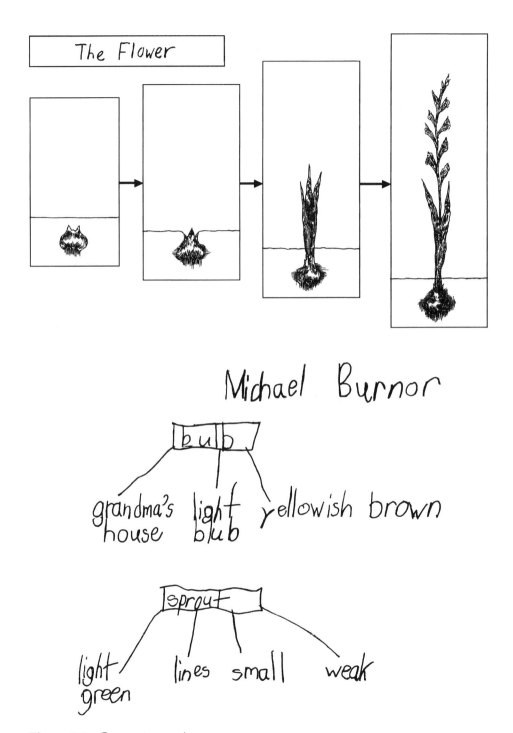

The Flower

Michael Burnor

bulb
- grandma's house
- light blub
- yellowish brown

sprout
- light green
- lines
- small
- weak

Figure 7-7 Concept organizer
Source: Flower illustration by F. Hernández.

146

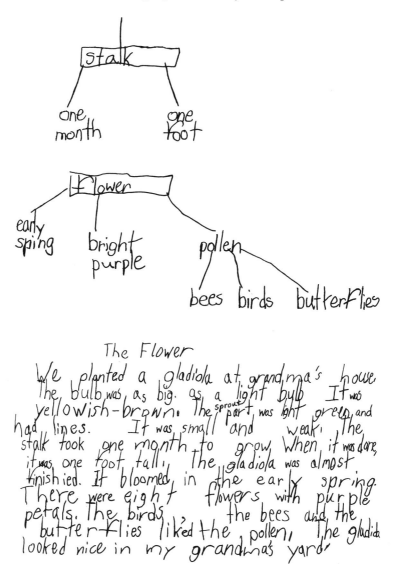

Figure 7-7, *continued*

reading series are not intrinsically bad," they are not the best way to begin (p. 115). Basal readers are not appropriate for students without literacy skills in their first language and only limited fluency in English. There are typically too many high-frequency words that are not familiar and unrealistic assumptions regarding the students' level of oral-language development. The frequency of irregular past-tense verbs, inclusion of "unnatural" sentences, and unfamiliar cultural content further contribute to the difficulties encountered by English language learners. For Gunderson as for others critical of basal reading series, the primary issue is that students be taught to read effectively and with strategies and materials appropriate to their level of language development. (Teachers required to use basal reading programs with English language learners may want to at least consider some of Gunderson's suggestions regarding adaptations to the traditional directed reading activities. Whereas Gunderson does not include basal reading instruction among the better alternatives available for teaching reading, the changes he suggests may at least help teachers to counter some of the negative aspects identified earlier.)

Au (1993, 48) characterizes instruction within traditional models as teacher centered, skills driven, decontextualized, and culturally biased. Literacy is taught as abstract skills and knowledge that can be transmitted to students for passive

Figure 7-8 Episodic organizer
Source: F. Hernández.

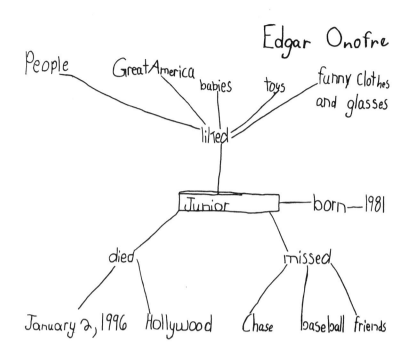

Edgar Onofre

People — GreatAmerica — babies — toys — funny Clothes and glasses

liked

Junior — born — 1981

died — January 2, 1996 — Hollywood

missed — Chase — baseball — friends

Junior

My grandfather's dog Junior, was born in 1981. He liked to run, lick people and play with toys and babies. When he was medium-sized Junior liked to go to GreatAmerica. In 1989, he liked to put on glasses and wear funny Clothes. When my dog was 105-dog years old, he went to Hollywood with my mom, my dad, and I. In January 2, 1996, Junior died. I missed Junior because he played Chase and base ball with me. He has a good friend.

Figure 7-8, *continued*

absorption. Little attention is given to the functions of literacy, social context, life experiences or cultural knowledge. Sirotnik (cited in Cummins, 1994) describes the hidden curriculum as

> a lot of teacher talk and a lot of student listening . . . almost invariably closed and factual questions . . . and predominantly total class instructional configurations around traditional activities—all in a virtually affectless environment. It is but a short inferential leap to suggest that we are implicitly teaching dependence upon authority, linear thinking, social apathy, passive involvement, and hands-off learning. (p. 314)

Despite years of controversy, no one method for teaching reading to native speakers of English has emerged as the "best method" (Gunderson, 1991, 20). Some researchers attribute reading failure at least in part to the use of basal reading programs; others find the personal characteristics of students and teachers to be more significant. In the midst of this debate, "it is no wonder that ESL students are not successfully learning to read" (p. 20).

In response to such concerns, advocates for changing the nature of literacy instruction often look to active, constructive processes that center on making meaning through interaction with texts, drawing on student knowledge and experiences as the basis for writing, providing culturally responsive instruction, and advancing critical literacy (Au, 1993). First and foremost, constructivist approaches are student centered. "Constructivist models of instruction assume that students will learn literacy by engaging in the full processes of reading and writing in a purposeful, largely self-directed manner" (p. 42). Literacy instruction is embedded in social and cultural contexts and proceeds from the global to the specific, from the whole to individual parts. "Through involvement in the full processes of literacy, and with the assistance of teachers, students gradually construct their own understandings of the hows and whys of reading and writing. In this sense, they learn to read by reading and to write by writing" (p. 42). This is consistent with research in the homes and communities of language minority students that shows that adults use literacy in a variety of ways in carrying out their everyday lives

In the final analysis, literacy instruction for students in multilingual classrooms is a more complicated task than in classrooms with only native speakers of English (Gunderson, 1991). To be effective, teachers need to consider a number of factors. These include literacy background in the primary language, language proficiency and literacy development in English, age, literacy needs and goals, cultural appropriateness, and reading materials.

Reading and Writing: Reciprocal Processes

As we have seen, literacy is much more than command of isolated language skills. "Literacy . . . is not synonymous with the ability to read (decode) or write (transcribe) per se. Rather it is a 'goal-directed, context-specific' behavior" (Flower et al, cited in Leki, 1993, 13). For the literate individual, reading and writing are meaningful, purposeful, and interactive. Current research strongly suggests the existence of a close relationship in the activities involved in creating and processing written text (Kaplan, 1987, 19). They are, in fact, dynamic reciprocal processes.

Reid (1993, 43) highlights a number of the findings from research on writing and reading. Both writing and reading

- are complex "processes of making meaning"
- involve thought patterns and linguistic habits that are similar
- are multifaceted processes that require many subskills
- build on learner's past experiences
- activate the learner's schemata related to the language, content, and form of a given topic
- are processes that rely on the learner's schemata to discover meaning
- are processes in which the learner generates and revises mental "drafts" of meaning

This reciprocity between literacy processes holds true for English language learners as well as native speakers (Leki, 1993; Reid, 1993). Focusing on the learner, Leki draws other parallels from the research on ESL reading and writing (pp. 9–10). Less skilled readers and writers tend to focus on text rather than meaning, on form rather than connections. When reading, they are unable to relate what they read to the preceding text. When writing, they find it difficult to operate beyond the immediate grammatical context of words and sentences. By contrast, more efficient second language readers use strategies differently, "interactively in reading," "recursively in writing" (p. 10). They display greater flexibility in applying strategies and greater sensitivity to communication and meaning. As Reid observes, "good writers are often good readers" (1993, 43).

How to help students make the most of this reciprocal relationship between language skills is central to critical literacy and teachers' effective use of literacy activities. These areas are explored in the sections that follow.

Vygotskian Perspectives

The educational implications of L. S. Vygotsky's ideas, particularly his notions regarding language and thought, have significantly impacted views on the schooling of language minority students (e.g., Faltis, 1993; Moll, 1990). Literacy instruction is no exception (e.g., Clay & Cazden, 1990; Y. Goodman & K. Goodman, 1990; Moll, 1989). For Vygotsky (1978), the best method for teaching reading and writing is through the natural use of these skills. "In the same way as children learn to speak, they should be able to learn to read and write" (p. 118).

Moll (1989) has explored the practical implications of Vygotsky's theoretical concepts—most notably the zone of proximal development—for teaching writing to second language students. With elegant simplicity, Vygotsky (1978) defines the ZPD as "the distance between the actual developmental level as determined by independent problem solving and the level of potential development as determined through problem solving under adult guidance or in collaboration with more capable peers" (p. 86). For Vygotsky, "good learning" is dynamic; good teaching anticipates potential advances in children's development.

Moll (1989) singles out three of Vygotsky's concepts for their special relevance to writing instruction. These are whole activity, mediation, and change. *Whole* activities do not reduce reading and writing into discrete skills and subskills. Rather, they capture the vital essence of what reading and writing entail by retaining all inherent and irreducible characteristics. Such activities reflect social and communicative goals that are conducive to creating a zone of proximal development. When teachers focus on isolated skills and subskills as synonymous with literacy, they constrain the intellectual level of lessons. In doing so, they also run the risk of underestimating the ability of second language learners by assuming that students "cannot engage in advanced English literacy activities until they master lower order basic skills, such as decoding" (p. 58). Díaz, Moll, and Mehan (1996) provide a moving account of how this happened to children reading in a Spanish and English language classroom.

Mediation reflects Vygotsky's belief that interaction between adults and children is at the heart of the educational process. "Central to his concept of the zone are the specific ways that adults (or peers) socially mediate or interactionally create circumstances for learning" (Moll, 1989, 59). Children learn by engaging in collaborative activities within social environments that are actively and mutually created by teacher and students. It is through social interaction that the teacher "creates and regulates those social systems for learning that we call lessons" (p. 59).

The teacher's role as a mediator is a critical one. Optimal learning is supported and facilitated by teaching that avoids unnecessary control or interference (Y. Goodman & K. Goodman, 1990, 236–238). As a mediator, the teacher enables the learner to maximize the possibilities within his or her ZPD. The teacher supports learning without attempting to control it, creating an environment that liberates rather than suppresses learners. Descriptions of classroom episodes with teachers in the role of mediator are typically characterized by pupils engaged in interactive activities in which they are encouraged to share knowledge, draw on their own experiences, and extend their capabilities. The teacher initiates, stimulates, supports, observes, and assists in ways that make it possible for learners to "own the process of their learning" (Y. Goodman & K. Goodman, 1990, 238).

Change is reflected in the progress made by children as individuals, independently and through collaborative activities (Moll, 1989, 59–61). The goal is a powerful one. At a conscious level, children become aware of how they manipulate literacy processes and learn to apply these insights in new activities and experiences. The emphasis is on literacy activities that are mediated jointly by teacher and students—activities "intended to help children express and obtain meaning in ways that will enable them to make this knowledge and meaning their own" (Moll, 1989, 60). Moll (1989) provides the following example to illustrate how the concepts apply in an episode from the classroom.

> The teacher asked the class if anyone wanted to share what they were writing, an activity that formed part of the students' writing routines. Lisa and Ernesto volun-

teered. The rest of the class moved to the front of the room. The teacher asked Lisa to read first and also asked, "Why are you doing this?" Lisa responded, "To see if it [the piece she has written] is o.k." Lisa then read a fairly lengthy story. After she had finished reading, the teacher asked, "What worked well?" Some of Lisa's peers responded that she let them know her characters by providing a physical description and used dialogue to describe the characters' thoughts. Another student commented that she did not start the story with the typical "Once upon a time . . . ," but rather with "The bus was coming . . . ," a much more interesting beginning. Others commented that by having her characters use different languages (Spanish and English) she interested her readers and defined her characters. (p. 64)

All three concepts are evident in this episode. First, based upon Moll's brief description of the writing task, it does appear to satisfy requirements for a whole activity. Second, the account suggests that the teacher in the role of mediator provided only the level of prompting required to facilitate interaction. Third, the children's responses reflected that they had "internalized" important insights as to how language is used in writing and how this affects readers (p. 64). Clearly, important changes are taking place through this collaborative activity.

Sociocultural Considerations

Writing is a cultural, social, cognitive, and linguistic process. In many basic and important ways, native speakers and second language learners have a great deal in common as they engage in writing activities (Hudelson, 1989; Peregoy & Boyle, 1993, 64–65). For example, students write for different purposes and different audiences. In the beginning stages, some children use drawing as a form of prewriting while others rely on illustrations to enhance their expression of ideas with written text. At higher levels of proficiency, student writing more closely approximates the native or target language. Native speakers and English language learners alike find it challenging to deal with the conventions of written language (e.g., grammar, spelling) and elements of the composing process (e.g., writing for fluency, audience, purpose).

Learners who are able to write in their primary language benefit from the transfer of understandings and skills (Peregoy & Boyle, 1993, 65). Experiences in the native language enable students to better appreciate the purpose and function of writing—it helps "learners understand what writing is and what writing can do" (Hudelson, 1989, 38). In addition, many of the insights and abilities developed in the native language can be applied to writing in the second, and a sense of competence in one language may even encourage students to try writing in another (Hudelson, 1989, 46). It is the similarity between writing processes in the first and second language that makes it possible for teachers to draw on strategies used with native speakers—process writing, for example—and to modify them for use with English language learners (Peregoy & Boyle, 1993, 65).

Because writing is a cultural, social, cognitive, and linguistic process, however, there are important differences between English language learners and native speakers that must be considered in writing instruction. Although some are rather obvious, others are more subtle. For example, it would not take teachers long to realize that second language learners do not have the same exposure to written text in English as native speakers do, and that they face constraints imposed by limitations in their command of vocabulary, syntax, and idiomatic expressions (Peregoy & Boyle, 1993, 64). It would be more difficult for teachers to recognize manifestations of differences such as those that exist across languages in rhetorical structure, that is, in the way that text is organized (Kaplan, 1987; Peitzman & Gadda, 1994). Studies of English composition reveal rhetorically distinct patterns in the writing of native speakers of Japanese, Chinese, Arabic, Spanish, Greek, Hindi, Samoan, Malagasy, and Native American languages (Grabe & Kaplan, 1989, 268–269). Various rhetorical modes are possible in any given language, but their frequency and distribution of use reflect clear preferences. What Kaplan describes as the "linear" coherence of textbook English expository paragraphs reflects an inductive or deductive structure that is not characteristic of paragraph and text development in other languages and cultures. Research indicates that the style of narratives in the first language influences the writing of English language learners with respect to setting, character, action, purpose, and language (Gadda, 1994, 44–46; Grabe & Kaplan, 1989).

As teachers become cognizant of the cultural differences in discourse and language socialization that students bring with them to the classroom, they ask what they can do. The response from Gadda (1994) is clear. Teachers need to identify teaching strategies that make it possible for students of all backgrounds to participate in the school's culture of literacy: "It's worth reflecting that the culture of the school is not the home culture of **any** student" (p. 54). Teachers need strategies that work effectively for all students but are especially appropriate for those "whose home cultures are at some distance from our schools' expectations about language use for academic purposes" (p. 70). To help teachers rethink their practice, Gadda offers general suggestions that are useful in guiding the selection and use of strategies (Figure 7-9). Teachers are encouraged to apply these recommendations as appropriate for the age and proficiency level of their students. The most generic would apply to all learners. Those specifically addressing aspects of academic competence are of particular concern for teachers of older learners with requisite language abilities.

Critical Literacy

Cummins (1989a), Ada, de Olave, and Zubizarreta (Ada & de Olave, 1986; Ada & Zubizarreta, 1989) are strong advocates of a pedagogy emphasizing critical literacy. In this context, *empowerment* "constitutes the process whereby students and educators collaboratively create knowledge and identity through action focused on personal and social transformation" (Cummins, 1992, 9). For literacy skills to empower language minority students, learners need to engage in reading and writing activities that also promote the development of critical thinking skills. Literacy and critical thinking skills are inextricably linked. In tandem, these skills will enable students to confront the complex issues that affect their lives. Cummins creates an image of the "empowered" learner as an "explorer of meaning, a critical and creative thinker" who is a contributor in the classroom and beyond.

Provide opportunities for a wide range of language use, both oral and written.
- Promote a wide variety of language use—oral and written—in teaching content areas.
- Capitalize on forms of speech used in the community for academic purposes (e.g., using rap songs to teach biology) (Heath, 1986).
- Provide instruction and guided practice specific to unfamiliar forms (Heath, 1986).
- Use collaborative activities that bring together students with greater and lesser abilities in a variety of language uses.

Discuss and contrast models of the kinds of writing that students are asked to produce.
- Provide at least two good models of the type of written text that students are expected to produce.
- Focus students' attention on relevant features of the text (e.g., for analytical writing, the teacher might use questions to draw attention to how the writer introduces a subject or issue, states a position, integrates the writing or ideas of others, and uses specific techniques to link ideas and connect text in order to achieve coherence).

Promote a critical attitude toward written texts.
- Provide opportunities for students to write analytically. For example, to maximize student access to challenging texts, the teacher might use the "into, through, and beyond" model. Students engage in activities that provide opportunities for them to "approach a text (into), interact with it (through), and write an analytical response to it (beyond)" (Brinton, Goodwin, & Ranks, 1994, 57).
- Provide activities that help students who regard texts "as uniquely authoritative *because* they are written" to become familiar with the traditional Western attitudes toward texts required for academic analysis (Gadda, 1994, 54).

Explain writing and academic conventions used in English.
- Make students aware of academic conventions (e.g., using and citing texts, providing documentation).
- Make students aware of writing conventions in English (e.g., using quotation marks).

Ask students to serve as informants about their own language use.
- Ask students about their writing when their conceptions are not consistent with expectations. For example, the teacher might inquire as to why a piece was begun or concluded as it was, what readers might already know about the topic, what the text is intended to convey, how students are to interpret what is said, how the writing will affect readers, and so on.

Figure 7-9   Teaching strategies that help students participate in the culture of literacy
Source: From "Writing and Language Socialization Across Cultures: Some Implications for the Classroom" by G. Gadda in *With Different Eyes: Insights Into Teaching Language Minority Students Across the Disciplines* (pp. 53–56) edited by F. Peitzman and G. Gadda, 1994, White Plains, New York: Addison Wesley Longman. Copyright © 1994 by The Regents of the University of California. Adapted by permission.

"They [students] read to learn rather than simply learn to read; they engage in creative writing both to collaboratively explore with teachers, parents and peers the horizons of their experience and to extend these horizons" (1989a, 72). Teachers can create an environment that fosters this type of learning "only if they themselves are empowered and critical thinkers" (Cummins, 1989a, 72).

Ada's framework provides an example of how second language learners can address the "broader issues of the social purposes for which language is used and the social relevance of the instructional content" (Cummins, 1992, 9). Inspired by

Freire, the reading process that Ada has developed emphasizes critical and creative thought focusing on issues that are real and of importance to the individual. The process consists of four phases (Ada & Zubizarreta, 1989; Cummins, 1989a, 1992).

In the *descriptive phase*, children demonstrate that they understand what is presented in the text. To check for understanding, the teacher asks questions that include *What happened? Where, when, how did it happen? Who did it? Why?* Since the answers to this initial set of comprehension questions can be found within the text, they provide an opportunity for children to recount and clarify what they have read (Ada & Zubizarreta, 1989, 12).

In the *personal interpretative phase*, children learn to relate information to their own feelings and experiences. This serves a twofold purpose. Self-esteem is enhanced as children develop an awareness that their personal interpretations are valued by others. Children also gain insights into learning as a process. They see that "true learning occurs only when the information received is analyzed in light of one's own experiences and emotions" (Ada, cited in Cummins, 1989a, 74). The teacher might ask questions such as *Has this ever happened to you? Have you ever felt like this? Have you ever had similar thoughts? How did what you read make you feel? Did you like it? Did it make you happy? Did it frighten you? What about your family?* These questions are important in validating the cultural and personal perspective that each child brings to the reading and in making the information more relevant (Ada & Zubizarreta, 1989, 12).

During the *critical multicultural phase*, students delve into a more critical analysis of the issues or problems that emerge in the reading. In this phase, the teacher asks students to draw inferences and make generalizations. Children of all ages can participate in this critical process, although the level of analysis will vary depending on experience and maturity. Teachers now use questions like *Could this have turned out differently? How would different people have reacted? Why? What are other alternatives? What would be the consequences? Is the decision fair or right? Does it benefit everyone?* According to Ada and Zubizarreta (p. 13), these questions help to enhance critical thinking skills by making students aware that in most situations, there are alternative courses of action, and that the choices they make can shape and transform their own reality.

The final stage, the *creative phase*, is the most important. The emphasis is now on translating the outcomes of the first three phases into concrete action. Discussion focuses upon change, as students explore alternative courses of action that can improve individuals' lives or work toward resolving a problem they have been asked to confront. The questions set the tone: "*What can you do to . . . ? How would you change (improve, alter, transform) . . . ? What are you going to do when . . . ? How would you prevent . . . ?* [italics added]" (Ada & Zubizarreta, 1989, 13). The kind of creative dialog that this fosters is important for students of all ages. Cummins (1989a) uses environmental pollution as an example. Once students have interpreted issues on a personal level and then critically analyzed the issues and their possible solutions, they can decide upon a course of action. Action may take the form of writing to local, state, or national government officials, writing to organizations or the local press, acting out particular themes through creative dramas or stories, and so on (p. 74).

Through this critical process, literacy is grounded in the experiences of students, making possible an expanded range of possibilities for personal and cultural identity formation and knowledge generation (Cummins, 1992). In the final analysis,

> ESL students engaging in the critical literacy process . . . have the possibility of actively voicing their own realities and their analyses of issues rather than being constricted to the identity definitions and constructions of "truth" implicitly or explicitly transmitted in the prescribed curriculum. When classroom interaction progresses beyond the descriptive phase, students engage in a process of *self*-expression; in other words, by sharing and critically reflecting on their experience they collaboratively construct a ZPD that expands options for identity formation. (pp. 8–9)

Literacy Activities

In multilingual classrooms, it is important to assess and adjust the learning environment to enhance literacy instruction and student performance (Au, 1993). Teachers can do this in different ways. They can start with students as a source of information. Research indicates that as early as kindergarten, students display considerable awareness of how they learn (Au, 1993, 136). Not only are students cognizant of what does and does not help them in reading and writing, they are fully capable of articulating and sharing their insights. Au implores teachers to "assume that students of diverse backgrounds have ample language ability and can learn to read and write well, given the proper circumstances" (p. 135). When students do encounter difficulties, teachers should focus on the classroom situation, analyzing the various aspects of literacy instruction. The following questions can serve as guidelines (pp. 135–136):

- "Did students find the activity interesting, motivating and meaningful?"
- Were students able to share their ideas about the activity?
- Were students' suggestions used to adjust the activity?
- Was the activity consistent with students' own goals for literacy learning?
- Did the activity provide the students with choices and options?
- Did the teacher provide students with instruction on needed skills?
- Were there opportunities for students to discuss how the activity relates to their lives outside of school?
- Was the type of interaction required to do the activity comfortable for students?
- Were students able to draw on strengths in their primary languages to help them to do the activity?

Summary

It is increasingly evident that the "great divide" once thought to exist between oral and written language has proven to be "considerably exaggerated and distorted" (Reder, 1994, 37). There is a great deal that teachers can do to ensure that English language learners develop the full range of oral and written language required to participate fully in schooling and society. To be most effective, language and literacy instruction must be sensitive to social, political, cultural, and linguistic influences and their implications. The development of language and literacy skills in a second language must be guided by an understanding of the purpose for which these skills are to be used—ideas, action, reflection, and experience, to borrow from Frank Smith (1988, 29).

To facilitate the constructive processes involved, teachers need to understand that what students know affects what and how they learn. For students from different social and cultural backgrounds, school literacy instruction may represent socialization into a different culture. Sociocultural factors influence the meaning that students assign to texts and their interpretation. How teachers respond to these influences is a powerful determinant in their students' development of language and literacy.

References

Ada, A. F., & de Olave, del P. (1986). *Hagamos caminos.* Reading, MA: Addison-Wesley.

Ada, A. F., & Zubizarreta, R. (1989). *Language arts through children's literature.* Emeryville, CA: Children's Book Press.

Au, K. (1993). *Literacy instruction in multicultural settings.* Fort Worth: Harcourt Brace Jovanovich College Publishers.

Brinton, D., Goodwin, J., & Ranks, L. (1994). Helping language minority students read and write analytically: The journey into, through, and beyond. In F. Peitzman & G. Gadda, (Eds.), *With different eyes* (pp. 57–88). White Plains, NY: Addison Wesley Longman.

Cantoni-Harvey, G. (1987). *Content-area language instruction.* Reading, MA: Addison-Wesley.

Chaudron, C. (1988). *Second language classrooms.* New York: Cambridge University Press.

Clay, M. M., & Cazden, C. B. (1990). A Vygotskian interpretation of reading recovery. In L. C. Moll (Ed.), *Vygotsky and education* (pp. 206–222). New York: Cambridge University Press.

Cummins, J. (1989a). *Empowering minority students.* Sacramento: California Association for Bilingual Education.

Cummins, J. (1989b). The sanitized curriculum: Educational disempowerment in a nation at risk. In D. M. Johnson & D. H. Roen (Eds.), *Richness in writing: Empowering ESL students* (pp. 19–38). White Plains, NY: Longman.

Cummins, J. (1992, March). *A critical approach to teaching English as a second language.* Paper presented at the TESOL Conference, Vancouver, BC.

Cummins, J. (1994). From coercive to collaborative relations of power in the teaching of literacy. In R. M. Ferdman, R-M. Weber, & A. G. Ramírez (Eds.), *Literacy across languages and cultures* (pp. 295–331). Albany: State University of New York Press.

Díaz, S., Moll, L. C., & Mehan, H. (1996). Sociocultural resources in instruction: A context-specific approach. In Bilingual Education Office, California Department of Education, *Beyond language: Social and cultural factors in schooling language minority students* (pp. 187–230). Los Angeles: Evaluation, Dissemination and Assessment Center, School of Education, California State University, Los Angeles.

Faltis, C. J. (1993). *Joinfostering: Adapting teaching strategies for the multilingual classroom.* Upper Saddle River, NJ: Merrill/Prentice Hall.

Ferdman, B. M., & Weber, R-M. (1994). Literacy across languages and cultures. In B. M. Ferdman, R-M. Weber, & A. G. Ramírez (Eds.), *Literacy across languages and cultures* (pp. 3–29). Albany: State University of New York Press.

Gadda, G. (1994). Writing and language socialization across cultures: Some implications for the classroom. In F. Peitzman & G. Gadda (Eds.), *With different eyes* (pp. 43–56). White Plains, NY: Addison Wesley Longman.

Goodman, K. (1986). *What's whole in whole language?* Portsmouth, NH: Heinemann.

Goodman, Y. M., & Goodman, K. S. (1990). Vygotsky in a whole-language perspective. In L. C. Moll (Ed.), *Vygotsky and education* (pp. 223–250). New York: Cambridge University Press.

Grabe, W., & Kaplan, R. B. (1989). Writing in a second language: Contrastive rhetoric. In D. M. Johnson & D. H. Roen (Eds.), *Richness in writing: Empowering ESL students* (pp.263–283). White Plains, NY: Longman.

Gunderson, L. (1991). *ESL literacy instruction: A guidebook to theory and practice.* Englewood Cliffs, NJ: Regents/Prentice Hall.

Hadley, A. O. (1993). *Teaching language in context* (2nd ed.). Boston: Heinle & Heinle.

Heath, S. B. (1983). *Ways with words.* New York: Cambridge University Press.

Hudelson, S. (1989). *Write on: Children writing in ESL.* Englewood Cliffs, NJ: Center for Applied Linguistics and Prentice Hall Regents.

Kaplan, R. B. (1987). Cultural thought patterns revisited. In U. Connor & R. B. Kaplan (Eds.), *Writing across languages: Analysis of L2 text* (pp. 9–21). Reading, MA: Addison-Wesley.

Krashen, S. D. (1981). *Second language acquisition and second language learning.* Oxford: Pergamon Press.

Larsen-Freeman, D., & Long, M. H. (1991). *An introduction to second language acquisition research.* New York: Longman.

Law, B., & Eckes, M. (1990). *The more than just surviving handbook.* Winnipeg, MB: Peguis Publishers.

Leki, I. (1993). Reciprocal themes in ESL reading and writing. In J. G. Carson & I. Leki (Eds.), *Reading in the composition classroom* (pp. 9–32). Boston: Heinle & Heinle.

Lindfors, J. W. (1987). *Children's language and learning* (2nd ed.). Englewood Cliffs, NJ: Prentice Hall.

Moll, L. C. (1989). Teaching second language students: A Vygotskian perspective. In D. M. Johnson & D. H. Roen, (Eds.), *Richness in writing: Empowering ESL students* (pp. 55–69). White Plains, NY: Longman.

Moll, L. C. (Ed.). (1990). *Vygotsky and education.* New York: Cambridge University Press.

Omaggio, A. C. (1986). *Teaching language in context.* Boston: Heinle & Heinle.

Palmer, A. S., Rodgers, T. S., & Olsen, J. W. (1985). *Back & forth: Pair activities for language development.* Hayward, CA: Alemany Press.

Pehrsson, R. S., & Robinson, H. A. (1985). *The semantic organizer approach to writing and reading instruction.* Rockville, MD: Aspen Publishers.

Peitzman, F., & Gadda, G. (Eds.) (1994). *With different eyes.* White Plains, NY: Addison Wesley Longman.

Peregoy, S. F., & Boyle, O. F. (1993). *Reading, writing, and learning in ESL.* White Plains, New York: Addison Wesley Longman.

Pierce, K. (1987). Clustering in first grade. In C. B. Olson (Ed.), *Practical ideas for teaching writing as a process* (p. 22). Sacramento: California Department of Education.

Ramírez, A. G. (1994). Literacy acquisition among second-language learners. In R. M. Ferdman, R-M. Weber, & A. G. Ramírez (Eds.), *Literacy across languages and cultures* (pp. 75–101). Albany: State University of New York Press.

Reder, S. (1994). Practice-engagement theory: A sociocultural approach to literacy across languages and cultures. In R. M. Ferdman, R-M. Weber, & A. G. Ramírez (Eds.), *Literacy across languages and cultures* (pp. 33–74). Albany, NY: State University of New York Press.

Reeves, K. (1987). Clustering on circles. In C. B. Olson (Ed.), *Practical ideas for teaching writing as a process* (pp. 22–23). Sacramento: California Department of Education.

Reid, J. M. (1993). Historical perspectives on writing and reading in the ESL classroom. In J. G. Carson & I. Leki (Eds.), *Reading in the composition classroom* (pp. 33–60). Boston: Heinle & Heinle.

Rico, G. L. (1987). Clustering: A prewriting process. In C. B. Olson (Ed.), *Practical ideas for teaching writing as a process* (pp. 17–20). Sacramento: California Department of Education.

Sánchez, F. (1989). *What is "primary language instruction"?* Hayward, CA: Alameda County Office of Education.

Scarcella, R. (1990). *Teaching language minority students in the multicultural classroom.* Englewood Cliffs, NJ: Prentice Hall.

Smith, F. (1983). *Essays into literacy.* Portsmouth, NH: Heinemann Education Books.

Smith, F. (1988). *Joining the literacy club.* Portsmouth, NH: Heinemann.

Urzúa, C. (1988). *Speak with a purpose: A resource book for teaching functional language to young people.* Lincolnwood, IL: National Textbook.

Vygotsky, L. S. (1978). *Mind in society* (M. Cole, V. John-Steiner, S. Scribner, & E. Souberman, Eds.). Cambridge, MA: Harvard University Press.

Walz, J. C. (1982). *Language in Education: Vol. 50. Error correction techniques for the FL classroom.* Washington, DC: Center for Applied Linguistics.

Williams, J. D., & Snipper, G. C. (1990). *Literacy and bilingualism.* New York: Longman.

8

Language and Literacy Development: Approaches and Strategies

As a teacher, I must first slow down in order to acknowledge the voices of my students—to take these moments to give value to what is being said no matter how loud or soft, gentle or angry, relevant or irrelevant it may seem.

Elementary teacher

If teachers set out to make learning a second language difficult, what would they do? With Frank Smith (1983) as a guide, this is what the classroom might look like. Teachers would teach words, expressions, and grammatical structures as discrete elements that must be mastered sequentially before proceeding to new learning. They would strive for early mastery of grammar and pronunciation rules, emphasizing "word-perfect" repetition and reading. This would, of course, permeate all instruction, capitalizing on every opportunity to improve oral and written expression. Insistence upon accuracy would be mandatory, corrections overt and immediate. It would be unthinkable to deviate from the textbook. There would certainly be no need to determine what students already know or to delve into topics of interest to them. Use of the primary language would be discouraged as detrimental to language development in English. Collaborative and cooperative learning would be minimized in favor of an emphasis on individual, independent work. It also would be critical to identify "problem language learners" early, making students acutely aware of the serious consequences that result from falling behind (adapted by Sánchez, 1990).

If this sounds all too familiar, it is probably because it describes the reality in many classrooms. To be effective, teachers committed to facilitating second language development need to look at language in new and different ways. They cannot forget that language is for communication, that it is purposeful and meaningful, and that it must be taught and learned in context. Whatever the purpose or function, language skills are integrated. Listening and speaking support the development of reading and writing, and vice versa.

Whereas teachers may adopt different views of language and employ a broad range of methods and approaches in promoting language development, there are certain basic assumptions that are particularly critical, especially for those working with children. In *What's Whole in Whole Language*, K. Goodman (1986) observes that what happens in school should support and expand upon what happens out of school, bringing together "the language, the culture, the community, the learner, and the teacher" (p. 8). Even those who may not agree with all of the tenets that underlie whole language approaches can appreciate the importance of adopting a view that emphasizes the relevance, purpose, and meaning of language, as well as respect for learners and their empowerment. K. Goodman asks, "What makes language very easy or very hard to learn?" and then proceeds to answer as follows (p. 8):

It's easy when

- it is real, natural, whole, sensible, interesting, and relevant
- it belongs to the learner and is part of a real event
- it has social utility, and purpose for the learner
- it is accessible to the learner, and the learner chooses to use it and has the power to do so

It's hard when

- it is artificial, dull, uninteresting, irrelevant, nonsense, and broken into bits and pieces

- it is imposed by someone else and belongs to someone else
- it is out of context and inaccessible
- it has no discernible purpose or social value, and the learner is powerless

With this general view of language in mind, we proceed on our exploration of language and literacy development. After completing this chapter, you will be able to

1. recognize major phases of development
2. consider a variety of approaches and strategies for language and literacy instruction appropriate to multilingual classrooms
3. identify skills and strategies specific to reading and writing related to content-area instruction
4. integrate learning strategies as an integral part of language and literacy development

Promoting Oral Language Development

Teachers should keep several basic assumptions in mind when considering activities to promote development of English language and literacy in multilingual elementary classrooms (Enright & McCloskey, 1988). The first assumption is that "the whole of language is greater than the sum of its parts" (p. 19). Language skills are integrated—part of a larger process of cognitive growth that involves concurrent development of listening, speaking, reading, and writing. This explains why language skills cannot be taught effectively only as separate, discrete skills to be learned in isolation. The second is that students learn best when language and literacy serve as vehicles for constructing meaning and expressing thoughts. Ideally, classroom language is comprehensible, authentic, functional, and relevant; the classroom atmosphere comfortable, supportive of student efforts to use new language, and accepting of errors as part of the process. Finally, fully developing language and literacy demands the ability to use language in different contexts for different purposes with different audiences. Second language development entails use of all the resources available to the learner (non-linguistic and linguistic, cognitive, affective, social, and environmental) as well as those in the native language and culture (pp. 19–26).

Enright and McCloskey (1988) explain how these assumptions relate to instructional decision making. The aim is to develop a set of learning activities that

- integrate exploration of subject matter areas using different thought and language processes
- are enjoyable, exciting, and interesting

- are meaningful, purposeful, important, and authentic
- build on prior cultural and linguistic experiences
- involve students in working collaboratively with peers, teachers, family, and community members toward mutual goals
- provide opportunities for success in a supportive and accepting environment (pp. 21–29)

To the extent possible, approaches and strategies presented in this chapter are consistent with this set of assumptions and guidelines.

Beginning and Intermediate Oral Language

To be effective, instructional strategies must be appropriate for English language learners. With this in mind, teachers may find broad, general guidelines useful in recognizing the two initial phases of oral language proficiency: beginning and intermediate (Peregoy & Boyle, 1993, 55–59). At the beginning level, "second language development starts immediately upon exposure to the new language" (p. 56). Although a child may be unable to understand or say anything at the outset, opportunities for social interaction provide the basis for listening comprehension. After a short period of time, which varies from a week to a few months, speech emerges naturally with the use of highly functional words and formulaic expressions. The key to participation is providing the social-emotional support required for acquisition and meeting the child's need to belong and feel safe and secure. Frequent use of small-group activities that encourage active involvement in low-risk tasks is recommended. Allowing children to express themselves nonverbally—through drawing or painting, for example—can make it possible for a child to become a contributing member of small groups during this phase.

By the time that English language learners reach the intermediate level, they are able to do more with the language they have (Peregoy & Boyle, 1993). Children are now able to handle face-to-face interactions, albeit with a grammatical system that is still evolving (e.g., use of unconventional verb forms and nonidiomatic expressions, limitations in vocabulary). Teachers can ask questions focusing on activities that the children are currently engaged in, questions that encourage children to discuss and elaborate. As they progress, intermediate students will be able to use the present and past tense to recall, identify, predict, and even summarize. Formulating and expressing their own ideas, however, will still be challenging. Teachers can continue to support language development by encouraging more active participation in collaborative group activities and with adaptations in content area instruction.

> More advanced intermediate students are capable of understanding steady streams of verbal instruction, but words should continue to be accompanied by charts, graphic organizers, concrete objects, and pictures to convey meaning. In addition, intermediate students can benefit from hearing the teacher use technical vocabulary, provided that it is introduced with concrete experiences, visual support such as graphs and pictures, and verbal explanations of meaning. (p. 59)

When they reach this point, students also will be able to benefit from many of the strategies presented in Chapter 9.

Stages of Production

Terrell (1981) characterizes initial language production in terms of four stages that include preproduction, early production, speech emergence, and in some derivations intermediate fluency (e.g., Fichtner, Peitzman, Sasser, 1994, 115). The questioning sequence in the science lesson on plants in Figure 8-1 illustrates the implications of Terrell's stages of production. (For more detailed information, refer to Krashen & Terrell's *The Natural Approach*, 1983.) Using this as a model, teachers can try to develop lessons that would involve students representing the stages described. The lessons should be evaluated based on the selection and appropriateness of questioning techniques addressing the different stages of language development.

At the *preproduction* stage, students have very limited comprehension skills (Terrell, 1981). Relying heavily on facial expressions, gestures, and visuals, students' understanding is limited to about 500 words. Beyond a simple yes or no, they are not yet able to respond verbally. In Figure 8-1, students at this level are asked to look and listen as the teacher makes ample use of pointing and pantomime to contextualize language use. When questioning, teachers emphasize comprehension with questions that do not require students to provide verbal responses. In addition to listening, pointing, and miming, students can perform actions—they can move, choose, match, act out, and draw, just to name a few (Williams & Cary, 1991).

As students enter the *early production* stage, they have developed limited comprehension skills and are able to respond to questions that elicit one- or two-word responses (Terrell, 1981). These include yes/no, here/there, and either/or questions as well as those requiring sentence completion. The students' 100-word productive vocabulary enables them to name, list, categorize, and label (Williams & Cary, 1991). In Figure 8-1, yes/no questions are used to check recognition of vocabulary related to the parts of a plant.

Students beginning to develop fluency are entering what Terrell defines as the *speech emergence* stage. Their comprehension skills are stronger, and they are able to respond to questions that demand longer phrases (three or four words) and simple sentences. With command of a 250 to 500 word productive vocabulary comes increased readiness for problem-solving activities and more content. Students are now ready to describe, retell, define, summarize, explain, role-play, recall, compare, and contrast (Williams & Cary, 1991). Figure 8-1 demonstrates how questions can be phrased to elicit short answers identifying parts of the plant and their functions.

Once students achieve *intermediate fluency*, their developing literacy skills and vocabulary will enable them to handle more challenging questioning strategies. Their comprehension and speech begin to more closely approximate those of a native speaker. They can be asked to analyze, state opinions, defend positions, create, debate, evaluate, justify, examine, read, and write in the second language (Williams & Cary, 1991). The students are challenged by the questioning strategies used in Figure 8-1. With appropriate modeling by the teacher, students can learn how to ask and answer higher-level questions that focus on content (Chamot &

Vocabulary:
plant, leaf, leaves, stem, vein, roots

Preproduction

Look carefully at the photograph, and **listen**. This photograph shows the different parts of a **plant**.

These are the **leaves** of a plant. (Point)

The thin lines on the **leaves** are called **veins**. (Point)

The **veins** (point) carry water through the **plant**. (Point)

This is the **stem** (point) of the **plant**.

At the bottom of the **stem** are the **roots**. (Point)

The **roots** (point) grow in the ground.

On this **plant** (point), these are the **roots** (point), and these are the **leaves**. (Point)

Follow a **vein** on a **leaf** with your finger. (Point, and lead action)

Pick the **plant** up by the **stem**.
(Point, and pantomime picking it up)

Speech emergence

What part of a plant is this? (Point to leaves)

What part of the leaves are these?
(Point to veins)

What part of the plant is this? (Point to stem)

What part of the plant are these?
(Point to roots)

What do the veins (point) do?

What does the stem (point) do?

What do the roots (point) do?

What are the roots on the plant?
(Point)

Point to and name some parts of a plant. (Point to various parts)

Early production

Are all the parts of a plant (point to different parts) the same?

Are these the leaves? (Point to roots)

Are these the leaves? (Point to leaves)

Are these the veins (point) in the leaves?

Do the veins (point) carry sunshine through the plant?

Do the veins (point) carry water through the plant?

Is this the stem? (Point to roots)

Is this the stem? (Point to stem)

Are these the roots? (Point to roots on plant)

Are these also roots? (Point to roots on onion)

Do the roots (point) of a plant grow above or below the ground?

Intermediate fluency

How are the veins of a plant and the veins of a human alike?

How are the veins of a plant and the veins of a human different?

How are the stem of a plant and the legs of a human alike?

How are the stem of a plant and the legs of a human different?

People sometimes trace their *family roots* to find out about their ancestors.

How do you think the phrase *family roots* started?

Which part of the plant do you think is the most important? Why?

Figure 8-1   Questioning strategies: Plants

O'Malley, 1994). This enables students to draw from previous knowledge while promoting understanding of new information.

Teachers who want a better picture of oral language development for specific English language learners in their own classrooms may want to use the Student Oral Language Observation Matrix (SOLOM) presented in Figure 8-2. Observation is a very powerful teaching tool, and the SOLOM has proven to be a useful guide for observing language development in a natural classroom setting. In addition to complementing information obtained through more formal assessment measures, the SOLOM enhances teachers' awareness of and insight into students' progress in developing comprehension, fluency, vocabulary, pronunciation, and grammar: "For the purpose of documenting language growth over time and for gaining a sense of how well students are getting along with English for classroom purposes, we believe that observational instruments such as the SOLOM matrix are more useful to teachers than tests that rely on an artificial sampling procedure" (Peregoy & Boyle, 1993, 55).

Approaches and Strategies

All of the activities described thus far in this chapter promote second language development. It is anticipated, however, that teachers will also want information about other approaches, strategies, and techniques. Teachers are reminded that they will need to use their own judgment as to which ideas are best for their particular students. Many are appropriate—sometimes with modifications—across grade levels and even for native speakers. The final determination as to whether a specific approach, strategy, or technique is suitable for a particular group of students in a given setting can best be made by the teacher.

Total Physical Response   Total Physical Response (TPR) is an instructional model predicated on the notion that "the assimilation of information and skills can be significantly accelerated through the use of the kinesthetic sensory system" (Asher, 1988, xi). As described by Asher (1981, 1988), TPR accelerates learning by presenting language through the imperative, that is, by using commands, thus enabling learners to internalize a new system much as they did when acquiring their primary language. The salient features of instruction include delaying production until students demonstrate comprehension, maximizing student intake, embedding grammatical features within commands, and postponing abstract concepts.

TPR activities emphasize learning through body movement, understanding before production. Typically, the teacher gives a command (e.g., stand up, walk, turn, stop, jump), models the action, and asks students to respond physically. Actions are subsequently linked to require responses in more complex sequences ("Stand, walk to the chalkboard, and write your name"; "Walk to me; give me the chalk; then return to your seat and sit down") (1981, 326). After 10–20 hours of initial instruction, students may feel ready to speak. Then, they too begin giving commands—to other students and to the teacher. Zany, silly, and even bizarre commands—"When Henry runs to the chalkboard and draws a funny picture of Molly, Molly will throw her purse at Henry!"—are used to maintain high levels of interest (1988, 3–2). When appropriate, commands and vocabulary can be written

SOLOM Teacher Observation
Student Oral Language Observaton Matrix

Student's name: _____

Language rated: _____ Grade _____ Date(s) _____

School _____ Teacher _____ Total score(s) _____

	1	2	3	4	5	Score(s)
A. Comprehension	Cannot understand even simple conversation	Has great difficulty following everyday social conversation, even when words are spoken slowly and repeated frequently	Understands most of what is said at slower-than-normal speed with some repetitions	Understands nearly everything at normal speed, although occasional repetition may be necessary	Understands everyday conversation and normal classroom discussion without difficulty	
B. Fluency	Speech so halting and fragmentary that conversation is virtually impossible	Usually hesistant; often forced into silence because of language limitations	Everyday conversation and classroom discussion frequently disrupted by student's search for correct manner of expression	Everyday conversation and classroom discussion generally fluent with occasional lapses while student searches for the correct manner of expression	Everyday conversation and classroom discussion fluent and effortless; approximately those of a native speaker	
C. Vocabulary	Vocabulary limitations so extreme that conversation is virtually impossible	Difficult to understand because of misuse of words and very limited vocabulary	Frequent use of wrong words; conversation somewhat limited because of inadequate vocabulary	Occasional use of inappropriate terms and/or rephrasing of ideas because of limited vocabulary	Vocabulary and idioms approximately those of a native speaker	
D. Pronunciation	Pronunciation problems so severe that speech is virtually unintelligible	Difficult to understand because of pronunciation problems; must frequently repeat in order to be understood	Concentration required of listener; occasional misunderstandings caused by pronunciation problems	Always intelligible, although listener conscious of a definite accent and occasional in-appropriate intonation pattern	Pronunciation and intonation approximately those of a native speaker	
E. Grammar	Errors in grammar and word order so severe that speech is virtually unintelligible	Difficult to understand because of errors in grammar and word order; must often rephrase or restrict speech to basic patterns	Frequent errors in grammar and word order; meaning occasionally obscured	Occasional errors in grammar or word order; meaning not obscured	Grammar and word order approximately those of a native speaker	

Figure 8-2 SOLOM teacher observation: Student Oral Language Observation Matrix

Source: Norm Gold, California Department of Education, Sacramento. Used with permission of the California Department of Education.

on the board for students to copy into their notebooks as reinforcement. The TPR approach works effectively with learners of all ages. Language teachers who use TPR also find that they can use the imperative in teaching other subjects as well. In fact, Asher (1988, 3–34) argues that there are important parallels between mathematics and language that make visual and tactile experiences especially critical for learners in both areas.

Affective Strategies   Whether under the guise of humanistic, affective, confluent, or some other name, teaching strategies and techniques that incorporate personal growth and interpersonal communication are powerful tools in language teaching at any level. On a personal level, students benefit in terms of self-esteem and self-actualization; learning about oneself can be motivational (Moskowitz, 1978). For the class as a whole, these activities contribute to building a sense of rapport and cohesiveness. Moskowitz emphasizes use of low-risk activities with themes that are safe for all students rather than threatening—positive, enjoyable, and thought-provoking rather than overly deep and personal. Along similar lines, Christison and Bassano (1981, 1987) recommend that interpersonal activities proceed from topics that are low-risk and nonpersonal (e.g., gathering information, reporting) to the sharing of personal feelings, beliefs, and values. For purposes of language development, activities should have a linguistic as well as an affective purpose.

The positive impact that these activities can have is captured in the words of a student:

> I discovered I had something to say. At first I was surprised that others really cared about listening to me. But after a while I realized that listening is a part of caring, and that the harder I listened to others, the harder they seemed to listen to me. Sometimes I was amazed at my own honesty and that of the others. Somehow, because of our "up front" sharing, we all became closer and learned to trust and care for each other. I'm amazed how my words could mean so much to me and to other people. They sort of tell me who I am, and who I am becoming. I just never thought words could be so powerful. In fact, I guess what I've learned the most is that I am the one who is powerful. (Galyean, 1982, 188)

From a cultural perspective, not all students will be equally at ease in sharing personal information, feelings, and preferences. It helps to remember that students have a right to pass when these activities are used. However, it is also important to remember that there are many models and such a wide range of activities available for integrating language and other content areas with students' feelings and experiences that good choices can be made as to which are most suitable for a particular group of students. Many of these activities also provide a useful vehicle for promoting cultural understanding as classmates gain insights into traditions, customs, and values different from their own. Galyean offers the example of an Israeli girl's response in a discussion of nicknames: "She'd always been called by her full name. In her religious practices, one's birth name is sacred and must not be changed" (1982, 179).

Teachers also can provide opportunities for students to explore personal identity through artistic expression. Bassano and Christison (1982) demonstrate the effectiveness of drawing activities that tap oral, kinesthetic, and visual expressive modes. Activities incorporating drawings and writing are quite versatile and easily adapted for use with beginning and intermediate learners of all ages. They have been used effectively to teach grammar and vocabulary and to facilitate expression in relation to personal situations, thoughts, needs, and values. The following examples are illustrative:

*   "Draw a picture of someone you have seen today who made an impression on you." (p. 78)
*   "Draw your two teachers. What do they look like? How do they feel? What do they do and say?" (p. 63)
*   "Invent a machine. Tell me what happens when you push the button, wind the crank, pull the lever, flip the switch and turn the wheel." (p. 58)
*   "Draw some Americans. Draw yourself. What do Americans say to you? What do you answer?" (p. 46)
*   "Draw a book. Give the book a title. Tell us what the book is about, what it is for, or what you can learn from it." (p. 91)

After completing the drawings and accompanying text, students are asked to share their work, usually in pairs or small groups.

Literacy Skills: Reading

In general, there is considerable support for the position that initial reading instruction should be in a child's primary language (Au, 1993; Gunderson, 1991). Research suggests that basic reading skills effectively transfer from one language to another (Gunderson, 1991) and that "quality literacy instruction in the native language facilitates overall academic achievement and the development of English-literacy skills" (Pérez & Torres-Guzmán, 1992, 42). As Gunderson observes, "In the best of all worlds, students would learn to read first in their own language" (1991, 23). (For additional information on methods, approaches, and strategies for promoting biliteracy skills, see Pérez & Torres-Guzmán, 1992, and Williams & Snipper, 1990.)

In most multilingual classrooms, however, the reality is that relatively few teachers are prepared to provide reading instruction in each child's primary language, particularly when several languages are involved. Consequently, children are often taught to read in English regardless of their primary language (Gunderson, 1991, 22).

In practice, it may not be possible to give students the opportunity to learn to read and write in their native language. Teachers and other adults in the school may not speak the students' native language, students may come from a wide variety of native

After completing the drawings and accompanying text, students are asked to share their work.

language backgrounds, and/or parents may prefer that their children be instructed in English. (Au, 1993, 148)

Nonetheless, Au insists that teachers in multicultural settings adhere to the basic guidelines of literacy instruction supported by research. Among the most important, she believes, are encouraging students to use their native language skills in learning to read and write in English (whenever possible) and building students' self-esteem by respecting the language and culture of the students' home. To this end, teachers will need to carefully identify the strategies and techniques that maximize their effectiveness with diverse populations. Excellent resources are available to assist teachers with literacy instruction, and the discussion that follows highlights several approaches and strategies effective with children and older learners.

Beginning and Intermediate Second Language Readers

The developmental phases of second language readers have been described as falling along a fuzzy continuum, one whose stages are not discrete and clearly identifiable: "Real children defy categorization" (Peregoy & Boyle, 1993, 119). To facilitate discussion of teacher decision making, however, Peregoy and Boyle provide developmental descriptions for beginning and intermediate levels of second language reading (pp. 119–139). At the beginning level, readers are learning to extract meaning from short, simple texts. Although able to recognize a limited number of sight words, they have not progressed beyond sentence-level texts.

In summary, beginners need to be immersed in reading and writing for readily perceived purposes. They need practice to solidify sound/symbol correspondences in

English and to remind them that English reads from left to right, top to bottom. Finally, they need enough practice to move them toward being able to read simple texts independently. (p. 120)

By contrast, readers at the intermediate level are able to comprehend different types of text and have developed command of a substantial vocabulary. They verbally negotiate meanings with peers and read with fluency. Despite these skills, however, extended texts with new vocabulary will still be difficult. A word of caution—Peregoy and Boyle (1993) advise teachers not to view their categories as rigid. Teachers know their students best and should trust their own judgment in determining what specific strategy is most appropriate for any learner.

For young children at the beginning level, strategies such as print immersion, word banks, and personal dictionaries are highly recommended (Gunderson, 1991, 59–60). Classroom environments filled with printed words and sentences immerse pupils in print. Word banks facilitate reinforcement of the first words that pupils learn, and personal dictionaries are useful as pupils with limited fluency expand their command of English vocabulary. At this level, Peregoy and Boyle (1993, 124–129) also encourage use of patterned books (books characterized by the repetition of phrases, refrains, and rhymes), illustrations (drawing out stories and poems in response to stories or poems read), and shared reading with Big Books. The latter are based upon Holdaway's use of oversized books with groups of children in ways that "capture" the personal experience of reading in the home. The questioning procedure modeled in Directed-Listening-Thinking Activity (DL-TA) is also effective in providing a scaffold that demonstrates how effective readers engage in making predictions.

Language Experience Approach

Gunderson (1991) observes that "no other method is recommended as often as is the Language Experience Approach" (p. 64). This is not surprising. Because students produce their own reading text through dictation, the language experience approach capitalizes on linguistic, cultural, and social strengths while matching student interests and concerns, background knowledge, and language proficiency (Peregoy & Boyle, 1993, 120). Dixon and Nessel (1983, 3) note that this approach has a number of important advantages. It integrates all communication skills in relevant reading material that directly reflects students' experiences, vocabulary, and language patterns. Self-esteem is also enhanced as students experience seeing their own language in print. The language experience approach—and the whole language philosophy that it embodies—has other, less tangible advantages as well. In the following statement, Linnea speaks for many teachers who use this approach.

> I just didn't know how much they could give. My feeling was that in the process of "reaching inside of children," trusting them as natural learners, and providing relevant, meaningful contexts for language learning, there was a confirmation of personal beliefs about the treasures in children's minds. (Traill, 1992, vi)

In addition, the language experience approach is very flexible. It works effectively with children, older students, and adults and can be used with individuals, small groups, or the entire class. Although the content of the dictation and subsequent discussion will vary according to age and interest, the basic procedures are appropriate for English learners at all age levels. "It is the level of oral skills that should determine lesson procedures, not the age of the student" (Dixon & Nessel, 1983, 7). The relationship between student proficiency, procedures, topics, and related activities is illustrated in Figure 8-3.

For students at the intermediate level, Peregoy and Boyle (1993, 173–174) recommend reading activities such as the cognitive mapping strategies discussed earlier and Directed-Reading-Thinking Activity (DR-TA). In a DR-TA, teachers ask students to actively engage in predicting what is going to happen in a story and then read to confirm their predictions. In his version of this strategy, Gunderson relies on three basic questions: "What do you think this story is about?," "What do you

	Student characteristics	Instructional procedures*
Stage 1	almost no oral English and no experience with any written language	key vocabulary; dictated pattern stories
Stage 2	some oral English and some fluency with written native language	story dictation; structured word lists
Stage 3	considerable oral English and fluency in oral and written native language	story dictation; story language revision

	Oral language/dictation topics	Reading-related activities
Stage 1	student's daily experiences; structured experiences of immediate utility	conversation; role-playing; listening to stories; word discrimination activities
Stage 2	student's daily experiences; American cultural events such as holidays or typical family celebrations; other American customs	read-along books; reader's theater; word recognition activities
Stage 3	student's daily experiences; new areas of learning such as other academic areas; areas of special interest the student is studying	rewriting of dictation; developing study skills; responding to literature

* These procedures may be used for lessons with individual students or for group instruction.

Figure 8-3   Language experience approach summary for English language learners

Source: From *Language Experience Approach to Reading (and Writing)* (pp. 6–7) by C. N. Dixon and D. Nessel, 1983, Hayward, CA: Alemany Press. Copyright © 1983 by C. N. Dixon and D. Nessel. Reprinted by permission.

think will happen next?," and "What makes you think so?" (p. 67). Taking the story section by section, students (preferably in small groups) predict what will happen and then read to find out. Used effectively with children and adolescents, this prediction process is a natural for reading aloud and independent reading (Peregoy & Boyle, 1993). It also has been adapted for use in other activities, such as stories on television (e.g., soap operas) and movies (Gunderson, 1991, 69).

Many strategies used in biliteracy approaches can be used effectively in multilingual classrooms. For example, Pérez and Torres-Guzmán (1992, 66) propose that creating meaningful and enabling literacy environments requires lessons generated from students' interests. In addition to observations, and interviews with students and their parents, they suggest that teachers draw insights from the types of books children select and their participation in discussions and reactions to readings. Teachers can take note of which themes are repeated in children's writing and in the stories they hear or read at home, how they respond to fantasy, and which activities they choose for themselves when options exist.

Multicultural Literature

There is considerable consensus in readings on literacy regarding the importance of reading literature aloud to children and incorporating literature as an integral element in literacy programs for English language learners (Au, 1993; Diamond & Moore, 1995; Gunderson, 1991; Heald-Taylor, 1989; Peregoy & Boyle, 1993). Literature is one of the key components in multicultural literacy programs for students from kindergarten through eighth grade. "Children shape their reality about themselves and others based on much of what they read" (Diamond & Moore, 1995, 11). Ideally, the literature that all children are exposed to is multicultural— literature that focuses upon a broad range of diverse cultural, ethnic, religious, regional, and social groups within the United States and in other countries. Multicultural literature influences children's attitudes, values, and beliefs and has a powerful effect on self-concept and self-confidence (Diamond & Moore, 1995). Multicultural literature is meaningful literature, literature that enriches children's knowledge of other people and cultures. By exploring emotions, needs, and desires, it heightens students' perceptions of underlying commonalties among people and helps children to better understand social issues and the need for social change.

For English language learners, literature provides an environment supportive of literacy development while providing exposure to the structure of narratives and literary language. Quality literature appropriate to student age and interest should be read aloud on a daily basis (Pérez and Torres-Guzmán, 1992). As a teaching strategy, the benefits are significant. From reading aloud, students also learn what fluent reading sounds like and how enjoyable an experience reading can be. Students learn to appreciate the language in books. They recognize aspects of writing style and the features of different genres. While engaged in making meaning, predicting, interpreting, and evaluating, children learn to think critically about the writing itself, authors' perceptions of the world, and issues important to them. In addition, quality literature is an effective way to introduce

English language learners to the "rhythm, syntax, and richness of the English language" through oral language patterns such as rhymes, refrains, story lines, and repeated patterns in predictable literature (Heald-Taylor, 1989, 30).

Teachers will also want to include folk literature as an integral part of multicultural literature. *Fairy Tales, Fables, Legends, and Myths* (Bosma, 1992) illustrates the variety of teaching ideas and lesson strategies that can be used in teaching folk literature. The rich legacy of folk literature that is available to all children provides an ideal vehicle for reading comprehension, vocabulary development, critical reading, writing, and creative activities.

Free Voluntary Reading

In *The Power of Reading*, Krashen (1993) asserts that "one of our major goals in language education should be to encourage free reading, to make sure it happens" (p. 33). Free voluntary reading is "one of the most powerful tools" available for promoting second language development with learners at the intermediate level (p. 1). Free voluntary reading encompasses both sustained silent reading (brief, regular periods of free reading) and self-selected reading (free reading incorporated within language arts instruction). Drawing on evidence from his own analyses of research studies, Krashen concludes that free reading promotes reading comprehension, writing, grammar, spelling, and vocabulary development in first and second language contexts: "Reading may be the only way to develop literacy skills" (p. 23). Reading emerges as the result of making meaning through interaction with text; it is not achieved through direct instruction, drills, and exercises. For English language learners, there is evidence that students who read more in their second language are able to write and spell better in that language. Free reading done outside of school also appears to predict literacy development.

Teachers can promote free reading in ways that complement sustained silent reading and self-selected reading. A strong advocate of print-rich environments, Krashen (1993) recommends classroom library corners and access to school and public libraries. "The richer the print environment, that is, the more reading material available, the better the literacy development" (p. 36). From kindergarten through college, students appear to read more if they are read to aloud. As readers, children are also responsive to the model provided by teachers and parents who display interest in reading for pleasure. When materials are appropriate, direct encouragement also appears to promote reading at the elementary school level.

For many teachers (and students), this endorsement of light reading is welcome news. "Perhaps the most powerful way of encouraging children to read is by exposing them to light reading, a kind of reading that schools pretend does not exist, and a kind of reading that many children, for economic or ideological reasons, are deprived of. I suspect that light reading is the way nearly all of us learned to read" (Krashen, 1993, 47–48). Teachers who were avid comic book readers in their childhood or teen romance enthusiasts in adolescence will be pleased to hear that this kind of light reading works. Comic books are useful in promoting adequate levels of language and literacy development while serving as a conduit to book reading and more advanced levels of proficiency. Although not as well researched, teen romances appear to parallel comics in their positive effect on reading development. Both are linguistically appropriate and comprehensible. However, there are limitations as to the level of attainment possible through light reading. "Although free voluntary reading alone will not ensure attainment of the highest levels of literacy, it will at least ensure an acceptable level" (p. 84). To achieve the highest levels of proficiency, students will require access to more sophisticated materials, for literacy is dependent to a great extent on "the kinds of texts that learners are exposed to, the way they are encouraged to respond to those texts, and the kinds of texts that they are expected to compose in particular discourse communities" (Eskey, 1993, 228).

Although Krashen and others provide evidence to support reading for pleasure, researchers such as Leki (1993) caution that it may not be an optimum strategy for all second language (L2) learners. For some older students, making pleasure reading a major goal of ESL reading classes may be unrealistic. "For all but the most proficient of our students, L2 reading is too difficult a chore to be engaged in simply for pleasure (Janopoulos, 1986), and to build proficiency in reading strictly through pleasure reading takes time our ESL students may not have" (Leki, 1993, 15). Again, teachers will need to exercise professional judgment in making decisions for their own students.

Phonics Instruction

Gunderson (1991) captures the essence of the dilemma that confronts many teachers working with English language learners, particularly older students:

> It seems that most people in the general public and, indeed, most teachers, both mainstream and ESL, believe that students should learn phonics skills. Time after time ESL teachers, most often those who teach older students, state that phonics skills should be taught and learned. Indeed, the belief that ESL students should learn to "crack the code" is quite pervasive among the public and in the teaching profession. (p. 82)

Phonics instruction is defined by Williams and Snipper (1990) as "teaching children the sounds of the alphabet so they can 'sound out' unfamiliar words during reading" (p. 14). Like Gunderson's, their examination of research reveals that phonics instruction is widely used and very controversial. Advocates believe that "comprehension begins with the print on the page" (p. 15), with the meaning of larger units such as sentences and paragraphs dependent upon the meaning ascribed to constituent words. For proponents of phonics instruction, success in reading is a cumulative process contingent upon the accurate "decoding" of sounds and words. Detractors argue that successful reading is not as dependent on phonics skills as it is on the more complex processes involved in predicting and synthesizing meaning from syntax, context, and purpose (p. 15). Phonics captures only a small part of what people do in the reading process and places undue emphasis on correct pronunciation at the expense of comprehension and fluency. This concern with error correction has had particularly negative implications for English language learners. Teachers monitoring student progress in reading-aloud activities concentrate on pronunciation and frequently interrupt students to address accuracy. These incessant interruptions interfere with English language learners' understanding of the text (pp. 23–24). Writing development is also affected.

We can, in fact, predict that such students will be inclined to concentrate on surface correctness rather than on global features associated with meaning. Not only will they find writing unpleasant, but their writing will lack the rhetorical features that essentially comprise the cues for comprehension. . . . [T]he real problem with nonmainstream writing is the lack of organization and elaboration needed to communicate a meaningful message, not the lack of surface correctness. (Williams & Snipper, 1990, 25)

Rather than deny what is a reality for many teachers and not address phonics instruction as part of this discussion, it seems more appropriate to at least provide some practical suggestions for teachers who adhere to this point of view or must teach within a system that mandates phonics instruction. For teachers considering phonics instruction, there is one important caveat: It does not work for all ESL students. "Only those with limited fluency in English and with a history of literacy training are able to cope with training in phonics" (Gunderson, 1991, 84). Younger English language learners may not benefit from phonics instruction because "it requires a kind of metacognitive activity they may not developmentally be able to do" (p. 115). Older learners, particularly those at the intermediate level, may derive benefit if they possess the level of literacy skills and English language proficiency required to deal with the metacognitive demands of letter-sound relationships.

Whereas there are many generalizations in phonics instruction, some are considerably more reliable than others. To the extent that phonics instruction is included as part of a literacy program, teachers are likely to discover that the more reliable patterns are generally the most useful for English language learners. In fact, Piper encourages teachers not to be afraid to provide some phonics instruction. "Many ESL students, convinced that English is totally unsystematic, will welcome the order suggested by these rules. Just a few rules which work most of the time will eliminate some of the guesswork involved in learning to read in English" (cited in Gunderson, 1991, 84). Among these are the following phonics implications identified by Piper as the most practical (Gunderson, 1991, 84):

1. Teach the rules first in relation only to root words. Then introduce suffixes and compounding.
2. Teach recognition of compound words. Do not focus on vowel digraphs that result from compounding.
3. Teach how unstressed vowels are pronounced. (For example, in suffixes, most vowels are pronounced the same as those in atten*ti*on and wait*e*d.)
4. Teach students that the pronunciation of *i* in *dried* and *happiest* is due to the pronunciation of *y* in the stem.
5. Teach the pronunciation of vowels followed by an *r* separately.

Gunderson provides a "Phonics Primer" that teachers may find useful in identifying some of the more reliable and useful phonics patterns. For example, the CVC (consonant-vowel-consonant) pattern is fairly reliable; in one reading series, Piper found it to be reliable 84% of the time. If students are introduced to the generalization that "CVC words have a short vowel sound" and given consonants and phonograms that are fairly reliable, then they can learn to recognize thousands of words (1991, 86):

Some Reliable Consonants:	b, d, f, g, h, j, k, l, m, n, p, r, s, t
Some Reliable Phonograms:	-ab, -ad, -ag, -am, -an, -ap, -at, -ed, -eg, -en, -et, -ib, -id, -ig, -im, -in, -it, -ob, -od, -og, -op, -ub, -ud, -um, -un, -ut

Gunderson suggests that students can take a phonogram such as *-an* and then add consonants to make as many words as they know. Games and other activities may follow. In general, going beyond patterns that are most highly regular is not recommended.

Literacy Skills: Writing

In this section, the focus is on second language writing. We begin by demystifying some myths about writing that affect how it is taught. This is followed by a discussion of sociocultural considerations and ways in which cultural, social, cognitive, and linguistic differences influence student writing. Descriptions of beginning and intermediate levels of second language writing provide the basis for a discussion of strategies and techniques for beginning English language learners and beyond (e.g., scaffolding, whole language, sentence activities, academic writing, and the writing process model).

Demystifying Writing

How teachers view writing has a profound effect on how they teach it. Teachers' assumptions influence "what is taught," "how it is taught," and "what the teacher values and responds to favorably in terms of written products" (Hudelson, 1989, 15). Of the beliefs that influence educational practice, perhaps the most critical is also the most basic: "what writing is" (what its nature is)(Edelsky, 1989).

Myths about writing and how it is learned are so pervasive that Smith (1983), Edelsky (1989), and others have taken the offensive to dispel some of the misconceptions. They do not assert that all teachers hold these beliefs, only that the way in which writing is commonly taught belies assumptions that need to be carefully examined. Illustrative of the issues involved are the 10 myths in Table 8-1 drawn from Smith's collection. They are contrasted with his corresponding view of reality.

Perhaps the most destructive aspect of these myths is that they undermine the essence of what writing should be.

> Written language is for stories to be read, books to be published, poems to be recited, plays to be acted, songs to be sung, newspapers to be circulated, letters to be mailed, jokes to be told, notes to be passed, cards to be sent, cartons to be labeled, instructions to be followed, designs to be made, recipes to be cooked, messages to be exchanged, programs to be organized, excursions to be planned, catalogs to be compared, entertainment guides to be consulted, memos to be distributed, announcements to be

Table 8-1   Ten myths about writing

Myth	Reality
1. "Writing is for the transmission of information." (p. 81)	Writing is more importantly "to create experiences and to explore ideas." (p. 81)
2. "Writing involves transferring thoughts from the mind to paper." (p. 82)	"Writing can create ideas and experiences on paper that could never exist in the mind." (p. 82)
3. "Writing is permanent, speech ephemeral." (p. 82)	"Writing can be reflected upon, altered, and even erased"—giving "the writer power to manipulate time." (p. 82)
4. "Most classrooms are reasonable places in which to expect children to learn to write." (p. 84)	"Most professional writers could not write" under "the physical and psychological constraints" imposed on most children in school. (p. 84)
5. "You must have something to say in order to write." (p. 85)	"You often need to write in order to have something to say." (p. 85)
6. "Writing should be easy." (p. 85)	"Writing is often hard work," requiring "concentration, physical effort, and a tolerance for frustration and disappointment." (p. 85)
7. "Writing should be right the first time." (p. 85)	"Writing generally requires many drafts" and editorial polishing. (p. 85)
8. "Writing can be done to order." (p. 85)	"Writing is often most reluctant to come when it is most urgently required." (p. 85)
9. "A writer is a special kind of person." (p. 83)	"There is only one difference between writers and people who do not write—writers write." (p. 83)
10. "People who do not themselves enjoy and practice writing can teach children how to write." (p. 87)	"Anyone who" teaches "children how to write must. . . demonstrate what writing can do and. . . how to do it." (p. 87)

Source: Smith (1983, 81–88)

posted, bills to be collected, posters to be displayed, cribs to be hidden, and diaries to be concealed. Written language is for ideas, action, reflection, and experience. It is not for having your ignorance exposed, your sensitivity bruised, or your ability assessed" (Smith, 1988, 29).

Teaching that is consistent with this view of what writing is and is not calls for a departure from what is traditional practice in many classrooms. The kinds of writing emphasized in schools are typically expository in nature, prompted by questions or assignments, and corrected by the teacher.

Participating in these kinds of writing assignments gives students certain impressions: that writing is done for someone and not for oneself; that the basic function of writing is to display one's knowledge to someone else; that writing consists of displaying one's knowledge by the use of specific structures and forms; that teachers know what those forms and structures are; and that it is the teacher's job to make sure that student writing conforms to those forms. This is a very different view of the writing process from the one suggested by Berthoff (1981) and many others, where the focus is on writing as a process of discovery, where writing is used as a way of working through what one means, and where the audience for writing (both teachers and peers) responds primarily to the writer's attempts to create meaning rather than to the forms and structures used. (Hudelson, 1989, 14–15)

Consistent with the latter perspective, the following sections explore writing instruction for English language learners.

Beginning and Intermediate Second Language Writers

To help guide teachers in making instructional decisions, Peregoy and Boyle (1993, 78–101) provide developmental descriptions of second language writers as beginning, intermediate, and advanced. The levels are characterized in terms of text type (fluency), organization, language use, style, and mechanics. Table 8-2 highlights features of writing at the beginning, intermediate, and advanced levels.

With beginning second language writers, the teacher's primary goal is to help pupils generate ideas and develop fluency. At this level, writers produce simple text—one or two brief sentences in length—that is very limited in vocabulary, grammar (e.g., present tense), and variety of sentence patterns. Peregoy and Boyle (1993) describe writers at this level:

> Beginning second language writers . . . may find writing laborious, producing very little at first. If so, organization is not a problem, because there is little on paper to organize. If beginners do produce a great deal, logical organization is apt to be lacking. . . . [B]eginning second language writers may use inventive spelling that includes elements from the spelling system of their first language. . . . [and they] may not have a good sense of sentence boundaries or of the conventional word order required in English. Thus, they are apt to make errors in grammar, vocabulary, and usage. In addition, they may exhibit grammatical and other infelicities common to native-English beginning writers. (pp. 79–80)

By contrast, writers at the intermediate level rely on a limited number of simple sentence patterns to produce longer text. Errors in punctuation, grammar, and usage are still common: "In fact, they may make more such errors than beginners because they are producing more writing—a positive sign of writing progress" (Peregoy & Boyle, 1993, 91). At this level, Peregoy and Boyle suggest that the teacher's main concern is to help students add form to fluid expression—that is, to foster use of organizational strategies (e.g., paragraphing, logical ordering of ideas), develop greater sentence variety, and improve grammar and spelling. At the advanced level, the English language learner is comparable to a student writing in his or her first language. The student produces paragraphs and longer discourse, recognizes different genres and their organization, displays command of grammar, vocabulary, and a greater variety of sentence patterns.

Table 8-2 Features of writing at different levels of development

Feature	Beginning Level	Intermediate Level	Advanced Level
Text type (fluency)	One or two short sentences	Several sentences	Paragraphs or longer discourse
Organization	No logical sequence or too short to require organization	Some sense of sequence	Standard for the genre
Grammar	Difficulty with basic word order; limited to use of present tense forms	Minor errors (e.g., -s on third person singular verbs)	Comparable to a native speaker
Vocabulary	Limited; may use primary language or request translation	Command of most words used to express ideas; unable to convey nuances of meaning	Word choice flexible; like a native speaker
Genre	No differentiation of form according to purpose	Form appropriate to purpose, but knowledge and choice of expository forms limited	Appropriate choice of genres; like a native speaker
Sentence variety	One or two sentence patterns	Several sentence patterns	Effective variation of sentence patterns

Source: From *Reading, Writing, and Learning in ESL: A Resource Book for K–8 Teachers* (p. 79) by S. F. Peregoy and O. F. Boyle, 1993, White Plains, New York: Addison Wesley Longman. Copyright © 1993 by Addison Wesley Longman. Adapted by permission.

Beginning and Beyond

For young children at the beginning level, writing needs to be an integral part of the learning experiences of English language learners (Hudelson, 1989). To achieve this end, time should be allocated for writing on a daily (or at least regular) basis. "ESL learners will not develop as writers if they do not have opportunities to write" (p. 48). The purpose for writing should be authentic and important to the children. It is essential that teachers (a) provide English language learners with initial encouragement so that children are willing to risk writing and are able to develop fluency and (b) respond to the message and meaning in children's initial efforts, rather than to correctness of form (pp. 48–49).

> Perhaps even more than native speakers, ESL learners need to be assured that it is acceptable to make guesses about how to write something, that it is natural to make mistakes, that it is okay to put something down even if it is not exactly what you want to express, that i[t] is better to construct some tentative ideas that can be improved rather than writing nothing at all. (p. 48)

Scaffolding   Literacy scaffolds are "instructional strategies that help students to read and write whole, meaningful texts at a level somewhat beyond what they could do on their own" (Peregoy & Boyle, 1993, 81). They are temporary frameworks that frequently provide beginning writers an element of predictability through repetition of language or routine. Peregoy and Boyle (pp. 81–90) provide the following activities as examples of literacy scaffolds:

- personal journals: personal writing to which the teacher does not respond unless asked to do so
- dialogue journals: a written conversation between individual students and the teacher
- buddy journals: a student conversation in writing
- life murals: a series of drawings (e.g., important events, people, and places in children's lives) that provide the structure for beginning composition
- freewriting: a process in which students put ideas on paper quickly, without regard to "form, coherence or correctness" (p. 89). They then write for five minutes on a word, phrase or sentence they like, and continue until a topic or theme they want to write about emerges.
- poetry writing: a simple formula for writing a poem is provided, a pattern that students can use as a model for their own creation (p. 83). (Also see Cecil & Lauritzen, 1994.)

Whole Language Strategies   Meaning is a powerful constant in most discussions of writing for English language learners. Meaning is inextricably embedded within writing, which is "simultaneously a social, psychological, and linguistic process for making meaning" (Edelsky, 1989, 168). Making meaning is empowering, for "writing is a mode of learning, facility in which gives students the power to create meaning and to affect those with whom they share their writing" (Gaies, 1989, xi–xii). There are even those who question whether meaning is something that can be taught. "Perhaps the one difficulty with the entire enterprise of teaching the construction of meaning, whether in reading or in writing, is that although it can be learned, in some important, very real sense, it cannot be taught" (Leki, 1993, 18).

Meaning is central to teachers who espouse writing instruction from a whole language perspective (Gunderson, 1991, 102). So are relevance, respect, and power (K. Goodman, 1986). Hence, many of the strategies and techniques highlighted throughout this book are consistent with whole language instruction. Teachers should have no problem finding resources providing whole language strategies that are appropriate for their students. In *Whole Language Strategies for ESL Students*, Heald-Taylor (1989) explores key whole language strategies—dictation, literature, process writing, and themes—that are particularly beneficial for English language learners in kindergarten through third grade. Teachers at all grade levels will find many practical ideas in texts by Ken and Yetta Goodman. *What's Whole in Whole Language* (K. Goodman, 1986) is a short introductory guide for parents and teachers. *The Whole Language Evaluation Book* (K. Goodman, Y. Goodman, & Hood, 1989) is loaded with contributions from teachers in a wide variety of classroom settings.

Sentence Activities   For intermediate level writers, Peregoy and Boyle (1993, 93–101) recommend strategies that develop the variety and complexity of sentence patterns, enhance the organization of ideas, and expand use of different genres. Show-and-not-tell, sentence combining, sentence shortening, and sentence models provide four examples of strategies that can be incorporated within the process writing sequence described later.

1. *Show-and-not-tell:* Students select a telling sentence, that is, a statement that makes a generalization. Then, rather than relying on a simple declaration, students are instructed to use showing sentences that are more powerful in providing specific information and descriptive detail. The following example is from an English language learner:

    Telling sentence: The band was noisy.

    Showing sentences: As the band played I felt the drummer was banging on my eardrums and the guitars yelled at me. I thought I would never hear right again. (Peregoy & Boyle, 1993, 94)

2. *Sentence combining:*   Students combine two or more short sentences into a longer sentence that conveys the same message.

3. *Sentence shortening:* Students rewrite and shorten sentences that are long and wordy. Arturo Jackson is credited with the idea of turning this activity into a game in which small groups compete to produce the shortest revision that retains the original meaning.

4. *Sentence models:* Students are introduced to a sentence model or select one from literature or their own writing. They use the model to generate their own sentences. These student examples are based upon models provided by Waddell, Esch, and Walker:

    If . . . , if . . . , if . . . , then *Subject Verb*

    If I was rich, if I could buy anything, I would buy my parents a house.

    Because . . . , because . . . , because . . . , *Subject Verb*

    Because it is rainy, because it is cold, because I feel lazy, I think I won't go to school today.

    When . . . , when . . . , when . . . , *Subject Verb*

    When I am home, when I am bored, when I have nobody to play with, I watch television. (cited in Peregoy & Boyle, 1993, 97)

The Writing Process

The writing process model has been effective in helping both first and second language learners develop writing fluency. Students progress through manageable tasks that integrate "oral language, reading, and writing at the service of the child's communication goals" (Peregoy & Boyle, 1993, 65). Process writing has been strongly recommended for English language learners at all levels, in all content areas, and for all types of writing (Au, 1993; Chamot & O'Malley, 1994; Peregoy & Boyle, 1993; Pérez & Torres-Guzmán, 1992; Roen, 1989). Dealing with second language writing as a process enables students to experience success.

The writing process model is also an appropriate way to help students deal with the differences between English academic prose and prose written in their native languages (Grabe & Kaplan, 1989; Reid, 1993). Studies in contrastive rhetoric reveal different rhetorical preferences in the presentation of written material across languages. As examples, Reid (1992) points to the tendency to begin academic text with an anecdote in Thai, to use elaboration in Romance languages, and to rely on philosophical statements in Arabic. By contrast, academic English, scientific and technical texts in particular, requires prose that is simple, direct, specific, and stripped down. Children learn to "tell 'em what you're gonna tell 'em, tell 'em, and tell 'em what you told 'em" (Reid, 1992, 212). This has particular implications for academically oriented students producing complex texts in a language that is not their first. The process approach to writing is useful in enhancing awareness of expectations associated with academic prose.

> We believe that writing instruction which stresses invention strategies and prewriting activities, which teaches planning, writing, and revising strategies as non-linear and cyclic processes, which employs collaboration and peer-group feedback, which includes conferencing and individual feedback, and which encourages multiple drafting is consistent with all that contrastive rhetoric implies. (Grabe & Kaplan, 1989, 275–276)

Stages of the writing process generally include prewriting, writing, sharing, revising, editing, and evaluating (California State University, Chico [CSUC], 1985; D'Aoust, 1987; Olson, 1987). These are represented in the conceptual model presented in Figure 8-4 and are described in the text that follows.

The first stage in the writing process—*prewriting*—consists of experiences, activities, and exercises designed to foster motivation and generate ideas for writing. In general, the younger and less experienced the writer, the more elaborate the prewriting activities (CSUC, 1985, 3).

Examples:

Clustering, brainstorming, retrieval charts, props, films, fantasizing, improvisational drama, field trips, interviews, and debating

The next stage—*writing*—involves putting ideas on paper. At this point, fluency takes precedence over correctness. By writing, students come to the realization that they write for different purposes and audiences. They learn to adapt their writing as they write for themselves, friends, peers, teachers, parents, and more distant readers. Students also write for different purposes, such as informing, persuading, entertaining, or complaining, for example (CSUC, 1985, 4–6).

Examples:

Writing for fluency: journals, diaries, learning logs, timed writing (noncompetitive and ungraded), dictation, listing, extensive reading, and notetaking

Figure 8-4   The writing process

Source: From "Teaching Writing as a Process" by C. D'Aoust in *Practical Ideas for Teaching Writing as a Process* (p. 9) edited by C. B. Olson, 1987, California Department of Education Publications, 515 L Street #250, Sacramento, CA 95814. Copyright © 1987 by California Department of Education. Reprinted by permission.

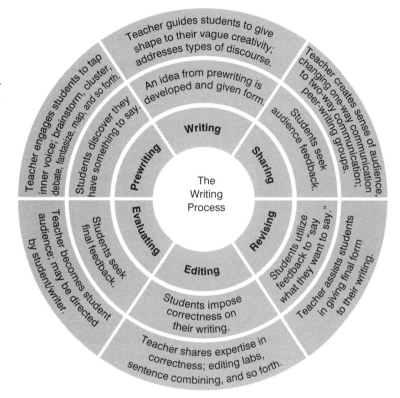

Writing for audience: two accounts of the same event for different audiences; letters for specific purposes, such as a get-well card, a complaint, or a letter to the editor

Writing for purpose: identifying different reasons for writing; identifying the intent of different pieces of writing

The third stage—*sharing*—provides opportunities for others to respond to student's words and ideas. Eliciting readers' reactions enables students to clarify their thinking and improve their writing. Sharing also fosters greater appreciation for the power of the written word (D'Aoust, 1987, 7–8).

Examples:

Peer-response groups, whole class response sessions, response sheets or forms, individual consultations

Revising involves rethinking, reviewing, and rewriting. Because writing is a recursive process, revising can occur at different points in the sequence, prompted by the writer's reconsideration of intent, effectiveness, organization, transitions, clarity, emphasis, and word choice. When revising follows sharing activities, feedback from peers or other readers provides an indication of how effectively meaning and intent have been communicated (CSUC, 1985, 7; D'Aoust, 1987, 8).

Examples:

Read-around groups, writing response groups, teacher-student conferences, analyses of student passages and published texts, writing on the same topic for different audiences, examples of revisions made by professional writers on their own texts

In *editing*, attention is focused on the refinement and conventions of writing. In refining their writing, students attend to presentation and clarity. They also deal with formal aspects such as writing conventions, accuracy, spelling, punctuation, grammar, and syntax (CSUC, 1985, 7–8).

Examples:

Proofreading, editing checklists, editing sessions, dictation, peer editing groups, sentence-combining activities, instruction focused on repeated errors, read-around groups, sentence-combining activities

By the time *evaluating* takes place, students are ready for final feedback on their writing. Although the teacher typically serves as audience and judge in assigning a grade at this point, self-assessment is also encouraged. Students need to clearly understand the purpose of and basis for evaluation. They also benefit from having input into the process (D'Aoust, 1987, 8).

Examples:

Clear statements of criteria for assignments and purpose of evaluation, whole-class assessment of sample papers, use of student-generated scoring guidelines for specific assignments

Publishing encompasses the broad range of possibilities for finished pieces of student writing (CSUC, 1985; Peregoy & Boyle, 1993). In addition to sharing with parents and peers, student work can be displayed in classroom libraries, on bulletin boards, in the community, and exchanged with other classes and schools via computer or by mail. Publishing contributes to students' sense of purpose and audience, fosters motivation, and promotes appreciation of the importance and value of writing.

Examples:

Class and school magazines; community newspapers; reading aloud to student or community groups; translations into other languages; recognition through contests, awards, and assemblies; presentations through video, local radio, or cable television (CSUC, 1985; D'Aoust, 1987; Olson, 1987)

Teachers interested in process writing will find that there are many resources available to assist them in their efforts. For example, *Practical Ideas for Teaching*

Writing as a Process (Olson, 1987) was produced as a collaborative effort by teachers and consultants involved with the California Writing Project, and is a rich source of information, applications, and ideas for teachers at all grade levels. Elementary teachers in grades 2–6 will find *Really Writing: Ready-to-Use Writing Process Activities for the Elementary Grades* (Sunflower, 1994) a useful compilation of practical ideas for narrative, descriptive, informative, and persuasive writing and more. Adolescent English language learners with advanced skills can benefit from group writing projects such as those in *The Writing Process* (Cramer, 1985). Through collaborative projects exploring topics such as "People and machines," "Food!," "The use of space," "Design a new product," and "A new series for television," students develop greater fluency, expressiveness, and accuracy.

Academic Content: Reading and Writing

The importance of integrating reading and writing throughout the curriculum is a consistent theme in the literature on teaching English language learners (Brechtel, 1992; Cecil & Lauritzen, 1994; Enright & McCloskey, 1988; Hudelson, 1989). There is general consensus that teachers should use strategies that (a) connect reading and writing through literary activities and (b) make reading and writing an integral part of content area instruction (Hudelson, 1989, 77). As Hudelson observes, children need to be exposed to different genres (e.g., stories, poems, limericks) that they can then use as literary models for creating texts of their own. Through thematic units and other activities, they also need to be encouraged to begin developing the academic writing abilities required in different disciplines.

Understanding reading material with academic content is often a challenging and difficult task for English language learners. To assist students in this critical area, teachers need to examine the appropriateness of the materials they are using and develop strategies that make the content more accessible to the second language reader. Although procedures for analyzing the content reading skills required by specific academic texts are available, content teachers do not regularly assess whether or not students have developed the reading skills demanded by the academic texts they use (Gunderson, 1991, 50). Not surprisingly, this results in English language learners using texts that are beyond their capacity to read and comprehend.

With this in mind, teachers may want to begin by examining the academic texts they are using relative to both reading skills and language. From a reading perspective, academic texts require specific skills, and among the most critical are the ability to:

- identify significant content
- discriminate between important and unrelated details
- locate the main idea in a paragraph and in lengthy segments of text
- distinguish between fact and opinion
- recognize topic sentences and responses to specific questions
- draw inferences from content

For literacy skills to empower language minority students, learners need to engage in reading and writing activities that also promote the development of critical thinking skills.

- evaluate content critically
- identify the author's purpose
- assess the accuracy of information
- use the table of contents, index, and appendices
- read and interpret tables, graphs, charts, maps, cartoons, diagrams, pictures, and formulas
- read and comprehend written problems, expository and descriptive material, argument, and categories
- adjust reading rate according to purpose or difficulty level
- scan for specific information and skim for important ideas
- understand new information (Gunderson, 1991, 50–51)

Gunderson suggests that teachers first look at a text to determine which of the skills listed are required and then frame questions to informally assess whether students have the requisite skills. "If the text focuses on main ideas, the assessment should have many questions on main ideas (e.g., 'Look at page six, read the paragraph about the Westward Expansion. What is the main idea of the passage?'" (p. 52). The teacher will then determine whether the student can function independently, whether the student will require special instruction to deal with content in the text, or whether the skills required are beyond the student's current level in reading and comprehension.

Once a determination has been made that the text is appropriate for students, teachers may want to look at the content again from a different perspective. Chamot and O'Malley (1994, 48) recommend that teachers analyze textbooks in order to identify the language demands of academic reading materials and to guide in the selection of language development activities. They emphasize consideration of the following features (p. 49):

- *Vocabulary* New vocabulary that is essential and familiar vocabulary that is used in a new way

- *Grammatical structures* New word forms and verb tenses, sentence structures, and other grammatical features

- *Discourse organization* The organization of paragraphs, sections, chapters, and/or units

- *Prior knowledge* Concepts that require preteaching and cultural assumptions that are not familiar

- *Learning strategies* Reading strategies and study skills related to note-taking, reference skills, and map, chart, and graph skills

There are strategies that teachers can use to make content reading more accessible to English language learners. One of the most frequently recommended techniques to promote reading, comprehension, and retention of content is SQ3R—survey, question, read, recite, and review (Adamson, 1993; Eskey & Grabe, 1988; Gunderson, 1991). According to Eskey and Grabe, the second language reader is often an insecure reader; for this reason, "pre-reading strategies— like the ancient and venerable SQ3R—are even more important than they are for the native reader, and the teacher must therefore coach the students in their use" (p. 229). The process used in SQ3R is described as follows:

1. *Survey* Survey the reading text, including table of contents, chapter title, subtitles and outline, captions and titles of graphic aids, summaries, questions, and key vocabulary.

2. *Question* Develop a study guide by formulating questions from the titles, subtitles, summaries, and graphic aids.

3. *Read* Read the text to answer the questions, taking notes and reformulating the questions as necessary.

4. *Recite* For each major section of a chapter, recite the answers to related questions orally or in writing without referring back to the text.

5. *Review* Upon completion, review the entire chapter, one section at a time, and related questions and answers (Gunderson, 1991, 149–150). In the version of SQ3R presented in Adamson (1993), use of collaborative small groups and dyads is recommended for the survey, question, recite, and review phases.

Additional techniques useful in helping English language learners with academic reading are presented in Figure 8-5. Adapted from Adamson (1993), these suggestions are particularly appropriate for older learners and can be modified and enhanced to meet specific needs.

By the time English language learners reach the secondary level, demands made on their writing abilities are varied and considerable. Expressive and personal writing are not sufficient to prepare students for academic writing assignments at higher levels (Reid, 1993, 42). Academic writing assignments do not emphasize personal or expressive writing; they emphasize research. Selection of topic is generally restricted and the text is expected to follow a specified rhetorical structure. At the secondary level and beyond, Reid (1992) recommends that students attend to specific aspects of academic writing. For example, they should examine assigned writing tasks for purpose, demands, and expectations related to

---

Predicting
- Provide the first and last lines of text and ask students to predict the content.
- Provide the title of the text and ask students to predict the content.

Brainstorming
- Briefly describe the main idea of the text and ask students to brainstorm for content.
- Briefly describe the topic of the text and ask students to brainstorm for vocabulary.

Identifying
- On the board, list relative pronouns in the text with the line and page on which they appear. Ask the students to scan the reading and identify the referent for each pronoun.
- On the board, list the numbers that appear in the text. Ask the students to scan the reading and identify what the numbers refer to.
- On the board, list selected key lines from the text. Ask the students to find the lines by scanning the reading.

Reviewing
- On the board, identify key words and phrases in order of appearance in the text that students have read. Use the words and phrases as prompts for retelling the content.
- With students working in groups, ask each group to create a short crossword puzzle using key vocabulary terms and then exchange with another group for solution.

Interacting
- Select key persons, places, and so on, that appear in the text and write each on a piece of paper. Pin a paper on the back of each student. Students interact with each other, asking questions that provide clues to the identity of the written word or words.

Questioning
- Select statements from the text and ask students to make up questions for which these would be appropriate responses.
- Ask students to make up questions of their own relative to the content of the text. As appropriate, incorporate selected questions in assessment activities.

Figure 8-5 Academic reading
Source: Adamson (1993, 169–170)

rhetorical conventions. Students need to be familiar with the basic format of (a) summaries (e.g., balance, objectivity); (b) English compositions (e.g., expository themes, argumentative essays, response papers); and (c) research papers (e.g., experimental and nonexperimental). It is also helpful for students to focus their attention on the syntax of academic prose (e.g., use of passive voice, personal pronouns, pattern of verb tenses) (pp. 213–216).

There are resources that teachers will find useful in addressing the academic writing needs of English language learners. Among these are *Academic Competence: Theory and Classroom Practice: Preparing ESL Students for Content Courses* (Adamson, 1993) and *Richness in Writing: Empowering ESL Students* (Johnson & Roen, 1989).

Language Learning Strategies

Another important way in which teachers can help students become more effective learners of language is by making them more aware of how they learn language. *Language learning strategies* are the strategies individuals use to approach the task of language learning. They are "specific actions taken by the learner to make learning easier, faster, more enjoyable, more self-directed, more effective, and more transferrable to new situations" (Oxford, 1990, 8). As students become more cognizant of the strategies they use, they are better able to expand their repertoire in order to enhance learning.

As learners, each one of us generates a set of strategies to deal with the task of language learning. Not surprisingly, some of us do so more effectively than others. Good language learners seem to be better at using a broader range of strategies than other students. They are described as less inhibited and more driven to communicate; they seem more willing to make mistakes in an effort to communicate, are more likely to guess and to do so correctly. In addition to being attentive to meaning, good language learners are also more focused on form and better able to analyze language to look for patterns (Rubin, cited in Oxford, Lavine, & Crookall, 1989). Good language learners approach language learning differently. They have a twofold vision of language as both a rule system and a communication tool. Such learners are active participants in the language learning process, learning to think in the second language and seeking out situations in which to use the strategies they command. Always modifying and expanding their understanding, good learners are also sensitive to the affective demands of the language learning process (Naiman, Frohlich, & Todesco, cited in Oxford et al., 1989). The basic problem facing teachers is that "the majority of students learning a foreign or second language do not inherently share the cognitive, strategy-related, and personality characteristics of good language learners" (Oxford et al., 1989, 36). Most students lack an awareness of language learning as a process. As a result, they are not cognizant of how strategies can facilitate language learning (Oxford et al., 1989).

As teachers become more aware of language learning strategies, they will discover that there are a variety of frameworks and approaches for classifying and

---

Direct Strategies

Memory strategies
- Creating mental linkages (grouping, making associations with previous learning, putting new words into meaningful contexts)
- Applying images and sounds (using imagery and semantic mapping, using key words and sounds to provide auditory and visual links)
- Reviewing well (using structured review in carefully spaced intervals)
- Employing action (using physical response or sensation)

Cognitive strategies
- Practicing (repeating, recombining, practicing sounds and writing, using routine formulas and patterns, practicing in natural settings)
- Receiving and sending messages (getting the idea quickly by skimming for ideas or scanning for specific details, using print and nonprint resources)
- Analyzing and reasoning (using deductive reasoning to apply general rules to specific situations, analyzing new expressions by determining the meaning of its component elements, comparing elements—sounds, vocabulary, grammar—across languages for similarities and differences, translating or transferring words, expressions, concepts or structures from one language into another)
- Creating structure for input and output (taking notes on the main idea or on particular points, summarizing or highlighting important information in a long passage)

Compensation strategies
- Guessing intelligently (using linguistic and other clues)
- Overcoming limitations in speaking and writing (switching to the mother tongue, getting help, using mime or gestures, avoiding communication partially or totally, modifying the message, selecting the topic, adjusting or approximating the message, coining words, using a circumlocution or synonym)

Figure 8-6   Strategies for language learning

Source: From *Language Learning Strategies: What Every Teacher Should Know* (pp. 18–21) by R. L. Oxford, 1990, Boston: Heinle and Heinle. Copyright © 1990 by Heinle and Heinle Publishers. Adapted by permission.

teaching language learning strategies (e.g., Benamer, 1993; Chamot & O'Malley, 1986, 1994; Oxford, 1990; Wenden, 1991; Wenden & Rubin, 1987). The approach developed by Oxford (1990), for example, encompasses three basic types of strategies used directly in processing language. These are memory strategies, cognitive strategies, and compensation strategies. *Memory* strategies help students to retain and recall new information (pp. 38–43). Also known as mnemonic devices, this set of strategies relies on groupings and mental associations based upon meaning. Associations may involve visual images, auditory links, or physical actions. According to Oxford, the mind is better equipped to store greater amounts of visual than verbal material. In fact, it appears that visual images actually promote the recall of verbal material. As a result, the connection between verbal and visual learning makes memory strategies powerful tools, particularly critical in the recall and retrieval of the extensive vocabulary required for fluency in any language. Some commonly used memory strategies are identified in Figure 8-6.

Cognitive strategies engage the learner in the manipulation of language (pp. 43–47). Practice with repeating, recognizing, recombining, and using lan-

---

Indirect Strategies

Metacognitive strategies
- Centering learning (doing an overview and making associations with concepts, principles, and material that is already known, paying attention to specific aspects of language or situation)
- Arranging and planning learning (finding out about the processes involved in language learning, organizing to ensure optimal conditions for language learning, setting long-term goals and short-term objectives, identifying the purpose of a language task, seeking practice opportunities)
- Evaluating learning (self-monitoring to identify errors in comprehension or production, self-evaluating to assess one's progress)

Affective strategies
- Lowering anxiety (using progressive relaxation, deep breathing, or meditation, using music and laughter to relax)
- Encouraging oneself (making positive statements that enhance self-confidence in the new language, taking risks wisely in language learning situations, rewarding oneself for good performance in the new language)
- Taking one's emotional temperature (paying attention to positive and negative signals given by the body, using a checklist to identify feelings, attitudes, and motivations related to language learning, keeping a language learning diary, expressing and discussing feelings about language learning with someone else)

Social strategies
- Asking questions (asking for clarification, verification, or correction)
- Cooperating with others (cooperating with peers and with proficient users of the new language to improve language skills)
- Empathizing with others (developing cultural understanding by learning about the new culture, becoming aware of the thoughts and feelings of other people)

---

guage is essential for acquisition to take place. Students need to know how to grasp the main idea rapidly, how to use available resources to enhance comprehension and production, and how to construct their own mental models of the new language. Some learners remain forever between the native and target language in the hybrid phase of interlanguage because they are unable to make effective use of analyzing and reasoning strategies. Among the most widely used cognitive strategies are those described in Figure 8-6.

Compensation strategies contribute to language learning by enabling students to use language in ways that compensate for limitations in knowledge (pp. 47–51). These are most often applied to gaps in a learner's command of grammar and vocabulary. Compensation strategies focus on the ways that learners use linguistic and nonlinguistic clues to guess meaning when listening and reading as well as the ways in which they overcome limitations in speaking and writing. That these are potent strategies is evident in Oxford's observation that learners adept in their use may communicate more effectively than those with superior command of vocabulary and language structures. A few of the most essential compensation strategies are highlighted in Figure 8-6.

The metacognitive, affective, and social strategies identified in Figure 8-6 are defined as indirect strategies in Oxford's model (pp. 135–147). They contribute to language learning by enabling learners to better manage the processes involved, by helping them to deal more effectively with their emotions and anxiety, and by facilitating interaction and cooperation. According to Oxford, direct and indirect strategies are complementary. The former involve the target language directly; the latter often do not (p. 135).

Teacher awareness of different language learning strategies is not enough. Chamot and Kupper (1989) found that the primary difference between more and less effective foreign language learners is in the variety and use of strategies. To address this situation, they suggest that teachers actively help learners identify the specific strategies they employ, assist them in using these more effectively, and provide opportunities for students to acquire additional strategies. Teachers may derive an unexpected benefit from providing strategy training. Oxford et al. (1989) observe that "through the presentation of strategies, many teachers begin to examine their own teaching strategies, as well as their underlying style preferences" (p. 37). When teachers begin to work with language learning strategies, they naturally select those most compatible with their own teaching style and preferences. In the process, however, many discover that their personal preferences are more compatible with those of some students than others. This increased awareness can provide the impetus teachers need to explore new ways of accommodating the diversity of learning styles and strategies represented in the multilingual classroom.

There are a variety of techniques that teachers can use, including observation, think-aloud procedures, and self-report interviews and surveys (Oxford, 1990, 193–200). (For an analysis of elicitation procedures, see O'Malley & Chamot, 1990.) Teacher *observation* can provide limited information on the use of strategies with outward manifestations that are evident through performance and interaction. Teachers can use notes or a checklist to focus observation of the entire class, small groups, or individual students. *Think-aloud* procedures ask students to verbalize their thinking processes while actively involved in a language task. As the name implies, "students 'think aloud' as they learn'" (Oxford, 1990, 195). Interviews and surveys allow time for reflection as students *self-report* on their strategy use in relation to a task, situation, and so on. Examples of the kinds of questions asked are included in Figure 8-7. As is evident, the SILL (Strategy Inventory for Language Learning) is most appropriate for high school students and adults. For English language learners who have not attained the level of proficiency required to respond in English, translations of the survey into languages such as Chinese, Japanese, and Spanish are either already available or soon will be (Oxford, 1990).

Summary

Learning activities that promote English language and literacy development are characterized as natural, interesting, purposeful, meaningful, and relevant. An optimal classroom environment is comfortable, supportive, and accepting. Beginning and intermediate oral language development is enhanced through the use of Total Physical Response activities and affective strategies.

Ideally, initial literacy instruction for children should be in the students' primary language. In reality, however, children are often taught to read and write in

This is a sample of items from Oxford's Strategy Inventory for Language Learning (SILL)—Version for Speakers of Other Languages Learning English. The items included provide examples of the variety of areas examined in assessing the learning strategies used by students. For a complete version of the SILL survey with accompanying worksheet, scoring procedures, and profile information, refer to Oxford (1990).

For each item, students are asked to select the response that best describes them.

1. Never or almost never true of me (very rarely)
2. Usually not true of me (less than half the time)
3. Somewhat true of me (about half the time)
4. Usually true of me (more than half the time)
5. Always or almost always true of me (almost always)

A. *Remembering language*

_____ I remember a new English word by making a mental picture of a situation in which the word might be used.
_____ I use rhymes to remember new English words.
_____ I physically act out new English words.
_____ I review English lessons often.
_____ I remember new English words or phrases by remembering their location on the page, on the board, or on a street sign.

B. *Using mental processes*

_____ I say or write new English words several times.
_____ I use the English words I know in different ways.
_____ I start conversations in English.
_____ I watch English language TV shows spoken in English or go to movies spoken in English.
_____ I write notes, messages, letters, or reports in English.

Figure 8-7 Assessing language learning strategies

Source: From *Language Learning Strategies: What Every Teacher Should Know* (pp. 293–296) by R. L. Oxford, 1990, Boston: Heinle and Heinle. Copyright © 1990 by Heinle and Heinle Publishers. Adapted by permission.

English regardless of their primary language. This makes the choice of approaches and strategies even more critical for teachers in multilingual classrooms. There are approaches and strategies that have proven to be effective for English language learners at different grade levels, among these the language experience approach, multicultural literature, and free voluntary reading.

As students learn to write in a new language, there are sociocultural considerations that need to be taken into account (e.g., command of vocabulary, syntax, and idiomatic expressions; rhetorical structure; knowledge of writing and academic conventions). To capitalize on the cognitive strengths that students bring to the writing task, teachers can use semantic organizers, scaffolding, whole language strategies, and other techniques. To assist students as thinkers and creators of text, process writing is strongly recommended for English language learners of all ages and for use across content areas. Language learning strategies will further enhance

_____ I look for words in my own language that are similar to new words in English.
_____ I try to find patterns in English.
_____ I find the meaning of an English word by dividing it into parts that I understand.
_____ I try not to translate word-for-word.
_____ I make summaries of information that I hear or read in English.

C. *Compensating for knowledge gaps*
_____ When I can't think of a word during a conversation in English, I use gestures.
_____ I read English without looking up every new word.
_____ If I can't think of an English word, I use a word or phrase that means the same thing.

D. *Organizing and evaluating learning*
_____ I try to find as many ways as I can to use my English.
_____ I notice my English mistakes and use that information to help me do better.
_____ I pay attention when someone is speaking English.
_____ I try to find out how to be a better learner of English.
_____ I look for people I can talk to in English.

E. *Managing emotions*
_____ I encourage myself to speak English even when I am afraid of making a mistake.
_____ I talk to someone else about how I feel when I am learning English.
_____ I notice if I am tense or nervous when I am studying or using English.

F. *Communicating with others*
_____ If I do not understand something in English, I ask the other person to slow down or say it again.
_____ I ask English speakers to correct me when I talk.
_____ I practice English with other students.
_____ I ask questions in English.
_____ I try to learn about the culture of English speakers.

Figure 8-7, *continued*

students' effectiveness by making them more aware of how they learn and better able to utilize memory, cognitive, and compensation strategies in the process.

As they develop literacy, students will read in order to learn and write in order to think. Empowered by the literacy skills they develop, students will become critical and creative thinkers, fully capable of contributing in the classroom, community, and society as a whole.

References

Adamson, H. D. (1993). *Academic competence: Theory and classroom practice: Preparing ESL students for content courses.* White Plains, NY: Longman.

Asher, J. J. (1981). The total physical response: Theory and practice. In H. Winitz (Ed.), *The annals of the New York Academy of Sciences: Vol. 379: Native language and foreign language acquisition* (pp. 324–331). New York: New York Academy of Sciences.

Asher, J. J. (1988). *Learning another language through actions: The complete teacher's guidebook* (3rd. ed.). Los Gatos, CA: Sky Oaks Productions.

Au, K. (1993). *Literacy instruction in multicultural settings.* Fort Worth: Harcourt Brace Jovanovich College Publishers.

Bassano, S., & Christison, M. A. (1982). *Drawing out.* San Francisco: Alemany Press.

Benamer, S. (1993). *Language learning strategy use among adult ESL/target language learners: A critical review of selected research literature.* Unpublished master's thesis, California State University, Chico.

Bosma, B. (1992). *Fairy tales, fables, legends, and myths: Using folk literature in your classroom* (2nd ed.). New York: Teachers College Press, Columbia University.

Brechtel, M. (1992). *Bringing the whole together.* San Diego: Dominie Press.

California State University, Chico. (1985). *Study guide: The writing process videotapes.* Chico: Author.

Cecil, N. L., & Lauritzen, P. (1994). *Literacy and the arts for the integrated classroom: Alternative ways of knowing.* White Plains, NY: Longman.

Chamot, A. U., & Kupper, L. (1989). Learning strategies in foreign language instruction. *Foreign Language Annals, 22*(1), 13–24.

Chamot, A. U., & O'Malley, J. M. (1986). *A cognitive academic language learning approach: An ESL content-based curriculum.* Wheaton, MD: National Clearinghouse for Bilingual Education.

Chamot, A. U., & O'Malley, J. M. (1994). *The CALLA handbook.* Reading, MA: Addison-Wesley.

Christison, M. A., & Bassano, S. (1981). *Look who's talking.* Hayward, CA: Alemany Press.

Christison, M. A., & Bassano, S. (1987). *Look who's talking* (2nd ed.). Hayward, CA: Alemany Press.

Cramer, N. A. (1985). *The writing process.* Cambridge, MA: Newbury House/Harper Row.

D'Aoust, C. (1987). Teaching writing as a process. In C. B. Olson (Ed.), *Practical ideas for teaching writing as a process* (pp. 7–9). Sacramento: California Department of Education.

Diamond, B. J., and Moore, M. A. (1995). *Multicultural literacy: Mirroring the reality of the classroom.* White Plains, NY: Longman.

Dixon, C. M., & Nessel, D. (1983). *Language experience approach to reading (and writing).* Hayward, CA: Alemany Press.

Edelsky, C. (1989). Bilingual children's writing: Fact and fiction. In D. M. Johnson & D. H. Roen (Eds.), *Richness in writing: Empowering ESL students* (pp. 165–176). White Plains, NY: Longman.

Enright, D. S., & McCloskey, M. L. (1988). *Integrating English: Developing English language and literacy in the multilingual classroom.* Reading, MA: Addison-Wesley.

Eskey, D. E. (1993). Reading and writing as both cognitive process and social behavior. In J. G. Carson & I. Leki (Eds.), *Reading in the composition classroom* (pp. 221–234). Boston: Heinle & Heinle.

Eskey, D. E., & Grabe, W. (1988). Interactive models for second language reading: Perspectives on instruction. In P. L. Carrell, J. Devine, & D. E. Eskey (Eds.), *Interactive approaches to second language reading* (pp. 223–238). New York: Cambridge University Press.

Fichtner, D., Peitzman, F., Sasser, L. (1994). What's fair? Assessing subject matter knowledge of LEP students in sheltered classrooms. In F. Peitzman & G. Gadda (Eds.), *With different eyes* (pp. 114–123). White Plains, NY: Addison Wesley Longman.

Gaies, S. J. (1989). Foreword. In D. M. Johnson & D. H. Roen (Eds.), *Richness in writing: Empowering ESL students* (pp. xi–xii). White Plains, NY: Longman.

Galyean, B. (1982). A confluent design for language teaching. In R. W. Blair (Ed.), *Innovative approaches to language teaching* (pp. 176–188). Rowley, MA: Newbury House.

Goodman, K. (1986). *What's whole in whole language?* Portsmouth, NH: Heinemann.

Goodman, K. S., Goodman, Y. M., & Hood, W. J. (Eds.) (1989). *The whole language evaluation book*. Portsmouth, NH: Heinemann.

Grabe, W., & Kaplan, R. B. (1989). Writing in a second language: Contrastive rhetoric. In D. M. Johnson & D. H. Roen (Eds)., *Richness in writing: Empowering ESL students* (pp. 263–283). White Plains, NY: Longman.

Gunderson, L. (1991). *ESL literacy instruction: A guidebook to theory and practice*. Englewood Cliffs, NJ: Regents/Prentice Hall.

Heald-Taylor, G. (1989). *Whole language strategies for ESL students*. San Diego: Dormac.

Hudelson, S. (1989). *Write on: Children writing in ESL*. Englewood Cliffs, NJ: Center for Applied Linguistics and Prentice Hall Regents.

Johnson, D. M., & Roen, D. H. (Eds.). (1989). *Richness in writing: Empowering ESL students*. White Plains, NY: Longman.

Krashen, S. (1993). *The power of reading*. Englewood, CO: Libraries Unlimited.

Krashen, S. D., & Terrell, T. D. (1983). *The natural approach*. Oxford, England/San Francisco: Pergamon Press/Alemany Press.

Leki, I. (1993). Reciprocal themes in ESL reading and writing. In J. G. Carson & I. Leki (Eds.), *Reading in the composition classroom* (pp. 9–32). Boston: Heinle & Heinle.

Moskowitz, G. (1978). *Caring and sharing in the foreign language class*. Rowley, MA: Newbury House.

Olson, C. B. (Ed.) (1987). *Practical ideas for teaching writing as a process*. Sacramento: California Department of Education.

O'Malley, J. M., & Chamot, A. U. (1990). *Learning strategies in second language acquisition*. New York: Cambridge University Press.

Oxford, R. L. (1990). *Language learning strategies: What every teacher should know*. Boston: Heinle & Heinle.

Oxford, R. L., Lavine, R., & Crookall, D. (1989). Language learning strategies, the communicative approach, and their classroom implications. *Foreign Language Annals, 22*(1), 29–39.

Peregoy, S. F., & Boyle, O. F. (1993). *Reading, writing, and learning in ESL*. White Plains, New York: Addison Wesley Longman.

Pérez, B., & Torres-Guzmán, M. E. (1992). *Learning in two worlds: An integrated Spanish/English biliteracy approach*. White Plains, NY: Longman.

Reid, J. M. (1992). Helping students write for an academic audience. In P. A. Richard-Amato & M. A. Snow (Eds.), *The multicultural classroom: Readings for content-area teachers* (pp. 210–221). White Plains, NY: Longman.

Reid, J. M. (1993). Historical perspectives on writing and reading in the ESL classroom. In J. G. Carson & I. Leki (Eds.), *Reading in the composition classroom* (pp. 33–60). Boston: Heinle & Heinle.

Roen, D. H. (1989). Developing effective assignments for second language writers. In D. M. Johnson & D. H. Roen (Eds.), *Richness in writing: Empowering ESL students* (pp. 193–206). White Plains, NY: Longman.

Sánchez, F. (1990). Twelve easy ways to make learning a second language difficult. *Instruction for language minority students*. Unpublished presentation handout.

Smith, F. (1983). *Essays into literacy*. Portsmouth, NH: Heinemann.

Smith, F. (1988). *Joining the literacy club*. Portsmouth, NH: Heinemann.

Sunflower, C. (1994). *Really writing: Ready-to-use writing process activities for the elementary grades*. West Nyack, NY: The Center for Applied Research in Education.

Terrell, T. D. (1981). The natural approach to bilingual education. *Schooling and language minority students: A theoretical framework* (pp. 117–146). Los Angeles: Evaluation, Dissemination and Assessment Center, School of Education, California State University, Los Angeles.

Traill, L. (1992). Foreword. In M. Brechtel, *Bringing the whole together* (pp. vi–vii). San Diego: Dominie Press.

Wenden, A. (1991). *Learner strategies for learner autonomy*. New York: Prentice Hall.

Wenden, A,. & Rubin, J. (1987). *Learner strategies in language learning*. Englewood Cliffs, NJ: Prentice Hall International.

Williams, C., & Cary, S. (1991). In S. Cary, *Sheltered English Instruction Workshops*, New Haven Unified School District (Grades K–6), Union City, CA, August 28–29, September 19, 1991.

Williams, J. D., & Snipper, G. C. (1990). *Literacy and bilingualism*. New York: Longman.

9

Teaching Content: Developing Academic Language and Competence

Every time the teacher talks, "it was like the water that flows over a duck's back with no feathers getting wet."

Chanhsinh Saechao

In many schools, teachers cannot assume that language minority students will receive academic support in their primary language and ESL until such time as they are ready for native-like instruction in English. As Richard-Amato and Snow (1992) observe, "support systems for language minority students in mainstream classes are often limited or missing. A surprisingly large number of these students may not have received instruction in English as a second language (ESL) at all" (p. 145). Relatively few receive native language instruction. As a result, teachers with limited or no specialized training in second language development find themselves teaching content in English to students who have not developed full proficiency in academic (if not communicative) language skills.

Unfortunately, many language minority students will fail to achieve academically when placed in classrooms in which instruction is not adapted to meet their needs (Adamson, 1993, xi). Even those receiving support in native language and ESL programs often find the transition difficult. Their experience may be like that described so aptly by Chanhsinh Saechao, a Mien immigrant: "Every time the teacher talks, 'it was like the water that flows over a duck's back with no feathers getting wet'" (cited in Y. Saechao, 1991).

This chapter focuses on teaching subject matter to language minority students, highlighting content area instruction in general, and areas such as mathematics, science, and social studies in particular. The discussion provides a distillation of theory and research, experience and strategies that enable teachers to enhance their effectiveness in teaching both content and language for academic purposes. Generally speaking, these strategies and techniques are used in grade-level classrooms in which instruction is designed for native speakers of English as well as in classrooms that are bilingual, ESL, "sheltered" (designed to provide English language learners at similar levels of proficiency with language-sensitive academic instruction in English), and adjunct (designed to match an ESL language class with a mainstream content area class so as to provide additional support for language and content development).[1] Teachers are reminded that even though some of the strategies and techniques are appropriate for students at all levels of proficiency, others demand greater levels of proficiency and should be used accordingly.

After completing this chapter, you will be able to

1. provide content-area instruction that is language-sensitive
2. promote academic competence

---

[1]The term "grade-level" classroom is borrowed from Enright and McCloskey (1988). "Sheltered" and adjunct classes are defined consistent with Adamson (1993) and Richard-Amato and Snow (1992, 145). Brinton, Snow, and Wesche (1989) further differentiate between sheltered and adjunct models on the basis of language proficiency. They indicate that the former is most appropriate for intermediate to high-intermediate levels, the latter for high-intermediate to advanced levels. Neither is regarded as appropriate for lower levels of proficiency due to the "inherent linguistic and conceptual complexity of academic subject matter" (p. 20).

3. recognize the importance of contextual support and use appropriate strategies to make instruction comprehensible

4. recognize some of the unique features of academic language in specific subject areas such as mathematics, science, and social studies

Language-Sensitive Content-Area Instruction

One of the primary goals in this chapter is to help teachers provide content-area instruction that is language-sensitive, that is, instruction that recognizes the language needs of students as well as the language demands of the content subject (Spanos, cited in Chamot & O'Malley, 1994, 176). In the process, students have access to academically demanding content and academic language that supports higher-order thinking skills. In this context, *language-sensitive* is preferred to other terms because it can be broadly used to encompass strategies and techniques that can be applied in a variety of classroom situations—grade-level, bilingual, ESL, and so on.

In this section, teachers will consider some of the basic features that characterize instruction that is language-sensitive. Specifically, the focus is on academic competence, contextual support, and ways of making instruction more comprehensible. Academic language in specific content subjects will be treated in the section that follows.

Focus on Content

Saville-Troike observes that English is simply a means to an end: in the final analysis, "the critical outcome . . . is how well (students) succeed in school" (cited in Adamson, 1993, 1). Academic competence is the key to achievement. Saville-Troike first used *academic competence* as a term encompassing those academic factors beyond communicative competence that are most critical in academic achievement. This is consistent with her view that "there is a qualitative difference between the communicative tactics and skills that children find effective for meeting their social needs and goals and those that are necessary for academic achievement in the classroom" (cited in Adamson, 1993, 4). Reading seems to be the most critical language skill in academic competence, followed by listening comprehension and writing (Adamson, 1993, 83). Although grammatical accuracy is of considerable concern to students and teachers, studies reviewed by Adamson reveal that grammatical accuracy does not appear to correlate with academic achievement (p. 107). This, he observes, is different from what educators expected: "We had thought that the most important factors in academic success were general language proficiency and sociolinguistic competence (knowledge of how to interact in socially appropriate ways). But Saville-Troike (1984) showed that specifically academic factors are necessary as well, and she introduced the term *academic competence* to include these factors" (p. 4). Clearly, enabling students to develop the ability to use English for academic purposes requires more than helping students master English grammatical structure or providing opportunities for social interaction.

Other factors—teacher, student, and instructional—have emerged as highly significant in determining whether students will ultimately succeed. Over time the concept of academic competence has been extended to encompass a variety of features based on insights drawn from theories, research, and classroom experience with effective academic instruction. The following topics represent some of the major areas identified in the literature. (Language learning strategies were discussed earlier and are not included here in order to avoid repetition.)

Academically Demanding Content and Higher-Level Thinking   First and foremost, language minority students need to engage in experiences with academically demanding content that promote thinking—the kind of thinking that empowers "students to take more control of their own education and their lives" (Barell 1991, xiii). This thinking process has been defined as

> the search for *meaning* (make sure problems "make sense"); the *adventurous* pursuit of alternative solutions, meanings, and perspectives; the attempt to base decisions or selections upon *reasonableness* (considering evidence); and the *reflection* metacognitively (thinking about thinking) on these processes to make them more conscious and bring them under our control. Thinking is conceived as creating one's own pathways, not following in others' footsteps. (p. xiv)

Thinking requires challenging, high-status knowledge that is studied in depth—content that provides students full access and multiple options. Language does not have to be an impediment. For example, teachers who have worked with sheltered instruction know that "a lesson can be linguistically simple but the content can be complex. . . . People think sheltered means remedial, but this is elevated content" (Schifini, cited in Biederman, 1987). According to Schifini, the emphasis on hands-on activities makes students less dependent on language that is unfamiliar. The emphasis on showing and doing rather than telling enables students to discover concepts by themselves. As Cummins (1989) has observed, "instruction that empowers will aim to liberate students from dependence on instruction in the sense of encouraging them to become active generators of their own knowledge" (p. 63). This is particularly critical for language minority students.

Authentic Oral and Written Texts   A full range of academic strategies and language functions in the second language can best be acquired in connection with authentic texts—oral and written—that reflect the kind of material that students actually need to master in the classroom context. Authentic texts are written and oral materials created for a purpose other than language teaching—natural texts with the structures, functions, and discourse features that students must learn (Brinton et al., 1989, 1). To be authentic, academic language experiences need to be integrated with content instruction. As proficiency in English develops, content needs to be studied in classrooms that provide appropriate contact with and exposure to native speakers (Adamson, 1993, 115).

Those who teach second language learners know that materials need to be adapted for students whose proficiency level precludes the use of materials in their original state (Brinton et al., 1989, 93). It is necessary, justifiable, and appropriate because "less proficient second language speakers *cannot* deal with real-life language 'in the raw'; otherwise, they would not need a second language support system" (p. 93). Once adapted, however, materials are no longer strictly "authentic." Care must be taken not to oversimplify the content and linguistic characteristics of the original.

Brinton et al. (1989) provide the guidelines for text selection in content-based ESL courses presented in Figure 9-1. Many of these suggestions are also useful for teachers in other settings to consider.

Relevant, Stimulating, and Coherent Materials, Tasks, and Curriculum   Content material should be relevant, interesting, and practical: "When students are interested in what they are learning, they learn it better" (Adamson, 1993, 9). Hence, consideration of students' prior school experiences, background knowledge, and individual learning styles is paramount. Curricula should be coherent

---

Authenticity of content and tasks
- Is the content material up-to-date?
- Does it provide adequate coverage?
- Are the activities appropriate to the content area?
- Do the tasks foster development of critical thinking skills?

Interest and difficulty levels
- Does the subject matter capture students' interest?
- Is the material suitable for students' level of proficiency?
- How difficult is the text in terms of vocabulary, structure, and syntax?

Accessibility
- Do students have the background knowledge required?
- Is cultural background a factor in accessing information?
- How dense is the information load?
- Is the writing style appropriate?

Text presentation and supplementary materials
- Are the materials clear and visually attractive?
- Does the presentation (e.g., layout, color, visuals, highlighting) enhance comprehension and retention of content material?
- Does the text's organization facilitate understanding of content and integration of skills?
- Does the text utilize different sources, text types, and media?
- What kinds of supplementary materials (e.g., visuals, films, audiotapes, videotapes) are available?
- Does the text accommodate a variety of learning styles?
- Are there study aids (e.g., glosses, questions, organizers) designed to enhance comprehension and retention of content material?

Figure 9-1   Guidelines for text selection
Source: Brinton, Snow, and Wesche (1989, 90)

and coordinated, enabling students to master content at a given level while preparing them to work beyond to the next level (Mesa, 1986; Hernández, 1992). Using math as an example, Mesa is critical of programs that do not prepare students in basic math courses for higher levels of study. Ideally, taking a basic course in mathematics should present students with multiple options, rather than channeling them in limited directions. To provide these options, there need to be stronger linkages between levels, such as basic math and algebra (and beyond). Providing a curriculum that is relevant, stimulating, and practical—one that also provides depth of knowledge within domains—has never been a more crucial factor in the academic achievement of language minority students (Berliner, 1990; Mesa, 1986).

As Dewey observed, "all knowledge, even the most abstract, is ultimately understood in terms of immediate, everyday experience" (cited in Adamson, 1993, 118). Like Adamson, Mohan draws on Dewey to emphasize that instruction for English language learners should proceed from the practical and experiential to the theoretical and expository:

> When education, under the influence of a scholastic conception of knowledge which ignores everything but scientifically formulated facts and truths, fails to recognize that the primary or initial subject matter always exists as a matter of an active doing, involving the use of the body and the handling of material, the subject matter of instruction is isolated from the needs and purposes of the learners, and so becomes just something to be memorized and reproduced upon demand (cited in Mohan, 1986, 102).

Multiculturation: Theme-Based and Learner-Centered Instruction   Thus far, culture has been taken into account in relation to context, content, and process. It is also important that teachers not forget the broader implications of the acculturation process that second language learners experience. One way of looking at this is through Cortés's vision of *multiculturation*—"the mutual acculturation of people, cultures and institutions" (1990, 14). His vision is to build a nation on the contributions of one and all, a community based on the positive commonalties that unite us—respecting, maintaining, and nourishing the constructive uniqueness that marks our diversity. This calls for several kinds of acculturation, among these acculturation that empowers and sensitizes. Acculturation that *empowers* enables all students to "develop socially-unifying knowledge, understanding, beliefs, values and loyalties, [and] effective English, advanced knowledge and empowering skills that will provide them with a reasonable chance of taking advantage of opportunities for reaching the fabled American dream" (p. 14). Acculturation that *sensitizes* helps all Americans "develop better intercultural understanding and become more dedicated to living with concern and sensitivity in a multiethnic society where racial, ethnic and cultural differences co-exist with national and human commonalties" (p. 14). Multiculturation is for all students.

The spectrum of issues encompassed by multiculturation is broad and varied, cutting across grade levels and subject areas (Enright & McCloskey, 1988; Hernández & Metzger, 1996). However, given the immediacy of certain concerns in the lives of language minority students (e.g., family, language, culture, school climate), some issues will be more relevant than others. This is why it is also imperative that instruction be theme based and learner centered. Meaningful themes are everywhere and will vary from one context to another. Themes can be drawn from the experiences and concerns of the students themselves, for students' voices are an essential guide in making decisions regarding their selection. Once identified, the themes can also serve as the basis for schoolwide and local community action projects (see Hernández and Metzger, 1996, on "Issues-education for Language Minority Students.")

Barell (1991) defines thoughtfulness as inseparable from thinking in the process of intellectual development. "It unites the head and the heart, thinking and feeling, the cognitive and the affective dimensions of living in our world" (p. xiv). To separate one from the other would do a "disservice to the complex nature of living" (p. xiv). Likewise, multiculturation has to be an inseparable part of genuine academic competence. It is the "cultural thoughtfulness" embodied in the promise of intellectual development that academic competence represents.

Contextual Support

If instruction is to be comprehensible, language must be contextualized (Cummins, 1996). When language is embedded in context, meaning is conveyed not only by the words themselves, but via situational and contextual cues as well. For example, gestures, facial expressions, and intonation all contribute to understanding the message expressed by a speaker. On occasion, nonverbal signals—a grimace or an action—may convey an idea so effectively that words seem superfluous.

In written text, language is typically embedded through the support provided by visuals such as photographs, diagrams, and illustrations. Being familiar with the situation in which language is used creates expectations that facilitate comprehension. Look at what cartoonists do. Much of the humor in the daily comic strips is conveyed through the juxtaposition of verbal and visual images. If you cover the pictures and read only the written text, the humor is often lost. Meaning is dependent on the situation and context conveyed visually. In daily routines, for example, children learn to anticipate what is going to be said or done. Students quickly learn to associate certain language with classroom procedures. They can predict what teachers will say when they begin the school day, take attendance, prepare the class for lunch or recess, and send them home at the end of the day. When essential information is not available, even simple tasks can become challenging and confusing (see Figure 9-2).

Cummins represents the extent to which language is embedded in context as falling along a continuum (Figure 9-3). At one end, there is ample contextual support. At the other, the absence of support requires that meaning be derived totally from the spoken or written word. As Cummins observes, "thinking and language that move beyond the bounds of meaningful interpersonal context make entirely different demands on the individual, in that it is necessary to focus on the linguistic forms themselves for meaning rather than on intentions" (1992, 19). In simple terms, it's the difference between a face-to-face conversation and a telephone call, between radio and television talk shows. In the classroom, the more embedded in

Let's look at what happens when written language is not presented in context. Take a piece of paper and complete steps 1 to 5.

1. Fold the piece of paper in half.
2. Fold down the upper corners until they touch in the lower center.
3. Fold the bottom up about 1/4 inch over the corners that are already folded down.
4. Then do the same on the opposite side.
5. Now describe what you made (Ittelson, 1989).

* * * * * * * * * * * * * * *

\What do you have in your hands? An airplane? A hat? Something different? Was the task difficult or confusing? Would it have helped if the instructions had been contextualized, with an example of what you were being asked to make, perhaps a model or picture showing what it was supposed to look like? What about illustrations taking you through the procedure step by step?

Now follow the directions below. Do you see the difference that putting language in context makes?

Hat

1. Take a square piece of paper and fold it in half to make a rectangle (Figure A).

Figure A

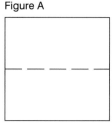

2. Fold the right corner of the rectangle to the middle of the paper (Figure B). Do the same thing with the left corner (Figure C).

Figure B   Figure C

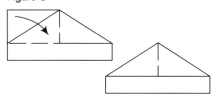

3. Fold up the front flap (Figure D). Do the same thing with the back flap (Figure E).

Figure D   Figure E

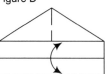
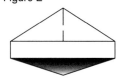

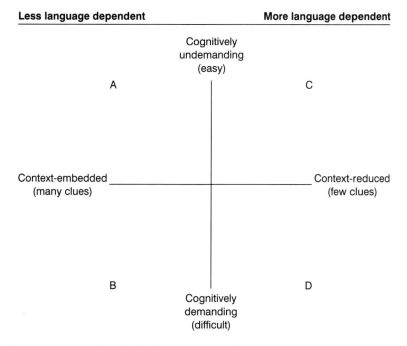

Figure 9-3   Annotated model of language proficiency

Source: From "Primary Language Instruction and the Education of Language Minority Students" by J. Cummins, 1996, *Schooling and Language Minority Students: A Theoretical Framework,* 2nd ed. (p. 10). Los Angeles: Evaluation, Dissemination and Assessment Center, School of Education, California State University, Los Angeles. Copyright © 1996 by Charles F. Leyba. Reprinted by permission.

context the language used for instruction is, the more comprehensible it will be for students in general and second language learners in particular.

In Figure 9-3, Cummins also directs teachers' attention to the difficulty level of tasks involving language. These range from the very simple and concrete (cognitively undemanding) to the most abstract and formidable (cognitively demanding), from activities involving automatized language to those demanding high levels of cognitive involvement. The tasks and skills falling in quadrant *D* (i.e., context-reduced and cognitively demanding) present the greatest challenge for teachers as well as students.

Cummins addresses the implications of embedded and disembedded thought and language.

> The more context-embedded the initial L2 [second language] input, the more comprehensible it is likely to be, and paradoxically, the more successful in ultimately developing L2 skills in content-reduced situations. A central reason why language minority students have often failed to develop high levels of L2 academic skills is because their initial instruction has emphasized context-reduced communication insofar as instruction has been through English and unrelated to their prior out-of-school experience. (Cummins, 1992, 21)

In the next section, techniques and strategies that can be used to contextualize communication and promote understanding of cognitively demanding content are considered.

Comprehensible Instruction

Classes that work for second language learners are characterized by the way they are organized for instruction and the way language is used in lessons (Wong Fillmore & Valadez, 1986, 670). Content area teachers typically work with language minority students in classroom situations described as mainstream (or grade-level), sheltered, and adjunct (Richard-Amato & Snow, 1992, 145). In these settings, specially designed language-sensitive instruction is critical in meeting the needs of language minority students. Adaptations can make challenging content accessible and meaningful for second language learners. A variety of linguistic and cognitive strategies can be effectively combined with modified curriculum and materials (Sánchez, 1989). Middle school teacher Kate Duggan describes her "conversion" to instruction that is language-sensitive as follows:

> I was a traditional mainstream teacher, and a pretty good one. But I came to sheltered techniques because I was faced with a situation in my school and I couldn't cope. I didn't know what was happening, but nothing I did in the classroom worked anymore. . . . What could I do that would show results? My lectures, having kids take notes wasn't working. I learned how to check for understanding. I became an actor in the classroom. My room is now filled with visuals. I act, I move. The kids work in groups producing visuals. It works! (quoted in Olsen & Mullen, 1990, 64–65)

Language-sensitive instruction provides the "bridge" connecting language and content that students who have already developed basic nonacademic English language skills need to succeed. On one side of the span, English language abilities are expanded to provide opportunities for academic language to develop. Attention is given to aspects of instruction such as comprehensible input, contextualization, and interaction. On the other side, cognitive development is enhanced as students are challenged by subject matter they understand and through active involvement in tasks that promote higher-level thinking. Expectations are high, and student success reinforces self-confidence and self-esteem. Students develop positive attitudes toward language and academic content. Language-sensitive instruction incorporates a variety of strategies and techniques such as those highlighted in the self-assessment in Figure 9-4.

As you read through Figure 9-4 (see pp. 212–213), keep in mind that cultural background may influence how students respond to questions like "Do you understand?" Students may be reluctant to admit that they do not understand, believing that it would reflect negatively on the teacher. Others may simply respond that they understand rather than admit that they really don't.

Language Development Through Content Area Instruction: Mathematics, Science, and Social Studies

In the previous section, you were introduced to a variety of generic strategies used across content areas to make instruction more comprehensible for second language learners. In this section, the focus narrows to consider ways of promoting English language development and academic competence in three specific content areas—mathematics, science, and social studies. Attention will also be given to the role of vocabulary development in content learning, the nature of academic language in each area, and finally, the interface between culture and content.

Vocabulary Development

Vocabulary development is critical for second language learners. Of all the linguistic factors that influence learning of subject matter content, knowledge of vocabulary is the most important (Saville-Troike, cited in Kessler & Quinn, 1987, 59). It even surpasses knowledge of grammar and syntax. Consider, for example, that until recently science textbooks (grades 6–9) introduce students to 2,500 new words each year—twice as many as in foreign language classes at the same grade levels (Hurd, Robinson, McConnell, & Ross, cited in Kessler & Quinn, 1987, 60). To master academic content in a second language, students must learn the key vocabulary.

Comprehension is influenced by the level of difficulty of vocabulary and can be enhanced by teaching the meanings of more difficult terms. For vocabulary instruction to enhance comprehension, it needs to provide students with

- repeated exposure,
- richly contextualized and meaningful information,
- connections with prior knowledge and experience, and
- opportunities for active involvement in the learning process. (Nation, 1990, 192)

Mohan (cited in Kessler & Quinn, 1987) emphasizes the importance of presenting new terminology and structures in the contexts in which they will be used rather than in lists of isolated vocabulary. It also appears that teachers can promote greater recall by relating the meaning of words directly to student experience through interactive activities than through techniques such as dictionary work and reading alone. Teachers need to remember that students who are physically involved in hands-on activities providing opportunities for interaction and discussion of concepts will acquire academic language more quickly.

There are many ways in which teachers can approach vocabulary development. Levine (1985) believes that vocabulary instruction must teach *visual* and *auditory* recognition of new words as well as *association of meaning*. She observes that much of the vocabulary used in the content areas is initially learned at the receptive level as the words are heard or encountered in readings. In the middle grades, Levine (1985, 235–237) suggests that teachers use techniques like the following to present new science and social studies vocabulary:

- Highlight six to eight new words on the blackboard, drawing attention to visual and sound cues. Encourage students to pronounce and repeat.
- Ask students to copy words on the list in order. Check for auditory and visual recognition.

Simplifying the language of instruction
- Do I speak naturally, but more slowly, and articulate clearly?
- Do I take longer pauses at natural breaks?
- Do I use shorter and less complex sentences (e.g., fewer compound sentences and subordinate clauses, simpler syntax)?
- Do I use simpler vocabulary and higher-frequency words?
- Do I use fewer idioms* and pronouns?
- Do I use appropriate cognates**?
- Do I limit the amount of new information in each sentence?
- Do I draw attention to key words?
- Do I provide redundancy by repeating, restating, and expanding upon ideas, defining key terms, and simplifying key vocabulary that is new or difficult?

Providing contextual clues
- Do I use gestures and facial expressions to help convey the meaning of what I say?
- Do I maximize opportunities to use visual aids (e.g., pictures, graphs, maps, slides), props, and realia?
- Do I use media such as videotapes and films?
- Do I maximize effective use of objects and manipulatives?
- Do I label objects, pictures, graphs, maps, and so on?
- Do I clarify the meaning of key terms that may not be familiar to students (e.g., describe what I am talking about in other words or act out the meaning)?

Checking for understanding
- Do I use confirmation checks (e.g., Is this what you're saying?, Do you mean———?)?
- Do I use comprehension checks (e.g., cards with yes/no or true/false choices, raising hands)?
- Do I use clarification requests (e.g., What do you mean by that?)?

Promoting communication
- Do I use a variety of question types such as
    "*wh-*" questions (who, what, where, etc.)?
    "proof" questions (How do you know that?)?
    "test" questions (So, in a democracy, the people elect their president, right?)?
    "referential" questions (seeking new information—What do you think this looks like?—instead of traditional "display" questions in which the teacher knows the answer)?
- Do I focus on topics and concepts, not structure; meaning, not grammar; function or purpose, not form (especially with students in the early stages of second language development)?
- When answering students' questions, do I respond simply and directly, avoiding explanations that are overly detailed?
- Do I correct for content or meaning?
- Do I model correct structural forms?
- Do I teach the language of instructions and procedures?
- Do I emphasize comprehension vocabulary as opposed to productive vocabulary when students are in the initial stages of language development?

Figure 9-4 Making instruction comprehensible: A self-assessment

Sources: Adamson, 1993; Brinton, Snow, and Wesche, 1989; Cantoni-Harvey, 1987; Chan and Chips, 1989; Chips, 1987; Martínez (cited in Mohan, 1986); Mohan, 1986; Richard-Amato and Snow, 1992; and Short, 1992.

- Do I give students the extra time they need to respond to questions in their second language?

Enhancing instruction
- Do I reduce teaching objectives, prioritizing to ensure inclusion of the most important?
- Do I provide a preview and a review?
- Do I identify key concepts and vocabulary?
- Do I synthesize and debrief at the end of lessons?
- Do I provide students with study aids such as tapes of content presented in lectures or comprehensive notes?
- Have I identified the linguistic demands of the subject area(s) I teach?
- Am I teaching students learning strategies appropriate to language and content?

Adapting instructional materials
- Do I adapt my use of materials to make information more accessible to language minority students?
- Do I use illustrations, charts, graphs, and other visuals to make materials more "user friendly"?
- Do I enhance students' understanding of processes using a series of pictures, a flowchart, or other visuals?
- In presenting information, do I consider the students' proficiency level and evaluate alternative formats for presentation?
- Do I build on students' prior knowledge, progressing from the familiar to the unknown, from the concrete to the abstract?
- Do I highlight specific text, emphasizing main points and important supporting information while deleting extraneous material (e.g., asides, superfluous examples)?
- Do I introduce new vocabulary through prereading activities and reinforce it through postreading activities?
- Do I control for new vocabulary by simplifying terms as appropriate and retaining key technical terms?
- Do I minimize the use of synonyms until students have mastered key concepts?
- In simplifying grammar for less proficient learners, do I use simple verb tenses (e.g., present, present continuous, simple past, simple future)?
- Do I use commands (imperatives) in directions and activities?
- In writing, do I use active voice, simplify word order, and avoid pronouns and relative clauses?

For students with higher levels of proficiency, lexical and structural simplification is not generally recommended, unless features such as excess embedding or lack of cohesion interfere with comprehension (Brinton et al., 1989).

---

* *Idioms* are defined by Bolinger (1975) as "groups of words with set meanings that cannot be calculated by adding up the separate meanings of the parts," such as "hold your horses," "kick the bucket," "rock the boat," and so on.

** *Cognates* are words from the same origin, similar across languages in form and meaning, such as the following cognates in English and Spanish: information/información; virtue/virtud; map/mapa. Teachers are reminded that not all words that appear to be cognates are. For example, *embarasada* does not mean *embarrassed* in Spanish. It means *pregnant*.

- Focus on the association of meaning by providing a brief contextualized explanation or demonstration.
- Reinforce learning using bingo grids, drawing, or labeling activities.
- Maximize the use of different modalities in providing experiences with the vocabulary. (Do not ask that students use the words in sentences.)

As learners, many of us have used mnemonic devices as a learning strategy to help us remember information. These are links or associations that facilitate recall and recognition. Several kinds of associations are often effective with new words (Cohen, 1990). Among these are linking the sound of a new word to one that is familiar and creating a mental image based on the meaning or structure of a word. Other techniques include grouping vocabulary by topic, visualizing the shape of the word, or associating a situation or physical action to the word. For older learners, word analysis, learning cognates, dictionary use, and practicing with flash cards are also recommended (pp. 21–37).

In the final analysis, teachers must consider whether the vocabulary development activities they use meet certain criteria. Teachers must ask themselves whether the language of instruction is embedded in context. Do the activities enable students to interact with the vocabulary within the context in which it is used? Do the activities provide opportunities for second language learners to interact verbally with other students? Classroom practices that meet these criteria include brainstorming, organizing material graphically by clustering or semantic mapping, categorizing, charting, stimulating discussion through the use of visuals, and providing a synopsis of key sections of text.

Academic Language

Academic language is special, characterized by special features that set it apart from the language used in everyday conversation. In this section, attention is focused on the nature of language in three content areas: specifically, the language of mathematics, science, and social studies. The purpose is to illustrate how the language of each subject area presents its own unique set of considerations and to model how teachers may approach the analysis of language in other areas. For example, art, music, and physical education are ideal for language-sensitive instruction. They provide ample opportunities for language development through activities that are naturally embedded in context and allow performance to be less dependent on language proficiency to a greater extent than in other academic areas (Cantoni-Harvey, 1987).

Mathematics   At the national level, the ultimate goal of mathematics instruction for all K–12 students is mathematical literacy (National Council of Teachers of Mathematics [NCTM], 1989, 5–6). Guided by an appreciation of the value of mathematics, mathematically literate students are confident practitioners, able to solve problems and to communicate and reason mathematically. As Chamot and O'Malley (1994) observe, this has implications for instruction that extend beyond the teaching of concepts and skills to encompass problem-solving that demands inquiry, critical thinking, communication, and context:

> In this type of instruction, students have opportunities to discuss authentic problems from their personal world that can be solved through mathematics, solve problems that require renewed effort when initial problem-solving attempts do not succeed,

solve problems in which cooperative group efforts generate success, and work on problems that require hypothesis-testing, data collection, evaluation, and generation and discussion of alternative solutions. (p. 226)

This type of instruction embodies the development of *mathematical power* as learners are empowered by their ability to apply logical reasoning and mathematical methods effectively to find solutions to real problems (NCTM, 1989, 5).

Many areas of mathematics are language dependent (Chamot & O'Malley, 1994). Solving word problems, for example, requires more than reading comprehension and computational skills. Some teachers contend that "teaching word story problems is one of the most difficult tasks in the elementary school curriculum" (p. 227). For English language learners, word problems are more difficult than computation. The reason is simple. Concept formation is more difficult when students are required to simultaneously process both the second language and the mathematical problem.

> Many word problems require formal operations or the ability to think abstractly and to manipulate concepts through language. If the student's thought processes are not automatic in the language in which the problem is expressed, but require deliberation due to confusion over unfamiliar meanings of words or phrases, the student's attempts to solve the problem will be delayed if not interrupted altogether. (p. 231)

The language of mathematics is described as precise, technical, and highly specialized (Cantoni-Harvey, 1987; Chamot & O'Malley, 1986, 1994; Dale &

Mathematically literate students are confident practitioners, able to solve problems and to communicate and reason mathematically.

Cuevas, 1987, 1992). Generally speaking, it is difficult for English language learners because words have a narrow range of meaning and are conceptually dense, that is, the words convey meanings that are very complex. It does not suffice for learners to recognize this vocabulary in isolation; rather, students must understand what the words mean in the contexts in which they are used, in the mathematical expressions in which they appear (Dale & Cuevas, 1987). To illustrate this point, Dale and Cuevas draw teachers' attention to specific aspects of mathematics vocabulary that must be mastered. Consider, for example, the complexity of terms such as *coefficient*, *least common multiple*, and *common denominator*. Add to these, words like *equals* and *set*. Notice that the meaning they have in everyday language changes when they are used in mathematics. Consider the many different ways in which operations like + and – are expressed. Just when a student has determined that + means *add*, he or she also discovers that in different contexts it also means *plus, combine, and, sum*, and *increased by*. Similarly, – can be expressed as *subtract from, decreased by, less, take away, minus, differ*, and *less than*. With little redundancy, students cannot rely on repetitions or expansions to decipher meaning; with contexts that are often abstract and limited in the clues they provide, students are more likely to become confused (Bruner, cited in Cantoni-Harvey, 1987, 130; Chamot & O'Malley, 1994).

Further complicating matters are what Dale and Cuevas (1987) describe as the salient characteristics of this mathematical language. For example, there is "the lack of one-to-one correspondence between mathematical symbols and the words they represent" (p. 15). The expression *fifteen divided by three* is not written in the same order in which it is normally said:

$$3 \overline{)\, 15}$$

Consider "the square of the quotient of a and b," which is $(a/b)^2$, and "the number a is five less than the number b" ($a = b - 5$) (pp. 15, 16). Other language features also present difficulties. These include the use of comparative structures (e.g., *greater than/less than, n times as much, as . . . as*), prepositions (e.g., *divided by* versus *divided into*), and logical connectors marking relationships between elements (e.g., *if . . . then, for example, because, but*, and *either . . . or*) (pp. 13–16). Teachers should realize that many of these structures are difficult for native speakers of English too. In fact, the ability to use logical connectors effectively distinguishes between students able to reason mathematically and those who cannot, regardless of their primary language (Dawes, cited in Dale & Cuevas, 1987, 16). Clearly, many of the special grammatical constructions used in mathematics are not typical of language used in everyday activities (Chamot & O'Malley, 1994).

Finally, students also encounter problems in dealing with semantic aspects of language (Dale & Cuevas, 1987, 18–19). Notice what happens with *a number* and *the number* in problems such as the following examples:

1. Three times a number is 2 more than 2 times the number.
2. The sum of two numbers is 18. If the first number is 2 times the other, find the number.

Solving these problems requires that students recognize whether they are dealing with one number or two. In the first example, *a number* and *the number* refer to the same quantity. The answer is 2. In the second, students must determine what the relationship is between *the first number*, *the other number*, and *the number*, and then express that in symbolic form: *the first number* is $2x$, *the second number* is x, the sum is 18, and *the value of x* is 6.

With immigrant and refugee students educated in other countries, teachers may also observe cultural differences (Chamot & O'Malley, 1994, 231–232). For example, in some Spanish-speaking countries students are taught to use different problem-solving procedures (switching the position of the divisor and dividend in division problems) and math symbols (a period instead of a comma in numerals that are multiples of 1 thousand and a comma instead of a period for decimals). Chinese immigrant students may prefer to rely on the memorization of rules and formulas to achieve accuracy and speed (Tsang, cited in Chamot & O'Malley, 1994, 232). In addition, the units of U.S. measurement (e.g., feet, yards, pints, quarts, ounces, pounds) and the corresponding importance accorded to fractions may be problematic for students who grew up with the metric system as their norm.

To provide a better overview of what is demanded of students at various grade levels, the basic listening, speaking, reading, and writing skills associated with mathematics instruction for grades 1–3, 4–6, and 7–12 are presented in Table 9-1. These are useful both in identifying some of the more language-dependent areas in mathematics and in developing appropriate academic language activities.

To enhance the effectiveness of mathematics instruction for English language learners, teachers can also

- ensure that students understand the language in word problems and that they can generate the symbolic translations used in problem solving
- provide students with explicit instruction on the sequence of steps* required for problem solution and then with opportunities for guided practice on their use
- ask students to verbalize the steps involved in problem solution
- make learning strategies an integral part of the problem-solving process
- use small groups (three to four students) to provide feedback, supply relevant background information, model effective problem solving, verbalize problem-solving procedures, and enhance student responsibility for learning (Chamot & O'Malley, 1994, 233–238)
- incorporate video-disc-based math programs such as The Adventures of Jasper Woodbury (grades 5–6) (Optical Data Corp., Warren, NJ)

Science   Scientific literacy is defined as "the knowledge and understanding of scientific concepts and processes required for personal decision making, participation in civic and cultural affairs, and economic productivity" (National Research Council, 1996, 22). To achieve science literacy, instruction must emphasize both scientific processes and content. Methods of inquiry and discovery are essential to understanding and appreciating scientific concepts and generaliza-

---

* Not in investigative problem solving.

Table 9-1

Language skills: Mathematics

Skill	Grades 1–3	Grades 4–6	Grades 7–12
Listening			
Understanding explanations without concrete referents	○	◑	●
Understanding oral numbers	●	●	●
Understanding oral word problems	○	◑	◑
Reading			
Understanding specialized vocabulary	○	◑	●
Understanding explanations in textbook	○	◑	●
Reading mathematical notations and equations	○	◑	●
Understanding word problems	○	●	●
Speaking			
Answering questions	●	●	●
Asking for clarification	●	●	●
Explaining how the answer was derived	○	◑	●
Writing			
Writing verbal input numerically	◑	◑	◑

less emphasis ⟶ more emphasis

○   ◑   ●

Source: Chamot and O'Malley (1986, 45)

tions. "Science should be taught as a way of systematically inquiring into questions or observations, not just as a body of declarative knowledge to be memorized. By inquiring into science and 'doing' science, students develop the ability to think scientifically" (Hyde & Bizar, cited in Chamot & O'Malley, 1994, 198).

The language of science is as precise, technical, and specialized as that of mathematics. Two frequent problem areas for students relate to vocabulary (Chamot & O'Malley, 1986, 1994). The first is the way in which common words change meaning in scientific contexts. As in mathematics, nontechnical terms acquire a new and highly specialized meaning. For example, consider how the everyday meanings of the following words compare with their scientific counterparts: *reaction, plate, element, compound, system, fault, work,* and *crystal.* The second is the use of words with Greek and Latin roots and affixes. These are particularly difficult for students whose primary language is not based on Greek or Latin origins. Chamot and O'Malley provide a classic example of the language that students must contend with:

The members of the kingdom Monera, the prokaryotes, are identified on the basis of their unique cellular organization and biochemistry. Members of the kingdom Protista are single-celled eukaryotes, both autotrophs and heterotrophs. (Curtis & Barnes, cited in 1986, 24; 1994, 195)

Methods of inquiry and discovery are essential to understanding and appreciating scientific concepts and generalizations

The language of science is complicated by other factors as well. Hurd (1991) refers to the overload of unfamiliar words that students are required to learn. "In a typical science course today, students encounter three to five new terms per day—words they have never seen before, never heard pronounced" (p. 34). In this regard, English language learners are among those most likely to benefit from changes that are now taking place in science education. Whereas the overload of topics and vocabulary is still characteristic of many traditional science courses and textbooks, this emphasis is expected to diminish with full implementation of the *National Science Education Standards* (M. Korte, personal communication, 1996).

The structure of language in science texts is another factor for teachers to consider. Sentences are long and complicated, embeddings are frequent, and definitions often difficult to discern (Chamot & O'Malley, 1986, 1994). Features such as passive voice, long noun phrases used as subjects or objects in sentences, *if . . . then* constructions, and expressions of causality further contribute to making texts more difficult. As students progress through the grades, textbook language becomes increasingly dense and decontextualized (Chamot & O'Malley, 1986, 25; 1994, 195). This increasing complexity is illustrated by a count of the number of pages devoted to the topic of inherited traits in science texts at different levels: 8 pages on inherited traits in humans in the sixth grade text, 43 pages on human heredity in a junior high life science text, and 91 pages in high school biology (Chamot & O'Malley, 1994, 194).

Table 9-2 describes the language skills associated with science instruction for grades 1–3, 4–6, and 7–12. These illustrate the kinds of academic language that is required to deal with scientific information and provide direction for developing appropriate academic language activities.

Most teachers tend to regard the content they teach, particularly in areas such as science and mathematics, as basically "neutral" from a cultural perspective. We

Table 9-2 Language skills: Science

Skill	Grades 1–3	Grades 4–6	Grades 7–12
Listening			
Understanding explanations without concrete referents	○	◑	●
Understanding demonstrations	○	◑	●
Following directions for experiments	○	●	●
Listening for specific information	○	◑	●
Working with a partner on an experiment	◑	●	●
Reading			
Understanding specialized vocabulary	○	◑	●
Understanding information in textbook	○	◑	●
Finding information from graphs, charts, and tables	○	◑	●
Following directions for experiments	○	◑	●
Finding information in reference materials	○	◑	●
Speaking			
Answering questions	●	●	●
Asking for clarification	●	●	●
Participating in discussions	●	●	◑
Explaining and demonstrating a process	○	◑	◑
Working with a partner on an experiment	◑	●	●
Writing			
Writing answers to questions	○	●	●
Noting observations	○	◑	●
Describing experiments	○	◑	●
Writing reports	○	◑	●

less emphasis ────────────────→ more emphasis

○　　　　◑　　　　●

Source: Chamot and O'Malley (1986, 26)

know, however, that this is often not the case. Culture influences the way teachers and students conceptualize and interact with content, and science is no exception. *Ethnoscience* has been defined by Kessler and Quinn (1987, 61) as the informal theories and procedures accepted by people within a culture as accounting for natural phenomena. It is how people explain the physical world. Whereas the influence of ethnoscientific perspectives on science-related thinking processes is not well understood, it does appear that these beliefs can influence how children conceptualize their physical environment. Among the Cree and Objibway people, for example, plants and animals are classified by function and use (Smith, cited in Kessler & Quinn, 1987, 62). This contrasts with the formal scientific classification system based on structure that is used in the schools. "While children universally carry out the process of classification, the system of classification made available to them is arbitrary. The classification systems of ethnoscience and formal science in this case are both valid, just different" (Kessler & Quinn, 1987, 62). Another example is the way in which the color spectrum is divided across cultures. Although people across cultures actually see the same colors, their languages may arbitrarily divide the color spectrum at different points with labels that do not correspond exactly with what English defines as purple, blue, green, yellow, and so on (Brown, 1986). For example, "the Shona of Rhodesia and the Bassa of Liberia have fewer color categories than speakers of European languages" (Gleason, cited in Brown, 1986, 45).

To bridge cross-cultural differences, teachers must recognize how culture can affect a learner's view of the physical world. Using questions such as those from Saville-Troike (1978) as a starting point, teachers can learn to identify potential conflicts between ethnoscience and formal science. The following sets of questions are illustrative (pp. 19–34):

- *Health and hygiene.* Who or what is believed to cause illness or death? How are specific illnesses or injuries treated? By whom? To what extent do individuals utilize or accept contemporary medical practices by doctors and other health professionals? If a student were involved in an accident at school, would any of the common first-aid practices be unacceptable? Who teaches children about certain topics (e.g., sex education)? At what age? Can they be taught by either a male or female teacher? In mixed groups?

- *Food.* What is eaten? What foods are taboo? What medicinal uses are made of food or categories of food? What are taboos or prescriptions associated with the handling, offering, or discarding of food?

- *History and traditions.* How and to what extent does the group's knowledge of history coincide with or depart from scientific theories of creation, evolution, and historical development?

- *Education.* Are there different expectations by parents, teachers, and students with respect to different subjects (i.e., science, health)? For boys versus girls? Are there experiments/investigations that violate the group's religious beliefs and practices (e.g., dissection of frogs, using human bones in a science lesson)?

- *Natural phenomena.* What beliefs and practices are associated with the sun, moon, comets, and stars? Who or what is responsible for rain, lightning, thunder, earthquakes, droughts, floods, and hurricanes? Are particular behavioral prescriptions or taboos associated with natural phenomena? What sanctions are there against individuals violating restrictions or prescriptions? How and to what extent do the group's beliefs about natural phenomena coincide with or depart from scientific theories? To what extent are traditional group beliefs still held by individuals within the community?

- *Pets and other animals.* Which animals are valued and for what reasons? Which animals are considered appropriate as pets? Which are inappropriate and why? What attitudes are held toward individuals or groups with different beliefs about animals?

English language learners are also subject to the same naive misconceptions and misinformation that characterize the thinking of other students their age. "Young children think that sugar ceases to exist when it is dissolved in water, and adolescents frequently use weight to predict that a cube of aluminum will displace less liquid than a steel cube of equal volume (Carey, and Linn, cited in Chamot & O'Malley, 1994, 197). Chamot and O'Malley observe that these perceptions are often persistent and resistant to change, even when contradicted by scientific information. Among the instructional approaches most effective in promoting a deeper understanding of science are those in which students are engaged in activities that require predictions, metareasoning, discovery learning, and discussion. Such activities demand that students test their ideas, develop more sophisticated problem-solving strategies, and examine contradictions in their thinking as they explore scientific concepts (Chamot & O'Malley, 1994).

To enhance the effectiveness of science instruction for English language learners, teachers can also

- build science units around themes that enable students to see the relationship between principles and processes, treat high-priority content in depth, and promote the relevancy of science to students' lives
- examine students' prior knowledge of science concepts through brainstorming, semantic mapping, charts, and visual representations
- select science activities and materials that provide active involvement through hands-on experiences with scientific processes and experimentation
- provide opportunities for students to engage in activities that promote development of academic language through listening, discussion, reading, and writing
- incorporate instruction in learning strategies (Chamot & O'Malley, 1994, 198–205)

Social Studies   Social studies instruction draws upon learning experiences from diverse disciplines to promote civic competence (National Council for the Social Studies [NCSS], 1994, vii, ix). Three basic goals embody what it means to be literate in the social studies: (a) knowledge within and across disciplines (b) democratic concepts and civic values, and (c) skills in social participation, critical thinking, and academic study (Chamot & O'Malley, 1994; NCSS, 1994). To be powerful, social studies teaching and learning must be *meaningful, integrative, value-based, challenging,* and *active* (NCSS, 1994, 11–12).

Given the heavy demand placed on higher-level literacy skills and the often abstract nature of generalizations and concepts, academic language is essential both to conceptual understanding and experiential learning in the social studies. One salient characteristic of the language of social studies is the complexity of the abstract concepts and knowledge—historic, geographic, cultural, and civic—embodied in the vocabulary (Chamot & O'Malley, 1986, 1994). For example, *democracy* and *representation* are more than just terms; "they stand for a complex set of ideas developed from a philosophy of government" (Chamot & O'Malley, 1986, 68; 1994, 259). For English language learners from countries where the political system is very different (or for those lacking prior knowledge for other reasons), there may be no direct transfer from the primary language and culture for these concepts and others, such as *balance of power*, *Constitution*, and *the Bill of Rights*. As a result, texts that appear to be simple grammatically or syntactically are likely to be very complex conceptually. The following example makes the point very clearly.

> Federalism means the division of governmental powers between the national and state governments. Both levels of government may act directly on citizens through their own officials and laws. Both levels of government derive their power to act from our Constitution. Each level of government has certain subjects over which its powers are supreme. Both levels of government must agree to changes in the Constitution. (Maryland State Department of Education, cited in Chamot & O'Malley, 1986, 68; 1994, 259)

With respect to grammatical structure, three features are particularly troublesome for students (Chamot & O'Malley, 1986, 1994). The first involves the way that phrases and clauses are embedded in long sentences. English language learners learn to look for the subject and verb early in sentences. In social studies texts, however, lengthy phrases and clauses can keep students from getting to the "heart" of the sentence early. When this happens, it becomes more difficult for them to grasp the meaning of what is said. The frequent use of cause-and-effect statements further increases the difficulty level. Consider this example from a third-grade social studies text: "Because there will be more people in the world in the future, we will need more land on which to build towns and cities" (Buggey, cited in Chamot & O'Malley, 68).

A second problem area results from the manner in which temporal relationships are expressed. Not only are complex structures used, but shifts in time may be difficult to follow, as in this excerpt from a sixth grade text: "'I *found* Rome a city of bricks and *left* it a city of marble.' Augustus *is supposed to have spoken* these words as he *lay dying*. He *was* Rome's first emperor, and *started* the first of its great building programs. He *claimed* that he *had had* over 80 temples *rebuilt*" (Marvin, Marvin, & Cappelluti, cited in Chamot & O'Malley, 1986, 69; 1994, 260).

The third troublesome feature identified by Chamot and O'Malley is the use of *they* as a referent to people and *it* as a referent to an event, fact, or conclusion mentioned earlier in the text. At the beginning of a sentence, pronouns can be troublesome for less proficient readers who are unable to figure out what is referred to in the preceding text.

To assist teachers in developing appropriate academic language activities, Table 9-3 describes the language skills required in social studies for grades 1–3, 4–6, and 7–12.

To enhance the effectiveness of social studies instruction for English language learners, teachers can also

Table 9-3
Language skills: Social studies

Skill	Grades 1–3	Grades 4–6	Grades 7–12
Listening			
Understanding explanations	●	●	●
Listening for specific information	○	◐	●
Reading			
Understanding specialized vocabulary	○	◐	●
Understanding information in textbook	○	◐	●
Finding information from graphs, charts, and maps	○	◐	●
Using a flexible reading rate (skimming and scanning)	○	◐	●
Finding information in reference materials	○	◐	●
Speaking			
Answering questions	●	●	●
Asking for clarification	●	●	●
Participating in discussions	●	◐	◐
Presenting oral reports	○	◐	●
Writing			
Writing answers to questions	○	●	●
Labeling maps, graphs, and charts	●	◐	○
Writing reports	○	◐	●

less emphasis ——————————————→ more emphasis
○   ◐   ●

Source: Chamot and O'Malley (1986, 70)

- build social studies lessons around content objectives that integrate conceptual learning with practical application
- build social studies lessons around content objectives that address thinking skills at various levels
- examine students' prior knowledge of social studies concepts
- provide opportunities for students to engage in activities that promote development of academic language specifically related to social studies topics while providing contextual support for learning abstract content (e.g., posters, maps, charts, models, illustrations, timelines, globes, films, videos, simulations, recordings, etc.).
- incorporate instruction in learning strategies associated with reading, vocabulary, listening, and reporting (Chamot & O'Malley, 1994, 263–270)

Summary

Making the curriculum accessible to second language learners is essential if language minority students are to achieve academically. Teachers must be able to provide content-area instruction that is language-sensitive and promotes academic competence. To this end, content needs to be academically demanding, while instruction promotes higher-level thinking. Students must have opportunities to interact with oral and written texts that are authentic and with materials, tasks, and curriculum that are relevant, stimulating, and coherent. Learning should be interactive, experiential, theme-based, and learner centered. In the final analysis, it should also facilitate the mutual acculturation process encompassed within multiculturation.

Language-sensitive instruction bridges language and content. Teachers can make use of generic strategies to make instruction more comprehensible. Instruction can be enhanced in many ways. Teachers can (a) simplify the language of instruction, (b) provide contextualization, (c) check for understanding, (d) promote communication, (e) employ techniques that enhance instruction, and (f) adapt instructional materials. Understanding the nature of academic language in specific subjects also contributes to the development of strategies that foster academic competence.

References

Adamson, H. D. (1993). *Academic competence: Theory and classroom practice: Preparing ESL students for content courses.* White Plains, NY: Longman.

Barell, J. (1991). *Teaching for thoughtfulness: Classroom strategies to enhance intellectual development.* White Plains, NY: Longman.

Berliner, D. (1990). *Research on teaching: Insight and promising direction.* Lecture presented at California State University, Chico.

Biederman, P. W. (1987, December 13). New tool in teaching the non-fluent. *Los Angeles Times.*

Bolinger, D. (1975). *Aspects of language.* New York: Harcourt Brace Jovanovich.

Brinton, D. M., Snow, M. A., & Wesche, M. B. (1989). *Content-based second language instruction.* New York: Newbury House.

Brown, H. D. (1986). Learning a second culture. In J. M. Valdés (Ed.), *Culture bound* (pp. 33–48). New York: Cambridge University Press.

Cantoni-Harvey, G. (1987). *Content-area language instruction.* Reading, MA: Addison-Wesley.

Chamot, A. U., & O'Malley, J. M. (1986). *A cognitive academic language learning approach: An ESL content-based curriculum.* Wheaton, MD: National Clearinghouse for Bilingual Education.

Chamot, A. U., & O'Malley, J. M. (1994). *The CALLA handbook.* Reading, MA: Addison-Wesley.

Chan, J., & Chips, B. (1989). Helping LEP students survive in the content-area classroom. *Thrust, 18*(6), 49–51.

Chips, B. (1987). The sheltered classroom—Tips for implementation. In F. Encinias, M. Martini, L. Mendez, S. Milesi-Davidson, C. Petzar, & T. Marinez (Eds.) *Methodology for the bilingual classroom* (Bilingual Teacher Training Program Manual). Riverside, CA: Riverside County Office of Education.

Cohen, A. D. (1990). *Language learning*. New York: Newbury House.

Cortés, C. E. (1990). E pluribus unum: Out of many one. *California perspectives: An anthology from the immigrant students project* (Vol. 1, pp. 13–16). San Francisco: California Tomorrow.

Cummins, J. (1989). *Empowering minority students*. Sacramento: California Association for Bilingual Education.

Cummins, J. (1992). Language proficiency, bilingualism, and academic achievement. In P. A. Richard-Amato & M. A. Snow (Eds.), *The multicultural classroom: Readings for content-area teachers* (pp. 16–26). White Plains, NY: Longman.

Cummins, J. (1996). Primary language instruction and the education of language minority students. *Schooling and language minority students: A theoretical framework* (2nd ed.) (pp. 3–46). Los Angeles: Evaluation, Dissemination and Assessment Center, School of Education, California State University, Los Angeles.

Dale, T. C., & Cuevas, G. J. (1987). Integrating language and mathematics learning. In J. Crandall (Ed.), *ESL through content-area instruction: Mathematics, science, social studies* (pp. 9–54). Englewood Cliffs, NJ: Prentice Hall Regents.

Dale, T. C., & Cuevas, G. J. (1992). Integrating language and mathematics learning. In P. A. Richard-Amato & M. A. Snow (Eds.), *The multicultural classroom: Readings for content-area teachers* (pp. 330–348). White Plains, NY: Longman.

Enright, D. S., & McCloskey, M. L. (1988). *Integrating English: Developing English language and literacy in the multilingual classroom*. Reading, MA: Addison-Wesley.

Hernández, H. (1992). The language minority student and multicultural education. In C. A. Grant (Ed.). *Research and multicultural education: From the margins to the mainstream* (pp. 141–152). London: Falmer Press.

Hernández, H., & Metzger, D. (1996). Issues-education for language minority students. In R. W. Evans & D. W. Saxe (Eds.), *Handbook on issues-centered education*. National Council for the Social Studies.

Hurd, P. D. (1991). Why we must transform science education. *Educational Leadership, 49*(2), 33–35.

Ittelson, L. (1989). Handout in guest presentation for EDUC 236 Introduction to Multicultural Education, California State University, Chico.

Kessler, C., & Quinn, M. E. (1987). ESL and science learning. In J. Crandall (Ed.), *ESL through content-area instruction: Mathematics, science, social studies* (pp. 55–87). Englewood Cliffs, NJ: Prentice Hall Regents.

Levine, L. N. (1985). Content area instruction for the elementary school ESL student. In P. Larson, E. L. Judd, & D. S. Messerschmitt (Eds.), *On TESOL '84: A brave new world for TESOL* (pp. 233-240). Washington, DC: Teachers of English to Speakers of Other Languages.

Mesa, R. P. (1986). Barriers to academic success for language minority students. In H. Mehan, H. T. Trueba, & C. Underwood (Eds.), *1985 Proceedings of the Linguistic Minority Project Conference: Vol. 2. Schooling Language Minority Youth* (pp. 60–65). Berkeley: University of California Linguistic Minority Project.

Mohan, B. A. (1986). *Language and content*. Reading, MA: Addison-Wesley.

Nation, I. S. P. (1990). *Teaching and learning vocabulary*. New York: Newbury House.

National Council for the Social Studies. (1994). *Curriculum standards for the social studies*. Washington, DC: Author.

National Council of Teachers of Mathematics, Commission on Standards for School Mathematics. (1989). *Curriculum and evaluation standards for school mathematics*. Reston, VA: Author.

National Research Council. (1996). *National science education standards.* Washington, DC: National Academy Press.

Olsen, L., & Mullen, N. A. (1990). *Embracing diversity* (California Tomorrow Immigrant Students Project Research Report). San Francisco: California Tomorrow.

Richard-Amato, P.A., & Snow, M. A. (Eds.) (1992). *The multicultural classroom: Readings for content-area teachers.* White Plains, NY: Longman.

Richard-Amato, P.A., & Snow, M. A. (1992). Strategies for content-area teachers. In P. A. Richard-Amato & M. A. Snow (Eds.), *The multicultural classroom: Readings for content-area teachers* (pp. 145–163). White Plains, NY: Longman.

Saechao, Y. (1991, Fall). Immigrant interview, course assignment in Education 236, Introduction to Multicultural Education. Unpublished manuscript.

Sánchez, F. (1989). *What is sheltered instruction?* (Pamphlet available from Alameda County Office of Education, Hayward, CA.)

Saville-Troike, M. (1978). *A guide to culture in the classroom.* Rosslyn, VA: National Clearinghouse for Bilingual Education.

Short, D. J. (1992). Adapting materials and developing lesson plans. In P. A. Richard-Amato & M. A. Snow (Eds.), *The multicultural classroom: Readings for content-area teachers* (pp. 145-163). White Plains, NY: Longman.

Wong Fillmore, L., & Valadez, C. (1986). Teaching bilingual learners. In M. C. Wittrock (Ed.), *Handbook of research on teaching* (3rd ed., pp. 648–685). New York: Macmillan.

P A R T

5 In the Final Analysis

10

Assessment and Evaluation

Education is not preparation for life;
education is life itself.

attributed to John Dewey

The conceptualizations of teaching and learning presented throughout this text represent a departure from some traditional views of curriculum and instruction. Changing theoretical views of language, learning, and cognition have replaced the notion that knowledge is an accumulation of factual information, a commodity that is transmitted through the process of education (García & Pearson, 1994, 337–338). Rather, contemporary theory and research view knowledge as

> the residual outcome of the process that occurs when learners construct meaningful interpretations of the data that they encounter in their transactions with the world and with other learners. Learning, along with the traditional linguistic concepts of comprehension and composition, is synonymous with constructing meaning. (p. 338)

By their very nature, these conceptualizations invite concomitant changes in how language and learning are assessed and how programs for English language learners are designed.

After completing this chapter, you will be able to

1. consider cultural and linguistic diversity issues involved in assessing learner outcomes
2. employ assessment practices that are consistent with contemporary theoretical views of language, learning, and cognition
3. examine the essential characteristics of schools that empower language minority students
4. do a self-assessment of program characteristics relevant to serving English language learners at your own school

Assessment

Educators are looking for new and different ways to "evaluate how students approach, pursue, and interpret meaning construction and problem-solving tasks" (García & Pearson, 1994, 338). As teachers search for their own answers, they need to be aware of problems with existing measures and approaches and cognizant of alternative assessment practices and their potential advantages and disadvantages. This section will focus on both of these areas.

Formal Assessment

In their extensive review of research on assessment and diversity, García and Pearson (1994) examine formal and informal, or alternative, forms of assessment. Well through the decade, formal tests continue to be defined by the standard of "a norm-referenced, multiple-choice test that samples performance or achievement in a well-defined curricular domain" (p. 341). These tests reflect bias with respect to norming, content, language, and culture. García and Pearson confirm what many teachers have learned through experience: that there are differences in how certain groups of students perform on formal tests (p. 340). Ethnic, gender, and class differences are consistently reflected in the outcomes. For example, African American, Latino, and Native American students and students whose primary language is other than English do not perform as well on formal tests as do other students. Two moderating factors—income and proficiency in standard English—appear to account for a significant portion of the discrepancy. Even Asian American students, who tend to excel on tests in mathematics, do not fare well on verbal measures. Teachers should also know that "the greater the use of a non-English language in the home, the lower the predictive validity of some of the most well known and respected psychometric instruments of mental ability" (Figueroa & García, 1994, 17).

Whereas many factors influence the test performance of students from diverse backgrounds, those related to language and culture are of special concern to teachers in multilingual classrooms. Years of research have revealed that "the bilingual is an integrated whole which cannot be decomposed into two separate parts. The bilingual is NOT the sum of two complete or incomplete monolinguals, rather, he or she has a unique and specific linguistic configuration. The coexistence and constant interaction of the two languages in the bilingual has produced a different but complete linguistic entity" (Grosjean, cited in Figueroa & García, 16). In reality, "it is almost impossible for a formal test to capture what bilingual students know in their two languages" (García, cited in García & Pearson, 1994, 347). The reason is simple. Formal language tests do not adequately capture the ways in which students acquire and use both languages (García & Pearson, 1994). As a result, English language tests appear to be rather insensitive measures of the content and strategic knowledge of bilingual students. The issue is more involved than deciding which language to use in testing, sometimes a difficult determination to make. Translating tests from one language to another is not a solution, because simple translation does not produce equivalence.

Bilingual students appear to do better when they are able to draw on the resources provided by both languages. García and Pearson cite research that suggests that bilingual students demonstrate greater comprehension of text in the target language when they are also permitted to use their primary language (be it English, Spanish, Navajo, Samoan, or Arabic) on an assessment task (p. 349). "Bilingual students frequently will demonstrate greater learning if they are allowed to choose their preferred language of response: their native language, English, or both" (p. 362). This option is the exception rather than the rule in formal assessment.

Other factors also affect the performance of students from diverse linguistic and cultural backgrounds (García & Pearson, 1994). One of the biggest problems for students is "speededness"—the inability to complete tests within time allocations. García's own work corroborates other research indicating that bilinguals require more time than monolinguals to process either of their two languages, and, not surprisingly, that they read more slowly in their second or weaker language. "Not only is the process potentially slower, it is also more amenable to blockage due to stress, task complexity or noise" (Figueroa & García, 1994, 17). When time limits for examinations are adjusted to the needs of monolingual students, bilingual students may be denied an opportunity to proceed at what would be a comparable pace for them. This is a disadvantage for high school and college students as well as for younger learners. There are broader social implications as well. Standardized tests

> reward the person who, by ability or inclination, reads and answers rapidly, and they punish individuals who read, decide and generally act in slow, careful, deliberative, methodical ways. Because so much of real life requires the latter traits, not the former ones, . . . the tests disadvantage people who possess the very traits that life often demands. (Velvel, 1993, 4)

Another set of problems that students encounter involves vocabulary (García & Pearson, 1994). On multiple-choice tests, for example, students are likely to encounter English vocabulary that is uncommon, yet critical for understanding. Knowing the correct answer is not enough if the student is unable to find the appropriate meaning among a series of distractors in a test item. The use of synonyms and paraphrases with unfamiliar terms or vocabulary whose nuances or connotations are obscure to second language students contributes to misinterpretations of text passages, questions, and distractors (p. 348).

Finally, G. Spindler and L. Spindler (1994) describe what happens from an anthropological perspective. Beyond test content and the correctness of answers, students may not grasp, perceive, or internalize the cultural complex upon which testing is predicated.

> Minority children often fail to acquire instrumental competence in test taking. The importance of tests in Anglo-oriented schools is not appreciated. The skills and motivations necessary for getting one's control of the content to be tested up (and then letting it drop); the significance of time in testing; and the need for hurry and tensed, focused excitement (even anxiety)—the whole pervasive complex of configurations of test-taking in our schools—is not understood nor are the motivations for meritorious performance under the imposed and quite artificial conditions of test-taking present. (p. 24)

Generally speaking, teachers are advised to be cautious in administering and using the results of formal, English-only tests administered to language minority students (Cohen, 1987; Cummins, 1984; Figueroa, cited in García & Pearson, 1994; García & Pearson, 1994). There is ample reason for concern. First, Figueroa reminds teachers that "we still do not know the optimal stage of second-language development at which to begin testing second-language students only in English" (cited in García & Pearson, 1994, 352). Teachers can only speculate as to how many of the language minority students currently being tested in English have actually attained the level of proficiency required to assess their performance fairly and accurately. This is especially true with respect to English language achievement scores. According to Figueroa, there is a "consistent discrepancy between low verbal IQ scores and high performance IQ scores of all bilingual populations, including Asian Americans": "To place too much stock in such [English language achievement] scores is to open the door to faulty inferences, misunderstandings, and decisions with negative consequences" (García & Pearson, 1994, 352).

Second, teachers are advised that standardized tests exert disproportionate curricular influence on instruction for low-income students (García & Pearson, 1994). It seems that teachers in low-income settings feel more pressure to "teach to the test" (p. 355). For example, federal eligibility and evaluation guidelines for compensatory programs such as Chapter 1 promote greater use of formal tests. In a survey of teachers in classrooms comprising primarily Chapter 1 students, teachers reported greater emphasis on testing, more changes in instructional planning to accommodate features of the test, more classroom time devoted to test preparation, and less on nontested subjects and skills. In a study involving 2,200 mathematics and science teachers, the teachers most likely to teach to the test were those in low-income settings (Center for the Study of Testing, Evaluation, and Educational Policy, and Rothman, cited in García & Pearson, 1994, 355). Commenting on the impact of high-stakes standardized testing in math and science, Madaus (1993) describes this as a "double whammy" for classrooms with large numbers of minority students. "They're being drilled extensively to get over the testing hurdle, but the tests really aren't measuring what the mathematics education community says is important" (p. 48).

Finally, "to say that tests will not be used to impede the progress of students of color is to deny the history of their use" (García & Pearson, 1994, 349). That testing and assessment is replete with educational equity issues is well documented (e.g., Cohen, 1987; Velvel, 1993; Wiggins, 1989). Looking to the future, Calfee (1993) cautions against efforts to achieve higher standards of educational achievement through externally mandated standardized tests based on uniform national standards. If these efforts are not based upon standards for curriculum, instruction, and schools, teachers and students will be doomed to duplicate the patterns of the last quarter-century.

> Only a minuscule proportion of students will attain the highest standards of educational achievement. They will be the children of the well-to-do, mainly from mostly white, English-only neighborhoods. Middle-class children will occupy the middle category. Because the middle class is shrinking, the proportion of students in this category will diminish. Students from depressed inner-city neighborhoods, from isolated rural areas, from the families of ethnic and linguistic minorities—the children of the poor—will be disproportionately represented in the bottom category. Because these children are increasing relative to the first two categories, national achievement will decline—further evidence that schools are failing their assignment. (p. 65)

Even alternative assessment practices (e.g., performance-based assessment) will fail to promote educational equity if they do not influence and support strong curriculum and effective teaching (Wolf, 1993, 78). Along similar lines, Figueroa and García (1994) assert that "authentic assessments must hold the instructional setting accountable and must also assess its impact on the learner" (p. 18). As an example, Herman and Winters's (1994) analysis of the limited research currently available on portfolio assessment indicates that findings thus far favor its use. "Well-designed portfolios represent important, contextualized learning that requires complex thinking and expressive skills" (p. 4). However, they caution that portfolio assessment has yet to be subjected to rigorous investigation of the technical quality necessary to support its efficacy as an assessment tool and its potential benefits for diverse populations.

Alternative Assessment

The term *alternative assessment* encompasses less traditional forms of assessment, such as authentic classroom assessment and performance assessment (García & Pearson, 1994). For purposes of this discussion, authentic classroom assessment is defined as focused upon student performance, oriented to classroom curriculum, and teacher designed and evaluated. Performance assessment, whether teacher developed or externally imposed, focuses directly or indirectly on performance. As García and Pearson observe, the usefulness of information generated through this type of assessment is contingent upon the quality and implementation of the classroom curriculum itself (pp. 355–357; 359).

Research on cultural, linguistic, and economic diversity provides teachers with some insights as to what assessment should offer students in multilingual classrooms (García & Pearson, 1994). Ideally, assessment would (a) allow the use of a wide variety of methods to assess and diagnose students displaying diverse styles of learning and thinking, (b) encourage building on cultural adaptations and reflect on cultural values, and (c) document what students know and can do in both languages. These, in turn, complement other criteria, such as the factors identified for authentic assessment of intellectual performance (Wiggins, 1993). The factors identified by Wiggins are consistent with the alternative assessment practices described in this discussion. They are summarized in Figure 10-1.

In working with second language learners, teachers will want to use multiple sources of information to evaluate student progress in language and academic development. As an assessment tool, portfolios exemplify one approach consistent with what Cummins (1989) describes as an interactive/experiential pedagogical orientation in which "thinking is manifested through active use of oral and written language for collaborative exploration of issues and resolution of the *real* problems that form the curriculum. . . . [T]he primary focus is on *process* rather than transmission of content" (p. 75). Portfolios enable teachers to observe student growth over time. They can also be used effectively to involve the learner as an active participant in the process (not just as the "subject" of evaluation efforts).

Mumme (1991) and Farr and Tone (1994) offer insights on the use of portfolios in evaluating language skills and content area performance (i.e., mathematics). In a content area, *portfolios*—to use Mumme's definition—represent a deliberate collection of work used to provide evidence of understanding and accomplishments. This includes everything from critical thinking and attitudes to the student's ability to express ideas and use language. The emphasis is on the student's productive work, that is, what the learner can do, not what he or she is unable to do. This is crucial if students are to develop confidence in their ability "to do mathematics." The documentation it provides is also invaluable in communicating with parents regarding student progress.

- *Problems/Questions* are engaging, worthy, and important. They demand that students use knowledge effectively and creatively.
- *Contexts* represent situations encountered in the field of study or in real life. Options, constraints, and access to resources are appropriate to the task rather than arbitrarily determined.
- *Tasks* are nonroutine and multistage. They are real problems that demand the ability to use a repertoire of knowledge, judgment, and skill.
- *Quality* in students' products and/or performance is required.
- *Criteria/Standards* are clear and explicit. This enables students to prepare, self-assess and self-adjust, as well as to discuss and clarify tasks and questions with teacher and/or peers.
- *Interaction* between student and teacher is embedded in the task (e.g., by asking the learner to justify responses and then address follow-up questions).
- *Judgment* on evaluation is based upon criteria that are clear and appropriate.
- *Patterns of response* emerge as students grapple with different aspects of situations. These reflect consistency that allows for "the assessment of *habits* of mind in performance." (p. 207)

Figure 10-1   Criteria for judging test authenticity
Source: Wiggins (1993, 206–207)

In mathematics education, Mumme (1991) sees a shift taking place in which the curriculum is moving away from emphasizing knowledge of facts and algorithms to stressing an understanding of mathematics. She describes what happens when students become "mathematically powerful" (p. 2):

- Student work reflects both collaboration and independent effort.

- Students are active learners (e.g., they investigate, analyze, evaluate, explore, invent, organize, predict, and visualize).

- Students apply their understanding of mathematics from different areas (e.g., geometry, measurement, algebra, and statistics).

- Students employ a variety of tools and techniques (e.g., computers, calculators, manipulatives).

- Students are able to communicate orally and in writing with different audiences and for different purposes (e.g., graphically, symbolically).

- Students develop and reflect attitudes such as curiosity, appreciation, confidence, and persistence). (pp. 2–3)

One reason for the power of portfolios is the degree to which the student can control or provide input in the assessment process. Farr and Tone (1994) contrast multiple-choice tests, performance, and portfolio assessment. Of the three, portfolio assessment has the potential to maximize student options and control over important factors, including topic, criteria for success, time, resources, collaboration, response, and question-and-response options (p. 10).

Assessment provides a picture of student growth and accomplishments on an ongoing basis.

The content of portfolios can effectively reflect the type of learning emphasized by the pedagogical changes that are taking place within mathematics and in other areas. Portfolios may include a wide variety of pieces. Mumme lists such items as written work (including journal excerpts, explanations, reflections on the portfolio itself); individual and group work; rough drafts and finished products; projects and investigations; diagrams, graphs, and charts; photographs of student work that does not fit in a portfolio; audio- and videotapes of student explanations and presentations; computer printouts and disks; and samples of work done at different times dealing with the same mathematical concept. These may be in English or the primary language. As these possibilities suggest, what actually goes into a portfolio is determined by the purpose (p. 5).

In making their own determination, teachers (perhaps in consultation with their students) will have to address questions such as What is the function of the portfolio? Who is the audience? Which aspects of the student's learning are to be assessed? What specific outcomes—knowledge, thinking, skill, process, product—are to be evidenced in the portfolio? How will materials be selected? What criteria will be used to evaluate the portfolio? How will self-reflection be incorporated? (Mumme, 1991; Stiggins, 1994).

Other strategies for monitoring student learning include student observation, conferences, projects, demonstrations, and exhibitions (Powell, Zehm, & García, 1995). Observation—even if only anecdotal records kept on the margins of a record book—can provide useful information as to how assessment strategies are working and how well students are learning. Regularly scheduled parent conferences offer an opportunity for parents and teachers to share observations and assessments of learning, particularly at the elementary level. Teachers conferencing with students provides similar opportunities with individual learners at all levels. Finally, students can reveal their ability to apply knowledge and skills and demonstrate creativity, responsibility, and initiative through performance on projects, demonstrations, and exhibitions (pp. 193–194).

Empowering Students

How to empower language minority students is a critical question for educators (Ruiz, 1991). Four school characteristics stand out as particularly critical in determining the degree of academic success of minority students (Cummins, 1986, 1989). The extent to which students are empowered or disempowered through schooling depends in part upon how educators see their role in relation to cultural and linguistic incorporation, community participation, pedagogy, and assessment. In this section, the focus is on these critical areas and their implications for teachers in multilingual classrooms.

Cultural and Linguistic Incorporation

According to Cummins (1989), a significant predictor of academic success for second language learners is the extent to which language and culture are incorpo-

Student work included in portfolios reflects both collaboration and independent effort.

rated into the school program. "Educators who see their role as adding a second language and cultural affiliation to students' repertoire are likely to empower students more than those who see their role as replacing or assimilating them to the dominant culture" (p. 61).

Schools can support primary language development in significant ways even when bilingual and heritage language programs are not feasible options. The following set of questions is based upon suggestions from the New Zealand Department of Education (cited in Cummins, 1989, 61).

- Does the school reflect the variety of cultural groups it serves by posting signs in the main office and other visible locations welcoming people in the different languages used within the community?

- Are students encouraged to use their primary language at school?

- Are there opportunities for students from the same ethnic group to interact with each other using their primary language (e.g., in selected cooperative learning activities)?

- Does the school recruit individuals who are able to tutor students in their primary language?

- Does the school provide books in different languages for use in the classroom and library?

- Does the school use the students' languages to convey information in newsletters and other official communications?

- Does the school provide signs that are bilingual and/or multilingual?

- Are pictures and objects representing the students' cultures on display?

- Do units of work incorporate languages other than English?

- Are students encouraged to submit written contributions for school newspapers and magazines in their primary language?

- Are there opportunities for students to study their primary language (e.g., in elective classes, through extracurricular clubs)?

- Are parents encouraged to assist in classrooms, in the library, on the playground, or through club activities?

- Are second language learners encouraged to use their primary language during assemblies, award ceremonies, and other official school functions?

- Are members of ethnic minority communities invited to serve as resource people and to meet with students formally and informally?

What do the answers to these questions tell you about your school? What steps are being taken to support primary language development and incorporate culture in your school program? What changes might you and other teachers at your school suggest?

Community Participation

When parents are treated as partners in the process of educating their children, the sense of efficacy they develop is conveyed to the children. This is then reflected in the children's academic achievement (Cummins, 1989). Not all forms of parent involvement and community participation are equal. The forms of parent involvement and community participation that are ineffective and even detrimental are those characterized by exclusion rather than collaboration. Teachers whose efforts are misguided are described as follows: "[They] tend to regard teaching as *their* job and are likely to view collaboration with minority parents as either irrelevant or actually detrimental to children's progress. Often parents are viewed as part of the problem since they interact through L1 with their children at home" (p. 63).

The forms of parent involvement that are effective are characterized by collaboration. Cummins cites a study conducted in the Haringey area of London's inner city as one example of how minority parents and teachers can work together effectively. In the two-year project, children's reading skills improved significantly when the children participated in a shared literacy program, reading aloud to their parents regularly at home. Many of the parents were not proficient in English, some were illiterate in their native languages (mainly Bengali and Greek). The students sharing this literacy experience with their parents outperformed another group of children working directly with a competent reading specialist. What makes this type of participation effective is that parents and teachers communicate and work closely together in a spirit of mutual respect (p. 62).

Pedagogy

Instruction that empowers students does so by promoting independent learning that enables them to "become active generators of their own knowledge" (Cummins, 1989, 63). Unlike the traditional pedagogical model that relies on teacher transmission of knowledge through highly controlled interaction with students, an empowerment model is interactive and experiential. It is based on the premise that "talking and writing are means to learning" (Bullock Report, cited in Cummins, 1989, 64). Instruction for which the answers to the following questions are "yes" would be consistent with such an empowerment model because students are encouraged "to assume greater control over setting their own learning goals and to collaborate actively with each other in achieving these goals" (p. 64).

- Is there real dialogue between student and teacher through oral and written modalities?
- Does the teacher guide and facilitate rather than control student learning?
- Is student-student talk in cooperative learning activities encouraged?
- Is there an emphasis on meaningful language use rather than correctness of form?

- Are language development and subject matter content treated in isolation or are they well integrated?
- Is there greater emphasis on higher-level thinking skills than factual recall?
- Does the way that tasks are presented promote intrinsic rather than extrinsic motivation? (adapted from Cummins, 1989, 64)

It is not possible to achieve a true multicultural orientation within a transmission model of pedagogy. "Transmission models exclude, and therefore, effectively suppress, students' experiences. Consequently, these teacher-centered approaches do not allow for validation of minority students' experiences in the classroom" (Cummins, 1989, 65). The interactive/experiential model is "culture-fair," since students are active participants in learning—"expressing, sharing, and amplifying their experience[s] within the classroom" (p. 65). Through involvement, learning becomes "an *active* process that is enhanced through *interaction*" (p. 65).

Assessment

Assessment based on traditional psychoeducational models disables minority students (Cummins, 1986, 1989). In a study he conducted, Cummins found that "although no diagnostic conclusions were logically possible in the majority of assessments, psychologists were most reluctant to admit this fact to teachers and parents" (1989, 66). There appears to be little reluctance, however, when it comes to attributing academic "problems" to the existence of presumed cognitive deficits and disabilities in language minority students. "This has had the effect of screening from critical scrutiny the subtractive nature of the school program, the exclusionary orientation of teachers towards minority communities, and transmission models of teaching that suppress students' experience and inhibit them from active participation in learning" (1989, 65). Over many decades, this "legitimization" of language as a deficit or disability has significantly contributed to the view of "language-as-problem" referred to earlier.

To counter this approach, psychologists and special educators can adopt an advocacy orientation. By becoming children's advocates they move beyond the narrow constraints of traditional psychoeducational assessment to develop a broader conceptual framework for assessment, one that considers the learning environment as a whole (Cummins, 1986, 1989). This would entail "scrutinizing critically the social and educational context within which the child has developed" (1989, 66). The scope of assessment would expand considerably.

> Assessment must focus on the extent to which children's language and culture are incorporated within the school program, the extent to which educators collaborate with parents in a shared enterprise, and the extent to which children are encouraged to use language (both L1 and L2) actively within the classroom to amplify their experiences in interaction with other children and adults. In other words, the primary focus should be on remediating the educational interactions that minority children experience. (p. 66)

Clearly, the link between pedagogy and assessment is an important one.

Program Goals, Design, and Self-Assessment

From a programmatic perspective, the goals for language minority students in multilingual classrooms can be defined in relation to the basic purposes of language proficiency—personal, social, and educational (California State Department of Education [CDE], 1990b, 1990c). Simply stated, program planning and implementation efforts must recognize students' need to communicate, to fully develop literacy skills, to acquire knowledge in the content areas, and to develop higher-level thinking skills. In the process of developing native-like levels of language proficiency, students will also learn to build bridges linking the languages and cultures of home and school.

> [The] program must portray linguistic and cultural diversity as positive elements in our society and reflect sensitivity to the experiences of limited-English-proficient students in their new environments. The instructional program should promote the importance of bilingualism and provide ample opportunities for students to succeed and demonstrate confidence and self-esteem in both English-speaking settings and in their primary language environment. (Curriculum Development and Supplemental Materials Commission, 1991, 2)

In designing programs that empower students in achieving these goals, teachers will also take into account *need, access,* and *quality* (CATESOL Position Statement, 1990). As we have seen, there is tremendous diversity within and among language minority populations and a corresponding range of educational needs. For example, students differ with respect to factors such as age; cultural and linguistic background; exposure to and knowledge of English; use of English in the home, school, and community; previous formal education; and, for immigrant and refugee populations, number of years in the United States. It follows that their needs in the classroom also will vary considerably. Providing a quality education requires that students have access to basic program components and receive appropriate evaluation, daily English language development instruction, and academically and linguistically appropriate content area instruction. Learners must develop both communicative and academic language skills. Critical thinking—including the affective and interactive dimensions of intellectual development—is also crucial.

How the goals are translated into an effective program is a basic issue for teachers in multilingual classrooms. Through research and evaluation studies, the features of effective language programs have been identified (e.g., CDE, 1985, 1990a, 1990b, 1990c). The problem is putting what educators know into practice. For example, Minicucci and Olsen (1993) report that at the secondary level, "only six out of 27 schools surveyed offer a full core program to LEP students. Over half of the high schools and one-third of the intermediate schools have major gaps in their offerings or no content offerings. This means that many California LEP students are not enrolled in required academic core content subjects. This serious lack of access limits their possibilities of high school graduation, further education, and career opportunities" (p. 18).

The self-assessment guidelines for multilingual classrooms in Figure 10-2 help teachers to identify a variety of program gaps—gaps in curriculum, instruction, school environment, parent and community involvement, communication between home and school, staff development, assessment, and auxiliary support. The questions represent a distillation of program characteristics drawn from different sources. They consolidate areas explored throughout the text, highlight many of the features that consistently emerge in the literature, and suggest important areas to be considered as part of a program evaluation. Recognizing the features of effective programs will enable teachers to transform insights into action—identifying a program's strengths and weaknesses and making plans to address the needs that emerge as most critical.

Teachers can use these questions to identify those areas that may be regarded as particular strengths and then to target aspects of a program that can and should be made more effective. Attention can also be focused on those features that are not presently incorporated in an existing program. Based upon this analysis, specific plans can be developed for making a program more effective (CDE, 1985).

Teaching in Multilingual Classrooms

It seems apropos to conclude this final chapter by reflecting one last time on good teaching. Teaching in multilingual classrooms is about good teaching just as it is in any classroom. In essence, good teaching is the kind of teaching that transcends grade level and subject area, language, culture, and socioeconomic class (Haberman, 1991). This message has been conveyed repeatedly and in different ways throughout the book.

Looking into your classroom, an observer of multilingual classrooms is likely to see good teaching

- Whenever students are involved with issues they regard as vital concerns . . .
- Whenever students are involved with explanations of human differences . . .
- Whenever students are being helped to see major concepts, big ideas, and general principles and are not merely engaged in the pursuit of isolated facts . . .
- Whenever students are involved in planning what they will be doing . . .
- Whenever students are involved with applying ideals such as fairness, equity, or justice to their world . . .
- Whenever students are actively involved . . .
- Whenever students are directly involved in a real-life experience . . .
- Whenever students are actively involved in heterogeneous groups . . .
- Whenever students are asked to think about an idea in a way that questions common sense or a widely accepted assumption, that relates new ideas to ones learned previously, or that applies an idea to the problems of living . . .
- Whenever students are involved in re-doing, polishing, or perfecting their work . . .
- Whenever teachers involve students with the technology of information access . . .
- Whenever students are involved in reflecting on their own lives and how they have come to believe and feel as they do. (Haberman, 1991, 293–294)

Curriculum

Does the program
- communicate its goals clearly to students, staff, and community?
- describe different levels of language competency in writing?
- monitor student progress in relation to program and lesson objectives?
- maintain high expectations and standards consistently across classrooms?
- take into account students' needs and expectations?
- enable students to make a smooth transition from one level or school to another?
- provide instructional materials that are age-appropriate and suitable for students' English proficiency levels?
- provide printed materials characterized by authentic language and situations?
- provide a variety of language experiences using different types of technology (e.g., videos, films, computers)?
- meaningfully relate English language development to the academic core curriculum?
- relate English language development to a broader language arts curriculum (elementary)?
- provide literate non-English speakers access to the core curriculum through instruction and materials in their primary language?
- integrate significant content representing all of the cultures in the district?

Instruction

Does the program
- view ESL/bilingual instruction as developmental rather than remedial or deficit oriented?
- provide teachers flexibility in choosing instructional methods?
- utilize a variety of approaches that are appropriate to students' age, language levels, and communicative needs?
- frequently provide activities that are student centered and activity based?
- use methods and materials that promote self-confidence and self-esteem?
- regard grammar and other components of language learning as means to enhance students' abilities to communicate in the second language rather than as ends in themselves?
- provide communicative language tasks organized around frequently used language functions having broad applications in many situations?
- promote oral language proficiency through a variety of group and individual listening and speaking activities?
- provide for peer interaction emphasizing cooperative experiences across language groups and proficiency levels and with native English speakers as appropriate?
- use various groupings—large, small, dyads—to explore ideas and values in literature and other readings (elementary level)?
- emphasize development of a wide range of thinking skills?
- use the writing process across subject areas?
- focus attention on content and fluency in writing before correctness of form?
- base instruction on effective, research-based classroom practices?
- incorporate students' home languages and cultural experiences into both curriculum and instruction?
- use information on student learning styles in planning instruction?

School environment
- Do teachers share responsibility for the instruction of second language learners by promoting English language development in all content areas?

Figure 10-2 Self-assessment for multilingual classrooms

Source: From *Handbook for Planning an Effective Foreign Language Program,* 1985; *Quality Criteria for Elementary Schools,* 1990; *Quality Criteria for High Schools,* 1990; *Bilingual Education Handbook,* 1990; California Department of Education Publications, 515 L Street #250, Sacramento, CA 95814. Copyright © 1985, 1990 by California Department of Education. Adapted by permission.

- Do teachers model the learning strategies that students need to use?
- Does the entire school share a commitment to the development of language and literacy skills for English language learners?
- Do curricular and extracurricular activities provide opportunities for students to interact in a positive manner with native speakers of English?
- Do students receive basic services *in addition to* those provided through categorical programs (e.g., Chapter 1, Migrant Education)?

Parent and community involvement/Communication between home and school
- Are parents encouraged to use their most fluent language when communicating with children at home?
- Is there frequent, systematic, and purposeful communication between the home and school?
- Are resources—people and materials—from the students' communities incorporated into the curriculum?

Staff development
- Do the school's inservice programs address second language development, cross-cultural communication, and strategies for teaching non-native speakers?
- Do the school's inservice programs promote the integration of language processes, thinking and concept development in ESL, and content instruction?
- Do the school's inservice programs provide training across curriculum areas that supports a shared commitment to meeting the needs of second language learners?

Assessment
- Do assessment practices include authentic holistic measures consistent with knowledge and skills instruction?
- Does the evaluation of student progress incorporate informal measures (e.g., individual and groupwork) as well as formal testing?
- Does the program give students credit toward graduation for all ESL classes, for work in the native language, or for demonstrated proficiency in subject-matter areas?

Auxiliary support
- Do the adults interacting with English language learners within the school expect the students to achieve academically?
- Does the school make an effort to recognize students' strengths and progress publicly?
- Does the school library contain a range of materials for beginning, intermediate, and advanced ESL students?
- Does the school library provide an extensive collection of materials in students' native languages that provides access to the core curriculum?
- Does the school library have personnel available to assist English language learners in the library?
- Does the school make guidance and health services accessible to students through native language support?
- Does the school make extracurricular activities accessible to students with little or no English language skills?
- Do school policies reflect awareness of the circumstances (immigrant/refugee status or migrant conditions) that some language minority students may face?
- Do school policies reflect sensitivity toward the effects such conditions may have on student learning?
- Do the teachers of other subjects modify their instruction (e.g., sheltered English) for second language learners?

Figure 10-2, *continued*

246

Summary

In evaluating learner outcomes, teachers should recall that the conceptualizations of teaching and learning presented throughout this text represent a departure from some traditional views of curriculum and instruction. Contemporary theory and research suggest changes in how language and learning are assessed. Formal assessment has its limitations. Alternative assessment practices hold promise. Use of multiple sources of information to evaluate student progress in language and academic development is sound practice.

How to empower students is a critical question for those teaching English language learners. Four essential areas to consider are cultural and linguistic incorporation, community participation, pedagogy, and assessment. Programs must recognize students' need to communicate, to fully develop literacy skills, to acquire knowledge in the content areas, and to develop higher-level thinking skills. Teachers will want to examine the features of programs within their own schools to ensure that they provide English language learners with full access to a quality education. In the final analysis, "education is not preparation for life; education is life itself" (Dewey, cited in *Bartlett's Familiar Quotations*, 1992, 577).

References

Bartlett's familiar quotations: A collection of passages, phrases, and proverbs traced to their sources in ancient and modern literature (16th ed.). (1992). Justin Kaplan (Ed.). Boston: Little, Brown.

Calfee, R. (1993). Standardized achievement tests are not the real answer. *The Long Term View*, 1(4), 64–67.

California Department of Education. (1985). *Handbook for planning an effective foreign language program*. Sacramento: Author.

California Department of Education. (1990a). *Bilingual education handbook*. Sacramento: Author.

California Department of Education. (1990b). *Quality criteria for elementary schools*. Sacramento: Author.

California Department of Education. (1990c). *Quality criteria for high schools: Planning, implementing, self-study, and program quality review*. Sacramento: Author.

CATESOL Position Statement on the Role of English as a Second Language (ESL) in Public School Grades (K–12). (1990). *CATESOL News*, 22(1), 4.

Cohen, A. (1987). *Tests: Marked for life?* New York: Scholastic.

Cummins, J. (1984). *Bilingualism and special education: Issues in assessment and pedagogy*. San Diego: College-Hill Press.

Cummins, J. (1986). Empowering minority students: A framework for intervention. *Harvard Educational Review*, 56(1), 18–36.

Cummins, J. (1989). *Empowering minority students*. Sacramento: California Association for Bilingual Education.

Curriculum Development and Supplemental Materials Commission. (1991). *California basic instructional materials in English as a second language and foreign language* (adoption recommendations of the Curriculum Development and Supplemental Materials Commission to the State Board of Education, draft). Sacramento: California Department of Education.

Farr, R., & Tone, B. (1994). *Portfolio performance assessment.* Fort Worth: Harcourt Brace College Publishers.

Figueroa, R. A., & García, E. (1994). Issues in testing students from culturally and linguistically diverse backgrounds. *Multicultural Education, 2*(1), 10–19.

García, G. E., & Pearson, P. D. (1994). Assessment and diversity. In L. Darling-Hammond (Ed.), *Review of research in education* (Vol. 20, pp. 337–391). Washington, DC: American Educational Research Association.

Haberman, M. (1991). The pedagogy of poverty versus good teaching. *Phi Delta Kappan, 73*(4), 290–294.

Herman, J. L., & Winters, L. (1994). Portfolio research: A slim collection. *Educational Leadership, 52*(2), 48–55.

Madaus, G. (1993). Interview. *The Long Term View, 1*(4), 3–4.

Minicucci, C., & Olsen, L. (1993). Caught unawares: California secondary schools confront the immigrant student challenge. *Multicultural Education, 1*(2), 16–19, 38.

Mumme, J. (1991). *Portfolio assessment in mathematics.* University of California, Santa Barbara: California Mathematics Project.

Powell, R. R., Zehm, S., & García, J. (1995). Field experience: Strategies for exploring diversity in schools. Upper Saddle River, NJ: Merrill/Prentice Hall.

Ruiz, R. (1991). The empowerment of language-minority students. In C. E. Sleeter (Ed.), *Empowerment through multicultural education* (pp. 217–227). Albany: State University of New York.

Spindler, G. D., & Spindler, L. (1994). What is cultural therapy? In G. Spindler & L. Spindler (Eds.), *Pathways to cultural awareness: Cultural therapy with teachers and students* (pp. 1–33). Thousand Oaks, CA: Corwin Press.

Stiggins, R. J. (1994). *Student-centered classroom assessment.* New York: Macmillan College Publishing.

Velvel, L. R. (1993). Introduction. *The Long Term View, 1*(4), 3-4.

Wiggins, G. (1989). A true test: Toward more authentic and equitable assessment. *Phi Delta Kappan, 70*(9), 703–713.

Wiggins, G. (1993). Assessment: Authenticity, context, and validity. *Phi Delta Kappan, 75*(3), 200–214.

Wolf, D. P. (1993). Assessment and educational equity. *The Long Term View, 1*(4), 76-79.

A P P E N D I X

Legal Responsibilities of Education Agencies Serving Language Minority Students

SYNOPSIS

This synopsis highlights key legislation, court rulings, and administrative regulations addressing language minority students and the legal responsibilities of educational agencies serving them.

A comprehensive discussion of the laws and rulings cited here can be found in *Legal Responsibilities of Education Agencies Serving National Origin Language Minority Students* (1988, 1993, 1995), written by James J. Lyons and available from the Mid-Atlantic Equity Center, 5454 Wisconsin Ave., Suite 655, Chevy Chase, MD 20815.

INTRODUCTION

As part of a national effort to secure equal educational opportunities for all American students, the three branches of federal government have acted during the last two decades to protect the rights of national origin minority students and those who are limited in English proficiency. A substantial body of federal law has emerged that establishes the rights of language minority students and defines the responsibilities of school districts serving them. This body of law has changed significantly in its scope and interpretation and continues to evolve.

Those who are responsible for state and local educational policies and programs can turn for guidance and direction to these laws and regulations. By doing so, they can ensure that the ever-increasing number of minority students they serve are provided with the educational opportunities guaranteed by a democratic society.

From the Mid-Atlantic Equity Center, 5454 Wisconsin Avenue, Suite 655, Chevy Chase, MD 20815, Dr. Sheryl J. Denbo, Director. Used with permission.

FEDERAL LAW

1868   *Constitution of the United States, Fourteenth Amendment*
"No State shall . . . deny to any person within its jurisdiction the equal protection of the laws."

1964   *Civil Rights Act, Title VI*
"No person in the United States shall, on the grounds of race, color, or national origin . . . be denied the benefits of, or be subjected to discrimination under any program or activity receiving Federal financial assistance."

1974   *Equal Educational Opportunities Act (EEOA)*
"No state shall deny equal educational opportunity to an individual on account of his or her race, color, sex or national origin, by . . . the failure of an educational agency to take appropriate action to overcome language barriers that impede equal participation by its students in its instructional programs."

COURT RULINGS

Supreme Court

1974   *Lau v. Nichols*
In a unanimous decision, the U.S. Supreme Court made the following rulings:

- Equality of educational opportunity is not achieved by merely providing all students with "the same facilities, textbooks, teachers and curriculum; [because] students who do not understand English are effectively foreclosed from any meaningful education."

- The Office for Civil Rights (U.S. Department of Education) has the authority to establish regulations for compliance with the 1964 Civil Rights Act.

1982   *Plyler v. Doe*
The Supreme Court ruled that the Fourteenth Amendment prohibits states from denying a free public education to undocumented immigrant children regardless of their immigrant status. The Court emphatically declared that school systems are not agents for enforcing immigration law and determined that the burden undocumented aliens may place on an educational system is not an accepted argument for excluding or denying educational service to any student.

Federal Courts

1974   *Serna v. Portales*
The 10th Circuit Court of Appeals found "undisputed evidence that Spanish surnamed students do not reach the achievement levels attained by their Anglo counterparts." The court ordered Portales Municipal Schools to design an educational plan that addressed national origin minority students' needs by implementing a bilingual and bicultural curriculum, revising testing procedures to assess achievement in that curriculum, and recruiting and hiring bilingual school personnel.

1978   *Cintron v. Brentwood*
The Federal District Court for the Eastern District of New York rejected the Brentwood School District's plan to restructure its bilingual program, finding that the

proposed plan "kept [Spanish-speaking students] separate and apart from English-speaking students in music and art in violation of the 'Lau Guidelines.'" The program also failed to provide for exiting students whose English language proficiency would enable them to understand regular English instruction.

1978 *Rios v. Reed*

The Federal District Court for the Eastern District of New York found Pastchogue-Medford School District's transitional bilingual program inadequate with regard to school professionals' knowledge of bilingual teaching methods, language assessment and program placement procedures, native language curriculum materials, and native language instruction. The court wrote, "While the District's goal of teaching Hispanic children the English language is certainly proper, it cannot be allowed to compromise a student's right to meaningful education before proficiency in English is obtained."

1981 *Castañeda v. Pickard*

The Fifth Circuit Court of Appeals formulated a test to determine school district compliance with the Equal Educational Opportunities Act (1974). The three-part test includes the following criteria:

1) THEORY: The school must pursue a program based on an educational theory recognized as sound or, at least, as a legitimate experimental strategy.

2) PRACTICE: The school must actually implement the program with instructional practices, resources, and personnel necessary to transfer theory to reality.

3) RESULTS: The school must not persist in a program that fails to produce results.

The "Castañeda Test" has been applied by courts in the following decisions:

1983 *Keyes v. School District #1*

A U.S. District Court found that a Denver public school district had failed to satisfy the second of the Castañeda Test's three elements because it was not adequately implementing a plan for national origin minority students.

1987 *Gomez v. Illinois*

The Seventh Circuit Court of Appeals found that state education agencies (SEAs) as well as local education agencies (LEAs) are required under the Equal Educational Opportunities Act (1974) to ensure that the needs of LEP children are met.

ENFORCEMENT POLICY

The Office for Civil Rights (OCR) of the U.S. Department of Education monitors school districts' compliance with Title VI of the Civil Rights Act (1964), reviewing procedures for the identification of limited English proficient (LEP) students and educational programs for national origin minority students. The OCR also investigates complaints of alleged noncompliance brought against school districts. Current OCR policy provides that school districts may use any method or program that has proven successful, or may implement any sound educational program that promises to be successful. This policy identifies four basic school district responsibilities (Office for Civil Rights Memorandum, May 25, 1970):

1. To take affirmative steps to rectify language deficiencies in order to open its instructional programs to language minority children who are limited-English-proficient;

2. To not place students in classes for the mentally retarded on the basis of criteria which essentially measure English language skills or to deny access to college preparatory courses as a direct result of failure of the school system to inculcate English language skills;

3. To not operate as permanent educational dead-ends any ability grouping or tracking systems which prevent national origin children from acquiring English language skills as soon as possible;

4. To adequately notify national origin parents of school activities which are called to the attention of all parents. Such notice in order to be adequate may have to be in a language other than English.

SUBJECT INDEX